# Java™ Database Programming

# Java™ Database Programming

**Brian Jepson**

WILEY COMPUTER PUBLISHING

John Wiley & Sons, Inc.

New York • Chichester • Brisbane • Toronto • Singapore • Weinheim

Executive Publisher: Katherine Schowalter
Editor: Philip Sutherland
Managing Editor: Angela Murphy
Text Design & Composition: Benchmark Productions, Inc.

This text is printed on acid-free paper.

*Library of Congress Cataloging-in-Publication Data:*
Jepson, Brian.
    Java database programming / Brian Jepson.
        p.    cm.
    "Wiley Computer Publishing."
    Includes bibliographical references  (p. ).
    ISBN 0-471-16518-2 (pbk.  :  alk.  paper)
    1. Java  (Computer program language)  2. Database design.
    I. Title.
    QA76.73.J38J47    1996
    005.74–dc20                                              96-36120

Printed in the United States of America
10  9  8  7  6  5  4  3  2  1

# Contents

| | | |
|---|---|---|
| **Preface** | | **ix** |
| **1.** | **Databases and the Java Programming Language** | **1** |
| | Java as a Database Applications Development Tool | 1 |
| | Ease of Maintenance | 2 |
| |     Connectivity to a Wide Range of Database Servers | 2 |
| |     Consistent API | 2 |
| |     Rapid Prototyping | 2 |
| | How Would People Use Java? Mythical Examples | 2 |
| |     Example One: Applet Happy | 3 |
| |     Example Two: Users on the Go | 3 |
| |     Example Three: Big-Time Corporate Intranet | 3 |
| | Using Java with Databases | 3 |
| |     Dynamic Data Structures | 4 |
| **2.** | **An Introduction to Databases and Database Design** | **9** |
| |     Table and Database Design | 9 |
| |     An SQL Primer | 14 |
| **3.** | **JDBC** | **27** |
| | The Banshee Screams for Database Meat | 27 |
| | Enough with the Buzzwords, History, and Pedagogy! What the %$&? Is JDBC? | 28 |
| | It Cuts Both Ways: Stored Procs and Database Independence | 29 |
| | Getting and Installing JDBC | 30 |
| | Getting Drivers | 31 |
| |     The tinySQL JDBC Driver | 31 |
| |     The mSQL JDBC Driver | 31 |
| |     The JDBC-ODBC Bridge | 31 |
| | Picking a Driver | 32 |
| | Installing tinySQL and the tinySQL textFile JDBC Driver | 32 |
| | Installing the mSQL JDBC Driver | 33 |
| | Installing the JDBC-ODBC Bridge | 34 |
| | Registering Drivers with java.sql.DriverManager | 35 |
| | Opening a Connection | 36 |
| |     JDBC URLs—tinySQL | 38 |
| |     JDBC URLs—the JDBC-ODBC Bridge | 38 |

JDBC URLs—the mSQL JDBC Driver                                        38
Running the Example Program                                           38
Issuing Update Statements                                            39
Issuing Update Statements, Part II                                   42
Performing a Query and Retrieving Results                            44
ResultSet Pitfalls                                                   47
Prepared Statements (no mSQL, no tinySQL)                            48
Callable Statements (no mSQL, no tinySQL)                            53
JDBC Escape Syntax                                                   56
Discovering Result Set Metadata                                      57
Discovering Driver Capabilities                                      57

**4.   Forward Into the Past: CardFileAbstract for JDBC            59**
Installing CardFileAbstract                                          62
Extending CardFileAbstract                                           63
public abstract void login(String[] argv);                          63
public abstract void getRow();                                       64
public abstract void delRow();                                       66
public abstract void nextRow();                                      66
public abstract void prevRow();                                      66
public abstract void save();                                         66
public abstract void update();                                      67
Running jdbcCardFile                                                 79

**5.   Fun with Widgets                                            81**
Hierarchical Data                                                    82
outline.java — Expanding the Tree                                    86
outlineMlTree.java—Extending outline.java to Use a Visual Component  100
Grids                                                               106

**6.   Inside the tinySQL Database Management System              123**
The Two Tiers                                                       124
tinySQL.java                                                        125
tinySQLException.java                                               161
tinySQLTable.java                                                   162
textFile.java                                                       165
textFileTable.java                                                  171
The Chrome Plated textFile of Destiny                              185

**7.   The tinySQL JDBC Driver                                    187**
The tinySQL JDBC Driver                                            188
tinySQLDriver.java                                                 189

textFileDriver.java                                                        194

tinySQLConnection.java                                                     196

   textFileConnection.java                                  208

tinySQLStatement.java                                                      210

tinySQLResultSet.java                                                      220

tinySQLResultSetMetaData.java                                              250

testTextFile.java                                                          261

That's It for the Other One                                                263

**8.  Extending tinySQL**                                                  **265**

   dbfFile—A Read/Only Interface to DBF Files               265

   dbfFileTable—The Implementation of the tinySQLTable      269

dbfFileDriver—The JDBC Driver for This Bad Boy                             282

dbfFileConnection—The JDBC Connection Object for dbfFile                   285

A Test Program for dbfFileDriver                                           287

Conclusion                                                                 289

**9.  .mSQL and MsqlJava**                                                 **291**

Getting mSQL                                                               292

Building and Installing mSQL                                              292

Starting mSQL                                                              295

Paying for mSQL                                                           295

Command-line Tools                                                        295

   msqladmin—A Tool for Managing Your Server                295

   msql—Issuing Queries and Creating Tables Interactively   296

Getting and Installing MsqlJava                                           296

   Testing the Installation                                 297

The Msql Class                                                            300

   Instantiating and Initializing an Object                 300

   Working with Tables and Issuing Queries                  300

CardFile.java—A Slightly More Complex Java Application                    301

**10.  Reimplementing the CardFile Application as an Abstract Class**     **327**

CardFileAbstract.java                                                     328

MsqlCardFile.java                                                         341

**11.  Connecting to Databases Using Applets**                           **353**

Pure Java JDBC Drivers                                                    353

Burns, Busts, and Bummers (No Rip-offs)                                   354

mSQL JDBC and Applets                                                     354

Weblogic's jdbcKona/T3                                                    355

JetConnect from XDB Systems                                               356

JDP                                                                       356

DataRamp                                                              357
It's Never Really the End                                             357

**Appendix A   MsqlJava API Reference by Example**                    **359**
Constructing the Msql Object                                          359
Connecting to the mSQL Server                                         360
Selecting a Database: public void SelectDB(String db)                361
Issuing a Query: public MsqlResult Query (String s)                  362
Working with Result Sets: public String [] FetchRow()                362
Closing the Connection: public void Close()                          365

**Appendix B   JDBC API Reference**                                   **367**
Instantiating a Driver                                                367
Using a Connection                                                    368
Working with a Statement                                              378
Working with a ResultSet object                                       384
The ResultSetMetaData Object                                          393
Working with PreparedStatements                                       397
Working with the CallableStatement                                    402
DatabaseMetaData                                                      404
ODBC/JDBC Escape Processing                                           433

**Appendix C   JavaLex and JavaCup Introduction**                     **435**
The JavaCup Grammar                                                   436
JavaLex Scanner Specifications                                        440

**Appendix D   JDBC/ODBC SQL Reference**                              **445**
Minimum, Core, and Extended Grammars                                  445
Conventions                                                           446
SQL Statements                                                        447
ODBC Scalar Functions                                                 462
SQL Components                                                        468

**Index**                                                             **473**

# However Big You Think You Are

*"He's the all-American bullet-headed Saxon mother's son"*
　　　　　　　—Lennon/McCartney, The Continuing Story of Bungalow Bill

It's been a long weekend. I've spent the last two caffeine-fueled days cranking out and revising eighty pages of programming examples and, when I've felt like it, some narrative to go along with it. Now it's eight o'clock on a Sunday evening, and I'm tossing back twelve ounces of Cider Jack. This is my first, but certainly not my last, drink of the weekend. Come to think of it, it's my first drink of the week.

I'm not drinking this Cider Jack for any sort of intoxicating effect, actually, and it's certainly not for the taste. Cider Jack is a great beverage, but I'm more of a malt and hops kind of guy. I'm tossing back this fine beverage to obtain a level of verisimilitude, because this is it's the same beverage which is served in unspeakable quantities to Brown and RISD students at the AS220 Cafe. This is where I would have normally spent most of my weekend, if not for various reasons. The first is that the AS220 cafe is closed one month a year, and this happens to be the month. The other reason is that, due to a combination of earning potential and intrigue, I have once again dragged myself out of my home state to take a job in New York City.

New York is one hell of a city, but as they say in Providence, "It ain't no Providence." Of course, they *would* say that in Providence. Nevertheless, I have forsaken a wonderful Rhode Island summer to spend time in New York, working on a most excellent Intranet project and writing a groovy book about Java. It's this last item I want to talk about. The book in your hands is the product of a summer's worth of sweat. I started the work in the Washington Square Hotel on Waverly and MacDougal, under flickering fluorescent lamps designed to keep costs down, while still flooding the rooms with illumination. The best parts of the book, however, were written in a TriBeCa sublet.

While this book has been a lot of work and very trying at times, I've had a great deal of fun bringing it to you. I finally got to do something I've always wanted to do: write an SQL database. You'll meet tinySQL later in the book; it's an SQL database engine written in 100% Java, my One Rainy Wish, written one rainy weekend in the Big Apple. Once I achieved that grail, the book started on an unstoppable roll.

## About the Web Site

All of the example code included with this book can be downloaded from `http://www.wiley.com/compbooks/`. In addition to listing all of the example code, this web page also contains links to the FAQ (Frequebntly Asked Questions) and related sites where you can download tools such as mSQL, the JDBC components, and other items of interest. Should you have any trouble with this site, or if you simply have questions concerning the book or software, you may email me at `bjepson@ids.net`.

In the tradition of Abbie Hoffman's Woodstock Nation, I think it's a good idea to mention some of the music that's helped to make this book a reality. Good music is important; the right tunes in the right mood can work wonders. It's kind of a "set and setting" thing.

- The Beatles, "Revolver" (English version), *Sgt. Pepper's Lonely Hearts Club Band*, and *The Beatles* (also known as, but not formally titled "The White Album")
- fIREHOSE, "if'n"
- Fugazi, "Repeater"
- The Grateful Dead, "Anthem of the Sun," *Grateful Dead* (first album), and *Live/Dead*
- The Jimi Hendrix Experience, "Axis: Bold as Love" and "Electric Ladyland"
- Van Morrison, "Astral Weeks"
- Pixies, "Surfer Rosa"
- Various Artists, *A Bitter Pill to Swallow: A Providence Music Sampler*
- The Who, "Quadrophenia"

Now that the self-indulgent part is almost over, I'll let you get ready for the book itself. I'd like to thank the editorial staff at John Wiley & Sons, Inc. who helped make this book a reality: Phil Sutherland, Kathryn Malm, Pam Sobotka, and Angela Murphy. They're the folks who are responsible for taking my gibberish and turning it into something coherent. Thanks also go out to the people of the SMT Computing Society for their moral support, and for the bail money they provided shortly after the incident at a laundromat involving three pigs, a stagecoach driver, and that now-infamous soap impression of Lenny Bruce. Special thanks goes out to Scott Schoen, Josh Marketos, Shawn Wallace, and my cat, Oscar, who provided good company and collaboration in various wild schemes (real and imagined). I'd especially like to thank my wife Pam, for putting up with my tapping away on the keyboard night after night, doodling in Etruscan, and all the while promising "just one more minute..."

# Chapter 1

# Databases and the Java Programming Language

## Java as a Database Applications Development Tool

*"One, Two, (Five) Three, Four"*

—The Beatles, "Sgt. Pepper's Lonely Hearts Club Band" (reprise)

Development tools fall in and out of favor on a daily basis. By now, you've probably heard a lot of hype about Java. It's touted as a robust, architecture-neutral, secure, simple, object-oriented, distributed, multithreaded, and dynamic development language. All of these characteristics make it very attractive as a database development tool. I could probably describe each one of these attributes and tell you why it makes Java great for database development. However, I believe it would be better to think about what developers look for in a database development tool and see how Java makes the cut. Don't worry; I won't drag this out any longer than I have to.

# Ease of Maintenance

Java's strong object-oriented nature makes it possible to develop components that can be incorporated into database applications. The package hierarchy makes it extremely easy to keep your components organized. In addition, the *javadoc* utility makes it simple to develop self-documenting code.

# Connectivity to a Wide Range of Database Servers

Shortly after Java arrived, a plethora of database connectivity software appeared for it. With the variety of database APIs (Application Program Interfaces) available for Java and drivers that use JDBC (Sun's API for database development in Java), it is possible to develop applications and applets that converse with many database server products.

# Consistent API

JDBC makes it possible to develop database-independent Java applets and applications. Many vendors support JDBC, including those who released database connectivity packages in the pre-JDBC days. Using JDBC, building applications that are portable to a wide variety of database server products is easy.

# Rapid Prototyping

I find that, to keep my clients happy, I must have a semi-working prototype in place as soon as possible. Users like to click the buttons and type in the fields, even if they do practically nothing. Java's object-oriented nature makes it easy to develop reusable components and leverage components authored by other developers. Once a developer has established a bag of tools, he or she can build prototypes rapidly.

Java includes many features beyond those listed above that make it an attractive tool for developing database applications. In case you're still not convinced that Java is the right tool for your database development, I'll supply a couple of hypothetical case studies.

# How Would People Use Java? Mythical Examples

Mr. Fiction and I were sipping coffees after a wonderful night of chicken at Riverrun in TriBeCa. Mr. Fiction had the Tarragon Chicken; I was in temporary heaven with my Chicken Pot Pie, which is, In My Humble Opinion, their signature dish. But we had to have them all pulled out for our dessert, a wonderful Savoy truffle. As we downed the java, we dreamed up the following case studies:

## Example One: Applet Happy

What solution would be for the benefit of Mr. Kite, owner of a small brokerage firm with a huge Web site? He's got a real-time feed of stock and commodities quotes that are dumped into an mSQL database. He's had a CGI script that allows users to search for specific quotes by date and product, but now he wants to deploy an applet that displays a graph of price movements in real time. Using mSQL-JDBC, or even the mSQL-Java library, Mr. Kite can quickly throw together data-rich applets that can be served to his ever-expanding client base.

## Example Two: Users on the Go

Maxwell Edison *is* the MIS department for a medical supplies firm. Despite the fact that he's taking night classes (majoring in medicine), he needs to develop a tool that allows his sales force to report in at the end of the day. Because the salespeople are always in different cities, they need to do this remotely, often from a hotel room.

Maxwell decides that it would be a good idea to have the salespeople dial in to a PPP server and use a custom application with embedded Java to send their daily information. Once this process is finished, the salespeople can dial in the next morning to update their application with the composite figures. This is done on the cheap, too! Each of the salesperson's laptops runs Windows 95, but the server is running Linux with mSQL as the database server!

## Example Three: Big-Time Corporate Intranet

Rita is the IT chief for a big Frobozz 500 corporation. It's her responsibility to come up with a single database application development tool that will work across Macintosh, Win32, and Solaris operating systems. She's inquired discreetly about products like FoxPro, Galaxy, Delphi, and Powerbuilder, but none of these products really inspire her confidence. She is drawn to Java because of its architecture-independence and ease of use.

# Using Java with Databases

To use Java as a client for one or more of the many database servers supported by a Java client class such as JDBC, you will need to become familiar with certain concepts. It is, of course, essential that you understand such things as the fundamentals of database design, the Structured Query Language (SQL), and methods for mapping information contained in database tables to Java's data structures and objects. The next chapter will deal with database fundamentals and SQL, but right now, I'll introduce you to a couple of dynamic data structures that will come in handy. Later chapters will deal with Java-based representations of database information.

# Dynamic Data Structures

When you work with databases, you will find that you need to have some sort of dynamic structures available. The Hashtable and Vector classes work in glorious concert to let you represent rows and columns in Java rather easily.

The Java program `Dynamic.java` instantiates a java.util.Vector object as rows. A Vector is simply a growable array of objects. In this example, each row contains a Hashtable. A Hashtable allows you to store values by keys, as in Perl's associative arrays. You can use the `put()` method to add an item by a key and the `get()` method to retrieve a value by a key. A key can be any Object, but in this case, we're using a String object.

An example of a simple Hashtable is a list of what everyone's drinking at a dinner party. Here's a little piece of code that does this:

```
import java.util.*;
public class Drinks {
   public static void main(String argv[]) {
      Hashtable beverages = new Hashtable();
      beverages.put("Vera",   "Ginger Ale");
      beverages.put("Chuck", "Rob Roy");
      beverages.put("Dave",   "Sloe Gin Fizz");
   }
}
```

Once you have done this, you can retrieve what Dave is drinking with:

```
String DaveDrinks = (String) beverages.get("Dave");
System.out.println(DaveDrinks);
```

Because the Hashtable can hold objects of any type, you need to explicitly cast the object returned by `get()` to a String when you assign it to an object of type String.

Here's `Dynamic.java`. Because I haven't shown you anything about databases yet, I'm cheating by putting some bogus data into the data structure. This example gives you an idea of one possible means for representing database tables in Java's data structures. You can get a row count from `rows.size()`, and you can retrieve each row with `rows.elementAt()`.

Because each object in Vector is a Hashtable, you can assign the Hashtable to a temporary object such as foo, then retrieve the values of that row by invoking `foo.get()` for each key.

```java
import java.util.*;

public class Dynamic {

  public static void main(String argv[]) {

    // a new Vector object to hold all the rows

    Vector rows = new Vector();

    // populate the data structure with some bogus
    // values that might appear in a table

    popData(rows, "Brian", "Jepson");
    popData(rows, "Mr.",   "Kite");
    popData(rows, "Mr.",   "Mustard");
    popData(rows, "Japhy", "Ryder");

    // process each row in the "table"

    for (int i = 0; i < rows.size(); i++) {

      // get the Hashtable that is contained in each row

      Hashtable foo = (Hashtable) rows.elementAt(i);

      // print out the row number - but add one to it
      // since the index offset is zero, but most
      // people are used to seeing records/rows start
      // at one.

      System.out.println("Row " + (i + 1));
```

**Continued**

```
         // since foo is the Hashtable for the current row,
         // you can get the column by invoking the get()
         // method with the name of the column you want.

         System.out.println("  first_name = " + foo.get("first_name"));
         System.out.println("  last_name  = " + foo.get("last_name"));

    }

    // exit cleanly

    System.exit(0);

}

// a convenience method to add items to the "table"

public static void popData(Vector rows, String first, String last) {

    // create a new Hashtable

    Hashtable columns = new Hashtable();

    // add the data to the new Hashtable

    columns.put("first_name", first);
    columns.put("last_name",  last);

    // add the Hashtable to the Vector

    rows.addElement(columns);

  }

}
```

And here's the output that this program produces:

```
Row 1
   first_name = Brian
   last_name  = Jepson
Row 2
   first_name = Mr.
   last_name  = Kite
Row 3
   first_name = Mr.
   last_name  = Mustard
Row 4
   first_name = Japhy
   last_name  = Ryder
```

Some of the examples in this book can be quite involved, especially when lots of Hash-tables and Vectors are involved. There's a lot of working source code in this book; it's a hands-on book, so you should read it within three feet of a computer at all times. I've made a sincere attempt to provide two levels of documentation: comprehensive documentation within the code, and more explicit narrative that accompanies it in the text of the book. I'm hoping that this approach will make a complicated subject clear to you.

# Chapter 2

# An Introduction to Databases and Database Design

*"I look at the floor, and I see it needs sweeping..."*
—The Beatles, "While My Guitar Gently Weeps"

As you work toward integrating Java and databases, you must understand more than how to connect to a database and execute commands. Your goal is to build a truly flexible system that can grow with your needs and be understandable to you and the people who maintain it. You will find it valuable to follow some of the principles that have guided database developers since the mathematician E.F. Codd published his theory for data modeling in relational database management systems in 1970. His foundation-setting theory was published in a paper entitled "A Relational Model of Data for Large Shared Data Banks" (*Communications of the ACM* 13, No. 6, June 1970) and is available on the Web at http://www.acm.org/classics/nov95/.

## Table and Database Design

A *table* is a collection of *rows*. Each row is broken down into one or more *columns*. A collection of tables is known as a *database*. A table is similar to a list you might jot down on any given day. Perhaps you are feeling particularly bored and extremely anti-social on a breezy summer day, so you take it upon yourself to catalog all the various stains on carpets and clothing throughout your house. Perhaps your list looks like this:

| Item | Type | Merlot | Ketchup | Jelly | Coffee | Unknown |
|------|------|--------|---------|-------|--------|---------|
| Handknit Sweater | Clothing | Yes | No | Yes | Yes | No |
| Couch | Furniture | No | Yes | No | Yes | Yes |
| Teddy Bear | Faithful Companion | No | No | Yes | Yes | No |
| Silk Tie | Clothing | No | Yes | Yes | No | No |

I'm sure you have more stains lurking in your house, but this should give you an idea of what a table might look like. Although you've managed to catalog many of the more important stains in your life, the relational model predicts that tables organized in this fashion will be difficult to work with. If you were to design your database table to mirror the structure of this list, you would start running into trouble when someone spilled a new, interesting substance on your couch; you would then need to add a column, altering the structure of the table.

**The Relational Model and the First Normal Form**  Codd's paper established the key guidelines of data normalization. *Data normalization* is a process that optimizes the way your data is represented in tables. Each step in normalization takes your data to a different *normal form*. As with horseshoes and grenades, more is always better, so it's important to normalize your tables to as many normal forms as possible. There can be as many as five normal forms depending on whom you believe; this chapter will explore only the first three, which are sufficient for most database development. I've met people who have gone beyond the third normal form. They usually have three eyes and can see 15 seconds into the future, which is really annoying.

For the database design to adhere to the first normal form, you must *eliminate repeating columns*. In the stain list shown previously, there is a column for the item, the type of item it is, and a column for each type of stain. That collection of stains is a perfect candidate for optimization (not to mention a high-tech cleaning agent). A repeating group of columns is a remarkably inefficient way to store data. For one, storage space is wasted; for each item, there must be a column for each possible stain, whether that item is squalid or untainted. Also, if an inebriated (or simply malicious) guest spills something different, like artichoke spread (mmm ... artichoke spread), the database structure must be physically modified. This is a big no-no: If specifications have been adequately drawn up for a system, no modification to table structure should be necessary unless significant new requirements arise. A different type of stain hardly qualifies as a "significant new requirement." After all, this database is about stains, so it should be able to handle lots of them.

For this table to conform to the first normal form, it needs to be split into two tables. A new table will be created, called STAIN. This table will contain the name of the stain, and two new columns. The first will be a stain ID, and the second will be an item ID. The original table, which will be referred to as ITEM, will lose all the stain columns, but it will gain a new one: item ID. The item ID will link the list of stains to the item. Here's the "new look" for the ITEM table:

| Item | Type | Item ID |
|------|------|---------|
| Handknit Sweater | Clothing | 1 |
| Couch | Furniture | 2 |
| Teddy Bear | Faithful Companion | 3 |
| Silk Tie | Clothing | 4 |

The STAIN table will look like this:

| Stain Name | Stain ID | Item ID |
|------------|----------|---------|
| Merlot | 1 | 1 |
| Jelly | 2 | 1 |
| Coffee | 3 | 1 |
| Ketchup | 4 | 2 |
| Coffee | 3 | 2 |
| Unknown | 5 | 2 |
| Jelly | 2 | 3 |
| Coffee | 3 | 3 |
| Ketchup | 4 | 4 |
| Jelly | 2 | 4 |

Organizing the table in this fashion may make it harder for humans to read, but it really makes things easy for the programmer when it comes time to add and manipulate data. The new columns that were added reveal some of the method in normalized data design. Each table in a well-designed schema (a *schema* is a collection of tables that are connected to each other in some way) should have a column that acts as a primary key. A *primary key* is a unique identifier, which is a column or group of columns whose values are *unique for each row in which it appears*. The ITEM table has the Item ID as primary key; no two rows can share the same Item ID in that table. The primary key in the STAIN table consists of two columns: Item ID + Stain ID. No two rows can have the same Item ID + Stain ID. The stain schema, which started out containing one horribly *denormalized* table, now consists of two tables, which are in the first normal form.

**Second Normal Form**   The primary key for the STAIN table (Item ID + Stain ID ) satisfies the requirement of the definition of a primary key; the value of the two columns will be different for each row. You may have noticed that the Stain Name repeats; it is a dependent value, and it is dependent on only one of the components of the multivalued primary key (the Stain ID). The application of the second normal form seeks to eliminate this type of condition, and in doing so, it eliminates redundant data. Right now, the Stain Name appears wherever a relationship is defined between stains and items. If one of the stain names is spelled differently, it can cause reporting anomalies, and you might not get the right count of stains. Even worse, if you ever identify the "unknown" stains, you would have to update all the records in the STAIN table, which is really doing double duty as a cross-reference table.

To bring the tables in this schema up to standard with the second normal form, you need to create yet another table. This will be called the STAIN XREF table, and it will contain only the Stain ID and Item ID. The STAIN table will now contain only the Stain Name and Stain ID. Here's how the STAIN table will look:

| Stain Name | Stain ID |
|------------|----------|
| Merlot     | 1        |
| Jelly      | 2        |
| Coffee     | 3        |
| Ketchup    | 4        |
| Unknown    | 5        |

Here is how the STAIN XREF table will look:

| Stain ID | Stain ID |
|----------|----------|
| 1 | 1 |
| 2 | 1 |
| 3 | 1 |
| 4 | 2 |
| 3 | 2 |
| 5 | 2 |
| 2 | 3 |
| 3 | 3 |
| 4 | 4 |
| 2 | 4 |

**Third Normal Form**  The third normal form has some things in common with the second normal form, but it is a little pickier. It seeks to eliminate any columns that are not at all dependent on the key. In the second normal form example, the column we eliminated was partially dependent on the key. Looking back at the ITEM table, note that there are three columns: Item Name, Type, and Item ID. Of these, only Item Name is dependent on the Item ID. The Type is independent of that. As proof, you can see that two items have the same type: the sweater and tie are both clothing. Again, you need to split tables. A new table called TYPE, containing a Type Name and a Type ID, will be created.  Further, the Item table will be updated to use a Type ID to express the relationship between items and types. Here's the TYPE table:

| Type Name | Type ID |
|-----------|---------|
| Clothing | 1 |
| Furniture | 2 |
| Faithful Companion | 3 |

And here's the revised ITEM table:

| Item | Type ID | Item ID |
|------|---------|---------|
| Handknit Sweater | 1 | 1 |
| Couch | 2 | 2 |
| Teddy Bear | 3 | 3 |
| Silk Tie | 1 | 4 |

The stain schema started out with one table. After it is taken to the third normal form, it now consists of four tables: ITEM, STAIN, STAIN XREF, and TYPE. As you learn about SQL, you will see how these tables can be defined, populated, and queried.

# An SQL Primer

SQL is a specialized language for set-based data access. Most database systems will be accessed using a dialect of SQL; all JDBC drivers will support a particular subset of the SQL standard. In the remainder of this chapter, the SQL examples will work fine with the isql utility (Sybase and Microsoft SQL Server), the msql utility (mSQL), or a command-line ODBC tool such as IODBC, which is available for Win32 systems and, ultimately, Unix systems, when I get around to porting it. You should consult your database product's documentation for specific information on using one of these utilities or on the counterpart for your database system, as you might encounter specific deviations from the norm, depending on your particular installation and architecture.

**Using SQL to Create Tables**   One of the first SQL Statements you will find useful is the CREATE TABLE statement. It is used to create an empty table within a database. Once you have created a table, you can use the INSERT statement to add data to it. The CREATE TABLE syntax looks like this:

```
CREATE TABLE tablename
   (column_name column_type [(column_width[, column_precision])]
   [,column_name, column_type [(column_width[, column_precision])]]
   ...)
```

Each table must have a name; the names that will be used in this example will be no longer than eight characters. This naming convention will conform to the limitations of some database products that run on PC platforms, such as many xbase products. Here's the first part of the definition for the ITEM table:

```
CREATE TABLE item
```

This needs to be followed by one or more column definitions, which must include the column name and the data type of the column. The number of SQL Data Types supported by each database product varies, and you will have to consult the documentation. The two data types used in these examples include *int* and *char*, which are supported by most database products. The default size and precision of *int* varies depending on the database product, and the size of a *char* column is explicitly set when you define the column. Here's the table definition for ITEM:

```
CREATE TABLE item
    (it_id int, it_name char(40), it_ty_id_ int)
```

Because the width of column names is limited to ten in some database products, these tables will be defined using names that are somewhat shorter than those seen earlier. Notice that each column in the item table starts with the prefix it_ (short for item). This can be useful when you build statements that reference columns from multiple tables. It allows you to determine from which table a column comes immediately. The it_ty_id_ column is a reference to the TYPE table, which you haven't seen yet.

You should be able to pass the previous SQL statement directly to your SQL query interface. Under a command-line query tool such as isql or IODBC, you must type GO on a new line and hit the Enter/Return key to issue the query. Under the msql command-line query tool, you must do something similar, but use \g instead of GO.

Here are the CREATE TABLE statements that define the tables STAIN, STAINXRF and TYPE:

```
CREATE TABLE stain
    (st_id int,
     st_name char(20))
CREATE TABLE stainxrf
    (sx_st_id_ int,
     sx_it_id_ int)
CREATE TABLE type
    (ty_id int,
     ty_name char(20))
```

One mark of the well-behaved database developer is the uncontrollable urge to document everything. With this in mind (and with the hope of making everything clear), I will provide a poor man's data dictionary. This lists each table and field and includes the long name from the tables that were defined in the database design primer:

| Table | Field | Description |
|---|---|---|
| item | it_id | Item ID |
| item | it_name | Item Name |
| item | it_ty_id_ | Type ID |
| stain | st_id | Stain ID |
| stain | st_name | Stain Name |
| stainxrf | sx_it_id_ | Item ID |
| stainxrf | sx_st_id_ | Stain ID |
| type | ty_id | Type ID |
| type | ty_name | Type Name |

**Using SQL to Add Data to Tables**  To add rows to a table, you must use the INSERT statement. The INSERT statement generally looks like this:

```
INSERT INTO table-name [(column-identifier [, column-identifier]...)]
  VALUES (insert-value [, insert-value] ...)
```

The INSERT statement requires the name of the table, a list of columns, and a list of values. The values must correspond to the columns in the list of columns. If you do not wish to specify the column list, you may omit it; in this case, all columns are assumed to be part of the INSERT statement, and the list of values must correspond to the columns as they appeared in the CREATE TABLE statement. Therefore:

```
INSERT INTO item (it_id, it_name, it_ty_id_)
  VALUES (1, 'Handknit Sweater', 1)
```

is equivalent to:

```
INSERT INTO item
  VALUES (1, 'Handknit Sweater', 1)
```

Such variants of the INSERT statement are called *positioned inserts*, and they can become rather dodgy when your table structure changes. Here's a series of INSERT statements that will populate the ITEM table:

```
INSERT INTO item (it_id, it_name, it_ty_id_)
    VALUES (1, 'Handknit Sweater', 1)
INSERT INTO item (it_id, it_name, it_ty_id_)
    VALUES (2, 'Couch', 2)
INSERT INTO item (it_id, it_name, it_ty_id_)
    VALUES (3, 'Teddy Bear', 3)
INSERT INTO item (it_id, it_name, it_ty_id_)
    VALUES (4, 'Silk Tie', 1)
```

The following SQL INSERT statements can be used to populate the TYPE table:

```
INSERT INTO type
    (ty_name, ty_id)
    VALUES ('Clothing', 1)
INSERT INTO type
    (ty_name, ty_id)
    VALUES ('Furniture', 2)
INSERT INTO type
    (ty_name, ty_id)
    VALUES ('Faithful Companion', 3)
```

The STAIN table is populated with the following SQL statements:

```
INSERT INTO stain
    (st_name, st_id)
    VALUES ('Merlot', 1)
INSERT INTO stain
    (st_name, st_id)
    VALUES ('Jelly', 2)
INSERT INTO stain
    (st_name, st_id)
    VALUES ('Coffee', 3)
INSERT INTO stain
    (st_name, st_id)
    VALUES ('Ketchup', 4)
```

```
INSERT INTO stain
    (st_name, st_id)
    VALUES ('Unknown', 5)
```

Finally, the cross-reference table, STAINXRF, can be populated with:

```
INSERT INTO stainxrf
    (sx_st_id_, sx_it_id_)
    VALUES (1, 1)
INSERT INTO stainxrf
    (sx_st_id_, sx_it_id_)
    VALUES (2, 1)
INSERT INTO stainxrf
    (sx_st_id_, sx_it_id_)
    VALUES (3, 1)
INSERT INTO stainxrf
    (sx_st_id_, sx_it_id_)
    VALUES (4, 2)
INSERT INTO stainxrf
    (sx_st_id_, sx_it_id_)
    VALUES (3, 2)
INSERT INTO stainxrf
    (sx_st_id_, sx_it_id_)
    VALUES (5, 2)
INSERT INTO stainxrf
    (sx_st_id_, sx_it_id_)
    VALUES (2, 3)
INSERT INTO stainxrf
    (sx_st_id_, sx_it_id_)
    VALUES (3, 3)
INSERT INTO stainxrf
    (sx_st_id_, sx_it_id_)
    VALUES (2, 4)
INSERT INTO stainxrf
    (sx_st_id_, sx_it_id_)
    VALUES (4, 4)
```

**Using SQL to Query Tables**  Now that you've got data in the tables, it wouldn't be fair if I didn't tell you how to retrieve some of that data. The SELECT statement allows you to pull data out of the tables, and so it would be perfect for making the cleaning crew's list of duties. When we ultimately use SQL in Java applets and applications, the results have to be processed one row at a time or stored in a data structure for later use (see "Dynamic Data Structures" in Chapter 1).

The most basic SQL SELECT Statement looks something like this:

```
SELECT column-list FROM table-list
```

The column-list is a comma-separated list of columns. It can also be replaced by "*", which represents all of the columns in the table or tables. The table-list is also separated by commas. Here's a simple example from the ITEM table, with one column and one table:

```
SELECT it_name
    FROM item
```

This would retrieve all of the items. Here's how the output might look from a command-line query tool, such as isql:

```
it_name
-------------------
Handknit Sweater
Couch
Teddy Bear
Silk Tie

(4 rows affected)
```

If you plan to include more than one table, or if you wish to limit the result set, you will need to get acquainted with the WHERE clause. This clause provides the capability to specify filter conditions. If you were to include the TYPE table, you would need to specify that the it_ty_id_ column in the ITEM table is a reference to the ty_id column in the TYPE table. The WHERE clause uses expressions like the following:

```
it_ty_id_ = ty_id
```

Multiple expressions in the WHERE clause can be separated by an AND. The OR conjunction may also be used, and expressions can also be grouped with parentheses to force precedence. If you feel that it improves the readability of your code, you can include the name of each table in the expression. When you do this, you must put the name of the table in front of the field name and separate them with the "." character (period, full stop):

```
item.it_ty_id_ = type.ty_id
```

Here's an example of an SQL SELECT statement that combines the ITEM and TYPE tables:

```
SELECT it_name, ty_name
   FROM item, type
   WHERE item.it_ty_id_ = type.ty_id
```

Here are the results of the above query:

```
it_name                                     ty_name
------------------------------------------- ---------------------

Handknit Sweater                            Clothing
Silk Tie                                    Clothing
Couch                                       Furniture
Teddy Bear                                  Faithful Companion


(4 rows affected)
```

If the WHERE clause does not specify a *join condition* for each table, strange things begin to happen. Each row in each table is matched with each row in each other table, producing what is known as a *Cartesian product*. For example, you might attempt to issue the previous query without any join expression (don't laugh, this sort of mistake is common—and a pretty good first guess for lots of people learning the ropes):

```
SELECT it_name, ty_name
   FROM item, type
```

You would get the following results:

```
it_name                                     ty_name
------------------------------------------- ---------------------

Handknit Sweater                            Clothing
Couch                                       Clothing
```

```
Teddy Bear                      Clothing
Silk Tie                        Clothing
Handknit Sweater                Furniture
Couch                           Furniture
Teddy Bear                      Furniture
Silk Tie                        Furniture
Handknit Sweater                Faithful Companion
Couch                           Faithful Companion
Teddy Bear                      Faithful Companion
Silk Tie                        Faithful Companion
```

```
(12 rows affected)
```

This result is probably not what you want at all. Note that there are three rows in the TYPE table and four rows in the ITEM table. Multiply the two, and you get 12. Notice how each item is matched once to each type. These results are not very useful, are they? Without some sort of join condition, it's hard to get useful results.

A join condition is a sort of filter. Filters in the WHERE clause may also be used to restrict the set of values that are returned. Here's an example that retrieves only those items that are clothing:

```
SELECT it_name
   FROM item, type
   WHERE item.it_ty_id_ = type.ty_id
   AND    type.ty_name    = 'Clothing'
```

Here are the results:

```
it_name
---------------------------------------
Handknit Sweater
Silk Tie
```

The Last Great Feature of the SQL SELECT statement that you will see involves the aggregate functions. The SELECT statement provides a GROUP BY clause, which causes all of the rows in the result set to be condensed into summary rows. The aggregate functions, such as MIN, MAX, SUM, and COUNT, can be used to return special calculated columns based on the summary values.

The following SQL SELECT statement can be used to get a list of all the types and how many items belong to the category represented by the type:

```
SELECT ty_name, total=COUNT(*)
   FROM item, type
   WHERE item.it_ty_id_ = type.ty_id
   GROUP BY ty_name
```

This statement produces the following results:

```
ty_name                total
---------------------- --------------

Clothing                   2
Faithful Companion         1
Furniture                  1
```

This SELECT statement also introduces the column label, which allows you to bind a column name to an expression in the select statement. Some implementations use the AS keyword, and the select statement would look like:

```
SELECT ty_name, COUNT(*) AS total
   FROM item, type
   WHERE item.it_ty_id_ = type.ty_id
   GROUP BY ty_name
```

In some implementations, the AS keyword is not required, so you could just as well say:

```
SELECT ty_name, COUNT(*) total
   FROM item, type
   WHERE item.it_ty_id_ = type.ty_id
   GROUP BY ty_name
```

Here's an SQL SELECT that will query all of the stains, items, and types:

```
select it_name, ty_name, st_name
   FROM item, type, stain, stainxrf
   WHERE it_ty_id_ = ty_id
     AND sx_it_id_ = it_id
     AND sx_st_id_ = st_id
```

And here are the results of that query:

```
it_name                             ty_name                 st_name
----------------------------------  ----------------------  ---------
Handknit Sweater                    Clothing                Merlot
Handknit Sweater                    Clothing                Jelly
Handknit Sweater                    Clothing                Coffee
Silk Tie                            Clothing                Jelly
Silk Tie                            Clothing                Ketchup
Couch                               Furniture               Ketchup
Couch                               Furniture               Coffee
Couch                               Furniture               Unknown
Teddy Bear                          Faithful Companion      Jelly
Teddy Bear                          Faithful Companion      Coffee
```

There's a lot more to the SQL SELECT statement—a lot more power under the hood. You've seen enough to get you through many of the examples in this book. Appendix D is an SQL reference that you might find helpful.

**Using SQL to Update Data in Tables**   You may find from time to time that you need to change the data in one or more rows. The UPDATE statement allows you to do this with ease. It can be used to update a single row or multiple rows. In each case, you will need to employ a WHERE clause, which is very similar to the one found in the SELECT statement. Without a WHERE clause, you will update every row in the table. If this is your intention, then by all means, make it so. The UPDATE statement takes this form:

```
UPDATE table-name
SET column-identifier = expression
    [, column-identifier = expression]
    [WHERE search-condition]
```

The search condition is optional; if you do not specify one, the entire table is updated. Here's an example that updates the TYPE table to prefix each ty_name with an asterisk (I'm not sure why you'd want to do this ...):

```
UPDATE type
   SET ty_name = "*" + ty_name
```

You can also specify a filter condition in the WHERE clause. An SQL UPDATE statement follows that only prepends the asterisk if that type occurs more than once in the ITEM table. This example also introduces a subquery. A *subquery* is a SELECT statement embedded in the UPDATE statement and bound to a column in the update table with the IN clause. A subquery can be pretty useful, especially when you want to include criteria from another table.

The HAVING clause, also introduced in the next example, is more or less like the WHERE clause, but it is used to filter the results of the query, whereas the WHERE clause is used to filter the query before the results are determined. Consequently, the HAVING clause is identical to a WHERE clause unless there is some sort of GROUP BY in effect.

```
UPDATE type
    SET ty_name = "*" + ty_name
    WHERE ty_id IN
    (SELECT it_ty_id_
        FROM item
        GROUP BY it_ty_id_
        HAVING COUNT(*) > 1)
```

The subquery in this UPDATE statement will select all of the rows in the ITEM table because there is no WHERE clause. But, it only chooses to emit those results (which are grouped by it_ty_id_) that have a count(*) greater than one. This distinction can have a tremendous impact on the performance of your system. If you issue a query that selects 20,000 rows but only emits 1, it can really slow things down!

Subqueries can be quite useful in many contexts. They may also be used in a SELECT statement's WHERE clause:

```
SELECT *
    FROM type
    WHERE ty_id IN
    (SELECT it_ty_id_
        FROM item
        GROUP BY it_ty_id_
        HAVING COUNT(*) > 1)
```

**Using SQL to Delete Rows from Tables** At some time, you may wish to delete rows from your tables. The DELETE statement looks like:

```
DELETE FROM table-name
    [WHERE search-condition]
```

Any of the search conditions shown for the UPDATE statement will work with the DELETE statement. Here's an example that will delete every stain from the furniture, which is a lot cheaper than hiring a cleaning service:

```
DELETE FROM stainxrf
    WHERE sx_it_id_ IN
    (SELECT it_id
        FROM item, type
        WHERE it_ty_id_ = ty_id
          AND ty_name = "Furniture")
```

You've seen a useful, if not comprehensive, explanation of some of the more common SQL statements and their features. For further study, however, see AppendixD, which is an SQL Reference. SQL is a powerful, set-based language that will let you manipulate your data in strange and exotic ways.

# JDBC

## The Banshee Screams for Database Meat

One of the biggest drags in database development can be the learning curve associated with each database package you encounter in your life (your life as a computer programmer, that is. After you retire and open a funky coffee shop/bookstore, it's all over; you can hire people to deal with your databases...). Each database vendor supplies a different, proprietary API. If you want to do any programming against one vendor's database product, you will need to learn your way around that API. This may seem pointless because, at a certain level, most database APIs offer the same features. They usually implement most of the features of the standard SQL, and sometimes a few features you didn't necessarily want. So why can't we all just get along?

Well, I'm sure you can see where this is going. Unless you live in a cave, you've probably heard about such things as DBI (Perl), ODBC (C/C++, Visual Basic, etc.), and JDBC (Java). All of these are APIs designed to provide database independence for developers. They define universal

27

means of issuing queries, retrieving result sets, and making discoveries about database metadata.

ODBC is an open standard developed by Microsoft; it has done really well, considering the difficulty Microsoft itself has had gaining acceptance and respect outside the Win32 community. Most people usually can't say the words "Microsoft" and "open standard" in the same sentence without causing permanent mental paralysis. It is rumored that all front ends to Cyc (http://www.cyc.com/) must filter out any sentence containing those words, or they will bring down Cyc. The resultant electronic mental constipation would cause an EMP that will affect electronic devices within a 300-mile radius.

Nevertheless, Microsoft did base ODBC on an open standard, and ODBC has been incredibly well received in the Win32 community, as well as in OS/2, Unix, and Macintosh circles. A variety of vendors supply ODBC driver managers and drivers for these platforms; both the DBI and JDBC are based on ODBC.

# Enough with the Buzzwords, History, and Pedagogy! What the %$&? Is JDBC?

I'm glad you asked. JDBC boils down to two things. First, it is a *call-level SQL API* for Java. All that means is that JDBC is concerned with executing SQL statements and sending you the results. Secondly, JDBC lets you write code that works with all JDBC-supported database products.

How does it do this? The JDBC driver classes are simply abstract classes with methods like `executeQuery()`, `next()`, and `getString()`. These commands execute an SQL query, retrieve a single row from a result set, and return a String object, respectively. It's the responsibility of the driver developer to implement each and every one of these methods in their driver. Within those classes, all of the ugly stuff that actually passed to the database product is dealt with. From your end, you need to make the JDBC calls, and the driver makes the vendor-specific calls on your behalf.

This approach insulates you from the vendor's API. Assuming the vendor's API isn't sick, bloated code, you shouldn't suffer any noticeable performance degradation due to the extra layer. Drivers that sit on top of an existing API don't need to contain a whole lot of code. You can experience this firsthand in Chapter 7.

# It Cuts Both Ways: Stored Procs and Database Independence

I was downing a glass of absinthe while talking with my good friend Srini Rao. We had somehow started a discussion of JDBC and database independence. We were in the last 25% (anyone who's worked with a Gannt chart knows exactly how much that means :) of a complex and stressful Web database project; I had suggested that we vent our frustrations by stomping a couple of mimes at the South Street Seaport. Fortunately, I was sidetracked by our discussion of JDBC.

"So, you're writing a book on JDBC, huh?" he asked.

"Well, it was gonna be just a book on Java databases, but it looks like JDBC is 'the word' as far as that's concerned."

"JDBC really wouldn't be that useful on a project like this...." I knew he was taunting me.

"What are you talking about, man?"

He went on to explain that in a major project like this, no one codes SQL statements on the front end; the front end is pretty much insulated from metadata, and all data is inserted and retrieved using stored procedures. *Stored procedures* are programs supported by many database servers, such as Sybase or Oracle. They're programs, written in the server's SQL dialect, that are compiled on the server and run on the server. They can return result sets just like an SQL SELECT statement, but they have a number of advantages over directly executed SQL.

The most important advantage in an environment like the Internet, or even on an Intranet, is the security advantage. To execute commands on your server, a remote applet or application needs to log into your server. If it is to update and retrieve data from tables, it needs permission to do so. A crazy person could write his or her own front end and trash the data by sending in his or her own SQL statements. And you know how important it is to keep crazy people away from your data.

With stored procs, you can actually *take away the right to modify data directly* and allow the user to have only what is known as *execute permission*. That means that the only interaction the user can have with the database is through stored procedures that you have written, which gives you a significant amount of control over what the user can do.

Even in these cases, I maintain that JDBC can be useful. It still divorces the developer from the business of learning database APIs; he or she can get on with the work of programming databases. JDBC supports stored procedures very well. Even in an environment where the front end is not issuing SQL statements and polling metadata, the ease and simplicity of JDBC provides enough of an advantage to make its use worthwhile.

# Getting and Installing JDBC

The JDBC driver manager is available from:

```
http://splash.javasoft.com/jdbc
```

From that URL, you may view some brief information about JDBC and download the latest version of the JDBC driver manager. The JDBC driver manager includes a series of classes that make up the JDBC driver manager (`java.sql.DriverManager`) itself and all of the abstract classes for the JDBC drivers. You may extract the archive anywhere you like, but you will need to add the `jdbc\classes` (on Win32) or the jdbc/classes (under Unix) directory to your CLASSPATH. The JDK 1.1 will include the JDBC classes, eliminating the need to download JDBC.

If you were a Win32 user who extracted the JDBC distribution to C:\LOCAL, it would have created the following directory (among others):

```
C:\LOCAL\jdbc\classes
```

You should add this directory to your CLASSPATH environment variable or move everything in that directory into a directory contained in one of your CLASSPATH directories.

If you were a Unix user who extracted the JDBC distribution to /usr/local, it would have created the following directory (among others):

```
/usr/local/jdbc/classes
```

You should add this directory to your CLASSPATH environment variable or move everything in that directory into a directory contained in one of your CLASSPATH directories.

Users of other operating systems (Macintosh, OS/2, Timex Sinclair) should follow their instructions for setting the CLASSPATH variable, which should be included with the JDK distribution.

# Getting Drivers

Well, before you can plug into a database system, you'll need to get your hands on a driver. A variety of drivers are presently available. As time marches on, more will become available. Here are a few drivers that you might find useful.

## The tinySQL JDBC Driver

The example code for this book includes an extremely lightweight SQL database engine written in Java called tinySQL. It also includes a JDBC driver. Many of the JDBC examples in this book will work with tinySQL. However, tinySQL is more of a learning tool, and it is not intended for use in a multiuser environment; it certainly wouldn't do as a production data server in its present incarnation. However, it's great for learning your way around SQL and JDBC, and it is small enough that you can become familiar with its source code quickly. At some point, it will grow and mature until it is the coolest thing since sliced marzipan.

To use tinySQL, which is merely an SQL layer to non-SQL data sources, you will need a tinySQL driver. The textFile driver, which allows you to use simple text files as databases, is included on the Java Database Programming website. Chapter 6 covers tinySQL in great detail.

## The mSQL JDBC Driver

If you have access to an mSQL server (see Chapter 9 for information on getting and installing mSQL), you can use George Reese's mSQL JDBC driver. You will need a machine running OS/2, Windows NT, Windows 95, or some flavor of Unix to run mSQL. Regardless of the server platform, the mSQL JDBC driver can be run from any Java-supported platform, provided you have access to an mSQL server. You can get the mSQL JDBC driver from:

```
http://www.imaginary.com/~borg/Java/java.html
```

## The JDBC-ODBC Bridge

Last, but not least, you can also use the JDBC-ODBC bridge, available from Sun and Intersolv at:

```
http://splash.javasoft.com/jdbc
```

The JDBC-ODBC bridge runs on either Solaris or Win32, and it requires that you have an ODBC driver manager and one or more ODBC drivers installed on each machine that runs your applets or applications. However, using WebLogic's T3Server, you can set up a server that will allow you to write Java applets or applications that can be run from any supported Java platform and that does not require the ODBC drivers to be installed on that machine. Chapter 11 explores this and related solutions.

# Picking a Driver

Depending on the operating system you use, you might not have much choice as to which JDBC driver you use. If you want to use JDBC-ODBC, you must run Win32 or Solaris. If you want to use mSQL-JDBC, you must have access to Unix, Win32, or an OS/2 box that runs mSQL. You can run the mSQL-JDBC client from any Java-supported OS on a machine that can connect to your mSQL server. If the computer on which you are running mSQL can support Java, then things should be pretty easy.

If you don't fall into any of the above two categories, or if you have trouble installing either of these drivers, you can still do quite a bit with tinySQL-JDBC. Even though it supports only a minuscule subset of ANSI SQL, you can still learn SQL and JDBC with it. Many of the examples in this book will work with it, and any exceptions will be noted.

# Installing tinySQL and the tinySQL textFile JDBC Driver

If you've extracted the example source code for this book, you've done most of the work needed to install tinySQL. You'll simply need to add two directories to your CLASSPATH; the eg\ch06 and eg\ch07 directories.

If you are a Win32 user and you extracted the examples to C:\USERS\DEFAULT, it would have created the following directories (among others):

```
C:\USERS\DEFAULT\eg\ch06
C:\USERS\DEFAULT\eg\ch07
```

You should add these directories to your CLASSPATH environment variable, separated by a semicolon, as in the following example:

```
CLASSPATH=c:\java\lib\classes;.;c:\book\eg\ch06;c:\book\eg\ch07
```

If you are a Unix user and you extracted the examples to /home/foobar, it would have created the following directories (among others):

```
/home/foobar/eg/ch06
/home/foobar/eg/ch07
```

You should add these directories to your CLASSPATH environment variable, separated by a colon, as in this example::

```
CLASSPATH=/usr/local/classes:.:/home/foobar/eg/ch06:/home/foobar/eg/ch07
```

Users of other operating systems should follow their instructions for setting the CLASS-PATH variable, which should be included with the JDK distribution.

Once you have done this and are running in a shell (Unix) or command window (Win32) that has inherited the correct CLASSPATH, you should be able to issue the command:

```
java textFile
```

If everything was installed correctly, you should see the following response:

```
textFile driver installed correctly.
```

You can test the JDBC driver for the tinySQL textFile engine with:

```
java   testTextFile
```

If everything was installed correctly, you should see the following response:

```
textFile JDBC driver installed correctly.
```

This indicates that the tinySQL engine, the textFile tinySQL driver, and the textFile JDBC driver were installed correctly. If you see some other response, review the previous instructions, check the FAQ (http://www.ids.net/~bjepson/javadb), or send me an e-mail (bjepson@ids.net) if you are still having problems.

# Installing the mSQL JDBC Driver

You can download the most recent version of the mSQL JDBC driver from:

```
http://www.imaginary.com/~borg/Java/java.html
```

Once you have extracted it, it will create the directory

```
mSQL-JDBC.x.y.z
```

where x.y.z is the current version of mSQL JDBC. A classes directory will appear under the one shown above; you should add the full path of that directory to your CLASSPATH.

The mSQL JDBC driver comes with two test programs: Select.java and Update.java. Both of these expect that you will have created a table called t_test in a database called Testdb. The table should be created with the following CREATE TABLE statement (make sure you are in the Testdb database when you run this):

```
CREATE TABLE t_test
    (test_id INT, test_val CHAR(30))
```

For more information on issuing mSQL queries, see Chapter 9. In order to run the tests, you will need to modify the following line in both Select.java and Update.java:

```
String url = "jdbc:msql://athens.imaginary.com:4333/Testdb";
```

You should replace the hostname (`athens.imaginary.com`) and the port number (4333) with the hostname and port number of your mSQL server. See Chapter 9 for information on installing and configuring mSQL. Once you have changed the programs, you can compile them with javac and run them with java (run Update first, so that Select will have something to query).

If everything is installed correctly, the examples should run without errors. If not, you may need to check the release notes for mSQL or mSQL JDBC. If you are completely stuck, check this book's FAQ (`http://www.ids.net/~bjepson/javadb`) or send me an e-mail (bjepson@ids.net).

# Installing the JDBC-ODBC Bridge

The JDBC-ODBC bridge is available from

```
http://splash.javasoft.com/jdbc
```

As its name implies, the JDBC-ODBC bridge is a driver that provides an interface to ODBC drivers. Many database packages come with ODBC drivers, such as FoxPro, dBase, Interbase, Sybase, and Oracle. You will need to install the 32-bit ODBC driver manager and 32-bit driver according to your vendor's instructions. The JDBC-ODBC bridge does not work with 16-bit drivers.

Once you extract the distribution, you should read the file:

JDBC-ODBC-RELEASE-NOTES

This file includes a section titled "installation," which explains how to install the Java classes and the native libraries that come with the bridge.

# Registering Drivers with java.sql.DriverManager

In order for the JDBC driver manager to know which drivers are available, you will need to "register" them. You can do this two ways. The first way, but one that requires configuration for each user, is to list the drivers in the "sql.drivers" system property. You can do this by editing the properties file in your .hotjava directory—note that this will affect only applets run under the appletviewer. If you want your Java application to pick up a driver from a system property, you will need to start it with the

```
-Dproperty=value
```

option, as in:

```
java -Djdbc.drivers=textFile mySQLApplication
```

The second way (and I think the better way) to register a driver is to include the statement

```
Class.forName("driver_name");
```

in your application. This statement will dynamically load each driver specified in such a fashion, and it allows the JDBC driver manager to load each one. You will notice that some of the examples include lines such as:

```
Class.forName("textFileDriver");           // the tinySQL textFile driver
Class.forName("jdbc.odbc.JdbcOdbcDriver");  // JDBC-ODBC bridge
Class.forName("imaginary.sql.iMsqlDriver"); // mSQL
```

This statement will cause the example to try to load each driver in succession until it finds one that can handle whatever JDBC URL you passed it. If, for some reason, you don't have one of the drivers installed, you should comment out the pertinent line, or you will receive errors when you try to run your program.

It's a good idea to comment out all but the one you will use because the JDBC driver manager will try to load each one, which can slow down your programs.

# Opening a Connection

Once you have installed JDBC and the drivers of your choice, you're ready to take that big step: making a database connection. Here's a little Java program that does nothing but connect to and disconnect from a data source. The connection is handled by Driver-Manager.getConnection(). It looks at the URL and asks each of the drivers you have loaded whether they are capable of handling the URL. If it finds a suitable driver, then it makes the connection. If it doesn't, then it throws an exception. Note that the Connection object is closed when you are through with it; this is good practice, as some drivers will require this in order to clean up properly.

```java
import java.net.URL;
import java.sql.*;


class jdbc_connect {

    public static void main(String argv[]) {

        // the url comes in from argv[0], so
        // error out if there was no url passed
        //
        if (argv.length == 0) {
            System.err.println("Usage:");
            System.err.println("");
            System.err.println("java jdbc_connect URL");
            System.exit(1);
        }

        try {

            // register all of the JDBC classes you might use
            // you can comment out or remove the ones you
            // are not using.
            //
            Class.forName("textFileDriver");          // the tinySQL textFile driver
```

```java
        Class.forName("jdbc.odbc.JdbcOdbcDriver");  // JDBC-ODBC bridge
        Class.forName("imaginary.sql.iMsqlDriver"); // mSQL

        String url = argv[0];

        // the user might have passed in a user name or password,
        // so try to read those in, as well
        //
        String user, pwd;
        if (argv.length > 1) {
          user = argv[1];
        } else {
          user = "";
        }
        if (argv.length > 2) {
          pwd = argv[2];
        } else {
          pwd = "";
        }


        // if we don't throw an exception here, then the
        // connection was made without a hitch
        //
        Connection con = DriverManager.getConnection(url, user, pwd);
        con.close();
        System.out.println("Connection successful.");
      }
    catch( Exception e ) {
        System.out.println(e.getMessage());
        e.printStackTrace();
      }
  }
}
```

Note that I load all three JDBC drivers. As mentioned earlier, if you did not install all of these drivers on your system, you will need to remove any `Class.forName()` invocation that loads an uninstalled driver. Once you have done this, you can recompile this program with:

```
javac jdbc_connect.java
```

## JDBC URLs—tinySQL

To execute the previous program, you will need to invoke it with a JDBC URL. The JDBC URL is composed of at least two parts; the first is the JDBC protocol indicator (`jdbc:`). Next, the subprotocol indicator must follow. After that, any other components are driver specific. In the case of the tinySQL driver, it is simply:

```
jdbc:tinySQL
```

## JDBC URLs—the JDBC-ODBC Bridge

The JDBC-ODBC bridge requires, at the bare minimum, a data source, as in:

```
jdbc:odbc:MY_DATA_SOURCE
```

Some data sources require additional arguments, such as user name and password, which are semicolon-delimited:

```
jdbc:odbc:MY_DATA_SOURCE;UID=bjepson;password=secret
```

You should consult your database vendor's documentation for additional parameters.

## JDBC URLs—the mSQL JDBC Driver

The mSQL JDBC driver has a slightly more complex URL. You must supply the hostname and port for the mSQL server. Most installations will use the root port, which is 1112. If the mSQL server is running as a mortal (non-root) user, it will usually use port 4333. After the hostname and port, you must supply the database name:

```
jdbc:msql://some.host.com:1112/my_database
```

## Running the Example Program

Once you have compiled jdbc_connect, you should run it with the following command:

```
java jdbc_connect URL username password
```

Although the JDBC-ODBC driver allows you to include the username as part of the URL, you can also pass it in on the command line, and it will get passed to the

`DriverManager.getConnection()`method, which will accept a username and a password along with the URL. Not all JDBC drivers allow you to put the username and password in the URL; in some cases, the `getConnection()` method may be the only way to send the username and password.

If you can execute jdbc_connect and it displays "Connection successful.", then you have successfully configured your system to execute queries against JDBC data sources.

# Issuing Update Statements

A certain set of SQL statements can be classified as updates, in that they are not expected to return rows. Although the SQL UPDATE statement falls into this category, the category and the UPDATE statement should not be confused, since INSERT, CREATE TABLE, and a variety of other statements are considered updates as well.

JDBC provides a method for issuing updates that expect no results. The Statement object, which is provided by the Connection object, provides an `executeUpdate()` method. To execute it, you will first need to obtain a Statement object. After you have made a successful connection, you can retrieve a Statement object with a line like:

```
Statement stmt = con.createStatement();
```

Then, you can issue updates until you are blue in the face:

```
stmt.executeUpdate("CREATE TABLE test (name CHAR(25), id INT)");
stmt.executeUpdate("INSERT INTO test (name, id) VALUES('Brian', 1)");
stmt.executeUpdate("INSERT INTO test (name, id) VALUES('Hank',  2)");
```

When you're done with the Statement object, you should close it, just as you do with a Connection object:

```
stmt.close();
```

The following Java application, `jdbc_update.java`, illustrates this by creating a table called test and inserting some rows into it. Notice how an attempt is made to drop the table before creating it; any exception is ignored, just in case the table doesn't already exist. The instructions outlined in the section titled "Opening a Connection" apply here because the same connection method is used. You should comment out or remove any `Class.forName()` references to drivers you have not installed.

```
import java.net.URL;
import java.sql.*;

class jdbc_update {

  public static void main(String argv[]) {

    // the url comes in from argv[0], so
    // error out if there was no url passed
    //
    if (argv.length == 0) {
      System.err.println("Usage:");
      System.err.println("");
      System.err.println("java jdbc_connect URL");
      System.exit(1);
    }

    try {

      // register all of the JDBC classes you might use
      // you can comment out or remove the ones you
      // are not using.
      //
      Class.forName("textFileDriver");              // the tinySQL textFile driver
      Class.forName("jdbc.odbc.JdbcOdbcDriver");  // JDBC-ODBC bridge
      Class.forName("imaginary.sql.iMsqlDriver"); // mSQL

      String url = argv[0];

      // the user might have passed in a user name or password,
      // so try to read those in, as well
      //
      String user, pwd;
      if (argv.length > 1) {
        user = argv[1];
      } else {
```

```
    user = "";
  }
  if (argv.length > 2) {
    pwd = argv[2];
  } else {
    pwd = "";
  }

  // make a connection to the specified URL
  //
  Connection con = DriverManager.getConnection(url, user, pwd);

  // get a Statement object from the Connection
  //
  Statement stmt = con.createStatement();

  // ignore any exception for DROP TABLE;
  // it will most assuredly throw one if
  // the table does not exist
  //
  try {
    stmt.executeUpdate("DROP TABLE test");
  } catch (Exception e) {
    // do nothing
  }

  // create a table
  stmt.executeUpdate("CREATE TABLE test (name CHAR(25), id INT)");

  // insert a couple of rows.
  stmt.executeUpdate("INSERT INTO test (name, id) VALUES('Brian', 1)");
  stmt.executeUpdate("INSERT INTO test (name, id) VALUES('Hank', 2)");

  stmt.close();
  con.close();
```

**Continued**

```
        System.out.println("Operation successful.");


      }
    catch( Exception e ) {
      System.out.println(e.getMessage());
      e.printStackTrace();
    }
  }


}
```

# Issuing Update Statements, Part II

It can be quite useful to determine the number of rows that an update statement affects.
The Statement object provides a method, `getUpdateCount()`, to do just that. It returns an
integer value after any sort of update operation that can be used to determine whether or
not and how many rows were affected by the operation. Here's a little example which does
just that. Note that neither the tinySQL JDBC driver nor the version of the mSQL JDBC
driver that's current as of this writing support this feature.

```
import java.net.URL;
import java.sql.*;

class jdbc_update2 {

  public static void main(String argv[]) {

    // the url comes in from argv[0], so
    // error out if there was no url passed
    //
    if (argv.length == 0) {
      System.err.println("Usage:");
      System.err.println("");
      System.err.println("java jdbc_connect URL");
      System.exit(1);
```

```
}

try {

  // register all of the JDBC classes you might use
  // you can comment out or remove the ones you
  // are not using.
  //
  Class.forName("textFileDriver");                // the tinySQL textFile driver
  Class.forName("jdbc.odbc.JdbcOdbcDriver");   // JDBC-ODBC bridge
  Class.forName("imaginary.sql.iMsqlDriver"); // mSQL

  String url = argv[0];

  // the user might have passed in a user name or password,
  // so try to read those in, as well
  //
  String user, pwd;
  if (argv.length > 1) {
    user = argv[1];
  } else {
    user = "";
  }
  if (argv.length > 2) {
    pwd = argv[2];
  } else {
    pwd = "";
  }

  // make a connection to the specified URL
  //
  Connection con = DriverManager.getConnection(url, user, pwd);

  // get a Statement object from the Connection
  //
  Statement stmt = con.createStatement();
```

```
        // issue a silly update
        //
        stmt.executeUpdate("UPDATE test SET name = 'Joe' WHERE name = 'Hank'");

        int cnt = stmt.getUpdateCount();

        stmt.close();
        con.close();

        System.out.println("Operation successful.");
        System.out.println(cnt + " row(s) affected.");

      }
    catch( Exception e ) {
      System.out.println(e.getMessage());
      e.printStackTrace();
    }
  }

}
```

# Performing a Query and Retrieving Results

Now that you've put some data into the table, it wouldn't be fair if I didn't let you get data out. The method used to execute a query looks pretty similar to `executeUpdate()`, except for its return value. Unlike `executeUpdate()`, `executeQuery()` returns a ResultSet object:

```
ResultSet rs = stmt.executeQuery("SELECT name, id FROM test");
```

To fetch the first row, you should invoke the `next()` method of the result set:

```
rs.next();
```

If there are any more rows, `next()` can be used retrieve them and prepare them for retrieval with one of the `get*()` methods. Because `next()` returns a Boolean value and does not throw an exception when there are no more rows, you can safely use `next()` to test for more rows in a while loop or similar situation. Once you have used `next()` to fetch at least one row, you can use one of the `get*()` methods, such as `getString()` or `getInt()`:

```
String name = rs.getString("name");
int    id   = rs.getInt("id");
```

Other methods are available for retrieving different data types (long, double, etc.) from the result set, and they are covered in greater detail in Appendix B, the JDBC Driver Reference. The following Java application, jdbc_query.java, queries the table that was created and populated in the previous example:

```
import java.net.URL;
import java.sql.*;

class jdbc_query {

  public static void main(String argv[]) {

    // the url comes in from argv[0], so
    // error out if there was no url passed
    //
    if (argv.length == 0) {
      System.err.println("Usage:");
      System.err.println("");
      System.err.println("java jdbc_connect URL");
      System.exit(1);
    }

    try {

      // register all of the JDBC classes you might use
      // you can comment out or remove the ones you
      // are not using.
      //
      Class.forName("textFileDriver");               // the tinySQL textFile driver
      Class.forName("jdbc.odbc.JdbcOdbcDriver");  // JDBC-ODBC bridge
```

**Continued**

```java
Class.forName("imaginary.sql.iMsqlDriver"); // mSQL

String url = argv[0];

// the user might have passed in a user name or password,
// so try to read those in, as well
//
String user, pwd;
if (argv.length > 1) {
  user = argv[1];
} else {
  user = "";
}
if (argv.length > 2) {
  pwd = argv[2];
} else {
  pwd = "";
}

// make a connection to the specified URL
//
Connection con = DriverManager.getConnection(url, user, pwd);

// get a Statement object from the Connection
//
Statement stmt = con.createStatement();

// Execute a query and get the result set
//
ResultSet rs = stmt.executeQuery("SELECT name, id FROM test");

// Display column headers
//
System.out.println("Name                          Id ");
System.out.println("========================= ===");
```

```
    // process each row
    //
    while(rs.next()) {

        // retrieve each column by name
        //
        String name = rs.getString("name");
        int    id   = rs.getInt("id");

        // display each row
        //
        System.out.println(name + " " + id);

    }

    stmt.close();
    con.close();

    }
    catch( Exception e ) {
        System.out.println(e.getMessage());
        e.printStackTrace();
    }
  }

}
```

# ResultSet Pitfalls

There are some pitfalls to avoid when working with ResultSets. Some drivers have trouble if you read the column values in a different order than they were specified in the query. If, for example, you issued

```
SELECT name, id
    FROM test
```

you could run into trouble with some drivers if you tried to do the following:

```
int    id   = rs.getInt("id");
String name = rs.getString("name");
```

Instead, you should take care to perform your get*() methods in the same order in which the columns appeared in the query, left to right:

```
int    id   = rs.getInt("id");
String name = rs.getString("name");
```

Also, you may read each column only once per row. Until you advance the row pointer with the next() method, you should not attempt to re-read a column. In this instance, you should assign the column value to a variable or object if you think you will need it more than once.

# Prepared Statements (no mSQL, no tinySQL)

Prepared statements are an advanced feature that JDBC drivers offer for such database servers as SQL Server and Oracle. Unfortunately, neither the mSQL JDBC driver nor the tinySQL JDBC driver offers these features. Prepared statements give you the ability to precompile an SQL statement that you will be issuing quite often; a prepared statement clearly has performance advantages because you don't need to compile it each time. It also allows you to define positional parameters, thus making your code somewhat more readable.

Like the Statement object, a PreparedStatement object is obtained from the Connection object:

```
PreparedStatement pstmt = con.prepareStatement(
                        "INSERT INTO test (name, id) VALUES(?, ?)");
```

Notice the two question marks (?) in the statement. When it comes time to execute this statement, you will need to assign values to these parameters. They are set with a method such as SetString() or SetInt(), as in:

```
pstmt.setString(1, "Ford");
pstmt.setInt(2, 1);
```

Once you have assigned each parameter, you can execute the query with:

```
pstmt.executeUpdate();
```

If the example were a query with a result set, you could also use `executeQuery()` and retrieve a result set for processing.

Here's a sample program (jdbc_prepared_statement.java) that uses elements from a multidimensional array to populate the test table with usernames and IDs. Because it is an array of String objects, the IDs must be converted to int values using `Integer.parseInt()`. After you run this, you might want to re-run jdbc_query to query the table and see the changes.

```java
import java.net.URL;
import java.sql.*;

class jdbc_prepared_statement {

  public static void main(String argv[]) {

    // the url comes in from argv[0], so
    // error out if there was no url passed
    //
    if (argv.length == 0) {
      System.err.println("Usage:");
      System.err.println("");
      System.err.println("java jdbc_connect URL");
      System.exit(1);
    }

    try {

      // register all of the JDBC classes you might use
      // you can comment out or remove the ones you
      // are not using.
      //
      Class.forName("jdbc.odbc.JdbcOdbcDriver");  // JDBC-ODBC bridge

      String url = argv[0];
```

**Continued**

```java
// the user might have passed in a user name or password,
// so try to read those in, as well
//
String user, pwd;
if (argv.length > 1) {
  user = argv[1];
} else {
  user = "";
}
if (argv.length > 2) {
  pwd = argv[2];
} else {
  pwd = "";
}

// make a connection to the specified URL
//
Connection con = DriverManager.getConnection(url, user, pwd);

// get a Statement object from the Connection
//
Statement stmt = con.createStatement();

// ignore any exception for DROP TABLE;
// it will most assuredly throw one if
// the table does not exist
//
try {
  stmt.executeUpdate("DROP TABLE test");
} catch (Exception e) {
  // do nothing
}

// create a table
//
```

```java
stmt.executeUpdate("CREATE TABLE test (name CHAR(25), id INT)");

// here's some sample data
//
String data[][] = {
                    {"Ford",           "100"},
                    {"Arthur",         "110"},
                    {"Trillian",       "120"},
                    {"Zaphod",         "130"},
                    {"Marvin",         "140"},
                    {"Benjy",          "150"},
                    {"Frankie",        "160"},
                    {"Slartibartfast", "170"}
};

// create a prepared statement to execute the update
//
PreparedStatement pstmt = con.prepareStatement(
                    "INSERT INTO test (name, id) VALUES(?, ?)");

// for each row in the data[][] array,
// add a row to the table using executeUpdate()
//
for (int i=0; i < data.length; i++) {

  // set the first parameter to a String,
  // the name of the person
  //
  pstmt.setString(1, data[i][0]);

  // set the second parameter to an int,
  // the ID of the person
  //
  pstmt.setInt(2, Integer.parseInt(data[i][1]));
```

**Continued**

```
        // execute the prepared statement. The parameters will
        // be inserted each time it runs.
        //
        pstmt.executeUpdate();

    }

    stmt.close();
    con.close();

    System.out.println("Operation successful.");

    }
    catch( Exception e ) {
      System.out.println(e.getMessage());
      e.printStackTrace();
    }

  }

}
```

Under Microsoft SQL Server, using the JDBC-ODBC bridge, the prepared statement is generated as the following stored procedure:

```
create proc #odbc#javated40236
   @P1 char(255), @P2 int
   as INSERT INTO test (name, id) VALUES(@P1, @P2)
```

Microsoft SQL Server does not follow the same prepared statement paradigm of ODBC, so ODBC actually creates the stored procedure itself. Because the parameters are not known when the statement is prepared, the stored procedure is not created until all parameters have been set, and the executeUpdate() or executeQuery() has been issued. Given vendor-specific versions of JDBC drivers, the prepared statement implementation may differ slightly more than one that follows ODBC, such as the JDBC-ODBC bridge.

# Callable Statements (no mSQL, no tinySQL)

The CallableStatement object allows you to easily work with stored procedures that return output parameters. Like the PreparedStatement, you must register parameters, but the CallableStatement introduces a new method, `registerOutParameter()`. This takes two parameters: the position of the output parameter, and the java.sql.Types type, which corresponds to the parameter's data type, as in:

```
cstmt.registerOutParameter(2, java.sql.Types.VARCHAR);
```

Here's an example that first drops and creates a stored procedure called test_sp. Then, a CallableStatement is created that executes the stored procedure and retrieves the output parameter. Note that this is Sybase or Microsoft SQL Server syntax in the stored procedure; the syntax for stored procedures will vary with your database product:

```java
import java.net.URL;
import java.sql.*;

class jdbc_callable {

  public static void main(String argv[]) {

    // the url comes in from argv[0], so
    // error out if there was no url passed
    //
    if (argv.length == 0) {
      System.err.println("Usage:");
      System.err.println("");
      System.err.println("java jdbc_connect URL");
      System.exit(1);
    }

    try {

      // register all of the JDBC classes you might use
```

**Continued**

```java
// you can comment out or remove the ones you
// are not using.
//
Class.forName("textFileDriver");              // the tinySQL textFile driver
Class.forName("jdbc.odbc.JdbcOdbcDriver");    // JDBC-ODBC bridge
Class.forName("imaginary.sql.iMsqlDriver");   // mSQL

String url = argv[0];

// the user might have passed in a user name or password,
// so try to read those in, as well
//
String user, pwd;
if (argv.length > 1) {
  user = argv[1];
} else {
  user = "";
}
if (argv.length > 2) {
  pwd = argv[2];
} else {
  pwd = "";
}

// make a connection to the specified URL
//
Connection con = DriverManager.getConnection(url, user, pwd);

// get a Statement object from the Connection
//
Statement stmt = con.createStatement();

// ignore any exception for DROP PROCEDURE;
// it will most assuredly throw one if
// the table does not exist
//
```

```
try {
   stmt.executeUpdate("DROP PROCEDURE test_sp");
} catch (Exception e) {
   // do nothing
}


// create a stored proc
//
stmt.executeUpdate("CREATE PROCEDURE test_sp " +
                   "  @id INT, " +
                   "  @name VARCHAR(50) OUTPUT " +
                   "AS " +
                   "BEGIN " +
                   "  SELECT @name = name FROM test WHERE id = @id " +
                   "END");


// set up a call to that stored proc
//
String sql = "{call test_sp(?, ?)}";
CallableStatement cstmt = con.prepareCall(sql);


cstmt.setInt(1, 1); // get the name for id = 1


// register the output parameter as a VARCHAR
//
cstmt.registerOutParameter(2, java.sql.Types.VARCHAR);


// execute the stored procedure
//
cstmt.executeUpdate();


// display the output
//
System.out.println( "Id 1 is: " + cstmt.getString(2) );


cstmt.close();
```

**Continued**

```
        stmt.close();
        con.close();

        System.out.println("Operation successful.");

    }
    catch( Exception e ) {
      System.out.println(e.getMessage());
      e.printStackTrace();
    }
  }

}
```

# JDBC Escape Syntax

Because each database product may provide an implementation of SQL that has its own nuances and idiosyncrasies, JDBC (like ODBC) provides an escape syntax that maps a standard JDBC syntax to vendor-specific syntax. If you use a driver that supports this syntax, you do not need to change the way you program using the JDBC API; you merely need to change the way you generate your SQL statements. The JDBC escape syntax provides a standard means of mapping stored procedure calls, scalar functions, date and time expressions, and outer join specifications to vendor-specific SQL. For example, the escape syntax for a scalar expression looks like:

```
{fn function-expression }
```

Here's an example that uses the COUNT() aggregate function within an escape terminator:

```
SELECT {fn COUNT(*)} AS total
    FROM test
    GROUP BY name
```

Unfortunately, tinySQL provides no support for aggregate functions, and the mSQL JDBC driver does not support the JDBC escape syntax, so you need to test such an example with a driver such as the JDBC-ODBC bridge.

# Discovering Result Set Metadata

In most cases, you will develop applets and applications with full knowledge about your result sets. You will probably know the size of each column, the data type, and other important information. However, in some cases, especially when SQL statements are issued "on-the-fly" or when you are developing with generic reusable components, some of the information regarding the result set may not be immediately available.

In situations such as this, it can be quite handy to have access to metadata, that is, data about data. It is possible to obtain a metadata object for a result set. To do this, simply issue a statement similar to the following (where rs is a ResultSet object):

```
ResultSetMetaData meta = rs.getMetaData();
```

Once you have the ResultSetMetaData object, you can use it to retrieve information about the result set. For example, you can get the number of columns in the result set with:

```
int numcols = meta.getColumnCount();
```

If you know the index of a column, you can find out its display size using `getColumnDisplaySize()`. This could come in handy if you are dynamically generating data entry screens:

```
int size = meta.getColumnDisplaySize(columnIndex);
```

A number of other methods are provided in the ResultSetMetaData object. These will be covered in detail in Appendix B, the JDBC Driver Reference.

# Discovering Driver Capabilities

The Connection object can return a DatabaseMetaData object when you invoke the `getMetaData()` method:

```
DatabaseMetaData meta = conn.getMetaData();
```

The Database MetaData object can return information that can help you determine the capabilities of the database or the driver. You can use find out which scalar functions are supported by the database by invoking the `getNumericFunctions()`, `getString-Functions()`, `getSystemFunctions()`, or `getTimeDateFunctions()` methods. Each of these returns a comma-delimited String object that lists the functions. The DatabaseMetaData object supplies a great deal of other information, which is covered in Appendix B, the JDBC Driver Reference.

# Chapter 4

# Forward Into the Past: CardFileAbstract for JDBC

Things being what they are, a book like this can't be a perfect mirror of the Karmic circle that keeps each of us going around and around. With that in mind, I'm going to recycle one of our future lives. As the Firesign Theater once told us, "The future can't wait; no place to hide!"

In the pages of this chapter, you'll see a very simple application fueled by JDBC. It's a simple mailing list system, which is based on the CardFile sample shown in later chapters. Before you can start fooling with it, though, you will need to create a table called `cardfile`. In order to do this, I have supplied an example program, `DDL.java`. You can run the compiled `DDL.class` file by specifying a URL to a JDBC data source, a user name, and a password, as in:

```
java DDL jdbc:odbc:MSSQL username password
```

If neither a user name nor a password is required for your data source, you may simply provide the URL, as in:

```
java DDL jdbc:tinySQL
```

Here's the code to DDL.java. It's a simple class, containing only the static method `main()`:

```java
/**
 *
 * DDL.java - Data Definition Language for Chapter 4 Examples
 *
 */

import java.net.URL;
import java.sql.*;
import java.lang.*;

class DDL {

  public static void main (String argv[]) {

     if (argv.length == 0) {
       System.out.println("You must supply a URL to a JDBC data source.");
       System.out.println("");
       System.out.println("Example:");
       System.out.println("java DDL jdbc:odbc:DATA_SOURCE_NAME;" +
                           "UID=userid;PWD=password");
       System.exit(0);
     }

     String url   = argv[0];

     // the user might have passed in a user name or password,
     // so try to read those in, as well
     //
     String user, pwd;
     if (argv.length > 1) {
       user = argv[1];
     } else {
       user = "";
     }
     if (argv.length > 2) {
       pwd = argv[2];
     } else {
```

```
  pwd = "";
}

try {

  // register all of the JDBC classes you might use
  // you can comment out or remove the ones you
  // are not using.
  //
  Class.forName("textFileDriver");          // the tinySQL textFile driver
  Class.forName("jdbc.odbc.JdbcOdbcDriver");  // JDBC-ODBC bridge
  Class.forName("imaginary.sql.iMsqlDriver"); // mSQL

  Connection con = DriverManager.getConnection(url, user, pwd);
  Statement stmt = con.createStatement();

  // The drops need to be included in these special
  // try...catch clauses. Since the tables might not
  // exist, an exception might be thrown which you
  // want to ignore.
  try {
    stmt.executeUpdate("DROP TABLE cardfile");
  } catch (Exception e) { }

  // create the tables
  stmt.executeUpdate("CREATE TABLE cardfile " +
                     "(name    CHAR(20), " +
                     " address CHAR(35), " +
                     " city    CHAR(20), " +
                     " state   CHAR(2), " +
                     " zip     CHAR(11), " +
                     " country CHAR(25), " +
                     " phone   CHAR(20), " +
                     " id      INT)");

  stmt.close();
```

**Continued**

```
        con.close();
        System.out.println("Tables were created successfully.");

    } catch (SQLException e) {

        while (e != null) {
            System.out.println("SQLState: " + e.getSQLState());
            System.out.println("Message:  " + e.getMessage());
            System.out.println("Vendor:   " + e.getErrorCode());
            e = e.getNextException();
            System.out.println("");
        }
    } catch (Exception e) {
        e.printStackTrace ();
    }
    }

}
```

# Installing CardFileAbstract

CardFileAbstract is an abstract class that provides a framework for a simple cardfile-style application. It displays a simple name, address, and phone number form within a Frame and allows you to skip from record to record, providing add, edit, and delete buttons. In its abstract state, it cannot be directly instantiated. You will first need to define several methods. These are basically concerned with getting data in and out of the database.

Before you can extend CardFileAbstract, you will need to add yet another directory to your ever-growing CLASSPATH. If you've extracted the example source code for the book, you're ready to add the eg\ch10 directory to your CLASSPATH.

For Win32 users who extracted the examples to C:\USERS\DEFAULT, the following directory (among others) would have been created:

```
C:\USERS\DEFAULT\eg\ch10
```

You should add this directory to your CLASSPATH environment variable, separated by a semicolon:

```
CLASSPATH=c:\java\lib\classes;.;c:\book\eg\ch06;c:\book\eg\ch07;c:\book\eg\ch10
```

For Unix users who extracted the examples to /home/foobar, the following directory (among others) would have been created:

```
/home/foobar/eg/ch10
```

You should add this directory to your CLASSPATH environment variable, separated by a colon:

```
CLASSPATH=/usr/local/classes:.:/home/foobar/eg/ch06:/home/foobar/eg/ch07:/home/foobar
/eg/ch10
```

Be sure to keep any directories in your CLASSPATH that were added in earlier chapters, or some examples may not work.

Users of other operating systems should follow their instructions for setting the CLASS-PATH variable, which should be included with the JDK distribution.

# Extending CardFileAbstract

Because CardFileAbstract is an abstract class, you need to define some of its methods in order for it to do anything at all. While CardFileAbstract does do quite a bit of work, it is mostly concerned with maintaining a visual front-end component. All of the database access is orchestrated through the abstract methods that will be implemented in `jdbcCard-File.java`. What follows is a discussion of each abstract method and what it is expected to do.

## public abstract void login(String[] argv);

This method is expected to establish a connection to the database. The only parameter is argv, which is an array of strings containing parameters. The way in which these parameters are used will vary on the implementation of CardFileAbstract. Other database APIs, such as mSQL-Java (the basis for mSQL-JDBC) or the tinySQL API (the basis for the tinySQL JDBC driver) do not require a URL as JDBC does, but they may require other parameters. For the purposes of JDBC, however, the first three parameters in the array will be considered significant. The first should be a URL, and the second and third should be a username and password, if they are required.

Because the CardFileAbstract is designed to be database API independent, there are no API-specific objects defined in it, such as a Connection or Statement object. In the jdbcCard-File example, you will see that the Connection and Statement objects are defined as fields of the jdbcCardFile object. The login() method that is defined in jdbcCardFile will interact with the Connection and Statement fields. The login() method is automatically invoked by the default constructor, which then displays the cardfile frame.

## public abstract void getRow();

This method is intended to retrieve a single row from the cardfile table. Once it has done that, it must update the data entry form. The means by which it retrieves rows is little less than straightforward; since JDBC does not provide scrollable cursors, you can't issue a call to skip to the previous record in a result set. You can go forward with next(), but that gets a little boring after you hit EOF.

In order to bypass this deficiency, a Vector is created by the getKeys() method. This Vector, cardfileKeys, is populated with the primary key (the "ID" column) from every row in the cardfile table. An integer index, currentRow, is drafted into service to track the current row within that Vector. Both of these are fields of the jdbcCardFile object.

If the first record in the cardfile table has a primary key of 10, the second has 20, and the third has 30, and the current record is 0 (Vectors are indexed starting at 0), then you can find out the primary key with:

```
cardfileKeys.elementAt(currentRow);
```

This will return 10, stored as a String object. Even though the ID is an INT value within the database, you can pass this value around in Java as a String. JDBC provides a lot of datatype independence. As long as you remember to wrap CHARACTER values in quotes and to not wrap INTEGER values in quotes when you send SQL Statements to the database, it really doesn't matter how you deal with the values in Java. Here's the SQL that gets passed to the database by getRow():

```
rs = stmt.executeQuery("SELECT * FROM cardfile WHERE id = " +
                       cardfileKeys.elementAt(currentRow));
```

Because it is expected that the ID value is unique within the cardfile table, this should return only one row. The current version of tinySQL does not enforce this sort of rule, so it will be up to you to make sure this rule doesn't get violated. However, when you implement something like this with a database such as mSQL, SQL Server, or Oracle, you should use the database system's features to enforce this rule. In SQL Server, you can put a unique index on the column, and in mSQL, you can define the column as a primary key in the Data Definition Language (DDL).

In order to update the data entry form, it is necessary to find out which columns correspond to which TextField object on the form. These TextField objects are instantiated and managed by CardFileAbstract, so your exposure to them will be limited. The CardFileAbstract object provides a Hashtable called columnmap. It is keyed by column name, and it contains references to the TextField, which corresponds to the column name. Within getRow(), a loop is set up that iterates over each column in the result set. The ResultSetMetaData object (meta) is used to get each column name. Then, the corresponding TextField is retrieved from the columnmap Hashtable. There might be some columns in the result set that are not in the columnmap; for example, tinySQL maintains a column called _DELETED on every table. Because some of these columns may not be in the columnmap, it's important to make sure the TextField that was retrieved was not null (if you try to get an Object from a Hashtable that doesn't exist, the Hashtable does not throw an exception; it merely returns a null). If a TextField object was retrieved from the Hashtable, then it's only a matter of setting its text to the value of the column via the setText() method.

```
for(int i = 1; i <= cols; i++) {


    String col_name = meta.getColumnName(i);


    // this gets the object (a TextField) from columnmap which
    // is keyed by the name of the column in col_name.
    //


    TextField tf = (TextField) columnmap.get(col_name);
    if (tf != null) {
        // here, we simply call the setText() method of that TextField
        // object to the value of the column.
        //
        tf.setText(rs.getString(i));
    }


}
```

This process occurs for each column in the result set. When it is finished, all of the TextFields on the data entry form should have been updated. This method is smart enough to verify that there actually are elements in cardfileKeys; if it is empty, it issues a call to `clearForm()`, which is the CardFileAbstract method used to blank out the form.

# public abstract void delRow();

This method, as its name implies, should delete a row in the cardfile table. It deletes the current row by sending the DELETE command to the database. The delete is qualified with a where clause. Like the `getRow()` method, it must determine the ID of the current row in order to restrict the delete to that row. Once it has performed the delete, it removes the row's ID from the cardfileKeys Vector and sets currentRow to 0, which should be the first element in the Vector. Finally, it calls `getRow()`, which will retrieve the currentRow, if there is one. Otherwise, `getRow()` clears the form.

# public abstract void nextRow();

The `nextRow()` method is called by CardFileAbstract in response to a user pressing the Next button. If the currentRow does not point to the last element in cardfileKeys, current-Row is incremented. If currentRow points to the last element, it is set to zero, which "wraps" the CardFile around to the top. Once the currentRow has been set, `getRow()` is called to update the form.

# public abstract void prevRow();

The `prevRow()` method is called by CardFileAbstract in response to a user pressing the Previous button. If the currentRow does not point to the first element in cardfileKeys, current-Row is reduced by one. If currentRow points to the first element, then currentRow is set to the index of the last element (cardfileKeys.size() -1 ), which "wraps" the CardFile around to the bottom. Once the currentRow has been set, `getRow()` is called to update the form.

# public abstract void save();

The `save()` method simply constructs an SQL INSERT statement. Here's where the example is a little weak; it relies on the user to enter a unique ID for the primary key. If you were to improve or extend this example, you would first want to modify the table structure to enforce the uniqueness of the ID column. Some database servers also make it possible to use a system-generated ID as well.

After the INSERT statement is issued, the ID of the new row is added to cardfileKeys, and it is set as the current row.

# public abstract void update();

The update() method is pretty simple; it sends an SQL UPDATE statement. The ID column is not part of the update; rather, it is used to specify the WHERE clause of the update. Only the row matching the current ID is updated.

Here's the source code to jdbcCardFile:

```
/**
 *
 * jdbcCardFile - implementation of CardFileAbstract for jdbc
 *
 */

import java.awt.*;
import java.lang.*;
import java.util.*;
import java.sql.*;
import java.net.URL;

public class jdbcCardFile extends CardFileAbstract {


  Connection con;         // the jdbc connection
  Statement stmt;         // the jdbc statement
  int currentRow;         // row number of the current row
  Vector cardfileKeys;    // A vector to hold all primary keys

  // the constructor
  //
  public jdbcCardFile(String[] argv) {
    super(argv);
  }
```

Here's the login() method. It gets invoked with the argv parameter, which might correspond to the parameter with which the main() method is usually called. Custom invocations of this method might use the argv parameter, as well.

```java
// logs you into the database and
// sets up a Connection
//
public void login (String[] argv) {

   if (argv.length == 0) {
      System.out.println("You must supply a URL to a JDBC data source.");
      System.out.println("");
      System.out.println("Example:");
      System.out.println("java DDL jdbc:odbc:DATA_SOURCE_NAME;" +
                          "UID=userid;PWD=password");
      System.exit(0);
   }

   // the Vector holds the primary key (customer ID) for
   // each row in the table. currentRow holds the index
   // of the one we are currently viewing.

   currentRow = 0;
   cardfileKeys = new Vector();

   try {

      // register all of the JDBC classes you might use
      // you can comment out or remove the ones you
      // are not using.
      //
      Class.forName("textFileDriver");                  // the tinySQL textFile driver
      Class.forName("jdbc.odbc.JdbcOdbcDriver");  // JDBC-ODBC bridge
      Class.forName("imaginary.sql.iMsqlDriver"); // mSQL

      String url = argv[0];

      // the user might have passed in a username or password,
      // so try to read those in, as well
```

```
        //
        String user, pwd;
        if (argv.length > 1) {
          user = argv[1];
        } else {
          user = "";
        }
        if (argv.length > 2) {
          pwd = argv[2];
        } else {
          pwd = "";
        }

        // make a connection to the specified URL
        //
        con = DriverManager.getConnection(url, user, pwd);

        // get a Statement object from the Connection
        //
        stmt = con.createStatement();

      } catch( Exception e ) {

        System.out.println(e.getMessage());
        e.printStackTrace();

      }

      // call getKeys() to populate cardfileKeys with unique identifiers
      // for all the keys in the table

      getKeys();

    }
```

The getRow() method is used by the other methods to retrieve a single row from the table and update the data entry form. As described earlier, the implementation here, which buffers primary key information, gets around the fact that JDBC lets you scroll forward, but not backward.

```java
/**
 * getRow()
 *
 * retrieve a row from the table, using the one indicated by
 * cardfileKeys.elementAt(currentRow)
 *
 */
public protected void getRow() {

  ResultSet rs;

  // if there are no rows to process, just clear
  // the form and return...

  if (cardfileKeys.isEmpty()) {
    clearForm();
    return;
  }

  try {

    // issue a select statement to get the row that is
    // pointed to by currentRow. Unless we have an
    // integrity violation, this should only be one
    // row.

    rs = stmt.executeQuery("SELECT * FROM cardfile WHERE id = " +
                            cardfileKeys.elementAt(currentRow));


    // get the result set's metadata
```

```
    //
    ResultSetMetaData meta = rs.getMetaData();

    // get the number of columns
    //
    int cols = meta.getColumnCount();

    // retrieve the row
    //
    rs.next();

    // loop until we reach the count of the number of columns
    //
    for(int i = 1; i <= cols; i++) {

      // get the name of the column from meta
      //
      String col_name = meta.getColumnName(i);

      // this gets the object (a TextField) from columnmap which
      // is keyed by the name of the column in col_name.
      //

      TextField tf = (TextField) columnmap.get(col_name);
      if (tf != null) {
        // here, we simply call the setText() method of that TextField
        // object to the value of the column.
        //
        tf.setText(rs.getString(i));
      }

    }

} catch (SQLException e) {
```

**Continued**

```
      e.printStackTrace();
    }
  catch (ArrayIndexOutOfBoundsException e) {
      e.printStackTrace();
    }
  }
}
```

The `getKeys()` method is used to populate the primary key buffer; this allows the CardFile to keep the most current data without having to check whether or not it has changed recently.

```
/**
 * getKeys()
 *
 * This populates the cardfileKeys Vector with unique identifiers
 * for all of the rows in the cardfile table. This lets us buffer
 * all of the rows, without storing the values for each column.
 * As a result, we only have to worry about dirty data if someone
 * changes a key, which of course, you would *never* do...
 *
 * Now, if someone else deletes or inserts a row, that's a
 * different problem. Handling that is an exercise left to
 * the reader...
 *
 */
public protected void getKeys() {

  ResultSet rs;

  try {

    // delete all the elements in cardfileKeys

    cardfileKeys.removeAllElements();
```

```
            // execute a query to get the id column for each of the
            // rows. Then, process each row and add the id column
            // to cardfileKeys

            rs = stmt.executeQuery("SELECT id FROM cardfile");

            while( rs.next() ) {
              cardfileKeys.addElement( rs.getString(1) );
            }

        } catch (SQLException e) {
            e.printStackTrace();
        }
}
```

The `save()` method will write out a new record to the database. It does so by constructing an SQL INSERT statement for the current record.

```
/**
 *
 * save()
 *
 * Save the record we are editing to the table
 *
 */
public protected void save() {

    // construct an INSERT statement, with values for each
    // column, including ID. Teaching this system to auto-
    // increment ID in a multiuser environment is an exercise
    // left up to the reader.
    //

    String sql = "INSERT INTO cardfile " +
```

**Continued**

```
               "   (name, address, city, state, zip, country, phone, id)" +
               "   VALUES (" +
                         "'" + txt_name.getText() + "', " +
                         "'" + txt_address.getText() + "', " +
                         "'" + txt_city.getText() + "', " +
                         "'" + txt_state.getText() + "', " +
                         "'" + txt_zip.getText() + "', " +
                         "'" + txt_country.getText() + "', " +
                         "'" + txt_phone.getText() + "', " +
                              txt_id.getText() + ")";

   try {

     // if the query doesn't throw an exception, we can add the newly
     // created ID to the cardfileKeys Vector, and set the currentRow
     // to the element that points to the new record
     //
     stmt.executeUpdate(sql);
     cardfileKeys.addElement(txt_id.getText());
     currentRow = cardfileKeys.indexOf(txt_id.getText());

     // call getRow() to refresh the form. This really shouldn't
     // be necessary, but it lets us know that the record was
     // saved correctly. Or not, as the case may be :-)

     getRow();

   } catch(SQLException e ) {
     e.printStackTrace();
   }


 }
```

The update() method will write out a changed record to the database. It does so by constructing an SQL UPDATE statement for the current record, regardless of whether or not the record changed. Altering the behavior of this program to respond to "dirty buffers" is an exercise left to the reader.

```
/**
 *
 * update()
 *
 * Send an update to the database
 *
 */
public protected void update() {

   // construct an UPDATE String for each of the columns
   // except for the ID. This is used as the criteria
   // for the update, so we probably don't want to
   // update it...

   String sql = "UPDATE cardfile " +
              " SET name    = '" + txt_name.getText() + "', " +
              "     address = '" + txt_address.getText() + "', " +
              "     city    = '" + txt_city.getText() + "', " +
              "     state   = '" + txt_state.getText() + "', " +
              "     zip     = '" + txt_zip.getText() + "', " +
              "     country = '" + txt_country.getText() + "', " +
              "     phone   = '" + txt_phone.getText() + "' " +
              " WHERE id = " + txt_id.getText();
   try {

      // send the query

      stmt.executeUpdate(sql);

      // call getRow() to refresh the form. This really shouldn't
      // be necessary, but it lets us know what the update did.
```

**Continued**

```
        getRow();

    } catch(SQLException e ) {
      e.printStackTrace();
    }


}
```

The `nextRow()` method advances the currentRow pointer to the next record, and calls `getRow()` to refresh the display.

```
// if the next button was pushed, then I want to
// increment currentRow. But, if that would push
// it out past cardfileKeys.size(), I will just
// wrap around to the beginning (zero).
//
public void nextRow() {

  if (currentRow + 1 == cardfileKeys.size()) {
    currentRow = 0;
  } else {
    currentRow++;
  }

  // call getRow() to update the form
  //
  getRow();
}
```

The `prevRow()` method advances the currentRow pointer to the previous record, and calls `getRow()` to refresh the display.

```
// if the user pushed the previous button, then
// I want to decrement currentRow. If currentRow
// already zero, then decrementing further would
```

```
// probably throw some evil exception, so I'll
// set it to cardfileKeys.size() - 1, which is the
// index of the last element.
//
public void prevRow() {

  if (currentRow  == 0) {
    currentRow = cardfileKeys.size() - 1;
  } else {
    currentRow--;
  }

  // call getRow() to update the form
  getRow();
}
```

The delRow() method deletes the current row. Like the update() and save() methods, it must construct an SQL statement to handle this.

```
/**
 * delRow()
 *
 * deletes the current row.
 *
 */
public protected void delRow() {

  try {

    // issue the query to delete the row

    stmt.executeUpdate("DELETE FROM cardfile WHERE id = " +
                       cardfileKeys.elementAt(currentRow));
```

**Continued**

```
        // Oh yeah, don't forget to remove the element from
        // cardfileKeys.

        cardfileKeys.removeElement(cardfileKeys.elementAt(currentRow));

        // let's just be lazy and return to row 0...

        currentRow = 0;

        // call getRow() to refresh the form with the current record.

        getRow();

      } catch (SQLException e) {
        e.printStackTrace();
      }
    }
```

Here's the `main()` method, which gets invoked if you run the compiled program from the command line.

```
    // our little friend main, who makes it all happen

    public static void main(String[] argv) {

        // make a new jdbcCardFile, pack() it and show() it.
        jdbcCardFile cardfile = new jdbcCardFile(argv);
        cardfile.pack();
        cardfile.show();

    }

}
```

# Running jdbcCardFile

Once you have correctly installed CardFileAbstract, you can change the directory to the Chapter 4 examples directory and execute jdbcCardFile with:

```
java jdbcCardFile URL USERNAME PASSWORD
```

Here the URL points to a JDBC data source, and USERNAME and PASSWORD contain a valid username and password, if required. Examples:

```
java jdbcCardFile jdbc:msql://imaginary.com:4333/Testdb bjepson mypasssword
java jdbcCardFile jdbc:tinysql
java jdbcCardFile jdbc:odbc:MSSQL bjepson mypassword
```

The jdbcCardFile application demonstrates some simple JDBC examples, yet it illustrates much of the functionality available through JDBC. You will revisit CardFileAbstract in later chapters, and you will learn other ways to extend and implement its functionality.

# Chapter 5

# Fun with Widgets

*"One... two... three... four... \*cough\* one... two"*

— the Beatles, "Taxman"

Some call them components, some call them controls. I like to say widget. "Widget widget widget." I think I'll keep saying it; on my own time, of course.

A *widget* is basically some sort of user interface component; it can be a field, a pull-down menu, a scrolling list, or something more sophisticated. It's that "something more sophisticated" that I'll deal with in this chapter. You'll see my favorite widget, the tree widget, sometimes called an outline or hierarchical view, and the grid widget, another of my favorites.

This isn't the first time I've been roped into writing about tree controls; I've implemented this in FoxPro 2.x, Perl/HTML, and now Java. The technique I use is based on one shown in an article contained in the Microsoft SQL Server Books On-line, called "Expanding Hierarchies." You would think that if I wrote about this many times, I'd probably just be cutting and pasting between chapters. cutting and pasting between chapters. Well, I can assure you that something like that wouldn't happen. Not only does cutting and pasting from earlier work undermine the value of what you're trying to say, but it introduces errors that even a good copy editor might miss. cutting and pasting between chapters. In this chapter, I promise only generic, reusable code (in whichever wonderful programming language that this book happens to be about), and no reusable text. cutting and pasting between chapters.

# Hierarchical Data

The problem of hierarchical data has been with human society for a long time. Ever since the first cavemen tried to parse the speech of their SubGenius overlords, ordinary humans have had a difficult time organizing hierarchical data into a usable form.

Hierarchical data is any table, the rows of which contain references to other rows in the same table. A good example is a corporate structure:

| Title | ID | Parent ID |
|-------|-----|-----------|
| Some sort of lobster-like creature | 100 | 0 |
| CEO | 110 | 100 |
| CFO | 120 | 100 |
| Regional managers | 130 | 110 |
| Accounting manager | 140 | 120 |
| Belligerent, drunken mimes | 150 | 130 |
| Grunts in the accounting department | 160 | 140 |
| The crazy guy who brought a gun in and threatened to blow everyone's head off | 170 | 130 |
| The crazy guy's buddy | 180 | 130 |

If you were to convert this into a hierarchical display, you would see it in the following format:

```
Some sort of lobster-like creature
    CFO
       Accounting manager
          Grunts in the accounting department
    CEO
       Regional managers
          The crazy guy who brought a gun in and threatened to blow everyone's
             head off
          The crazy guy's buddy
          Belligerent, drunken mimes
```

Here's a program that will create a table called tree and populate it with the sample data shown previously. It should look similar to the DDL.java in the previous chapter. You can execute the compiled code by specifying a URL to a JDBC data source, a username, and a password, as in:

```
java DDL jdbc:odbc:MSSQL username password
```

If neither a username nor a password is required, you may simply provide the URL:

```
java DDL jdbc:tinySQL
```

```
/**
 *
 * DDL.java - Data Definition Language for Chapter 4 Examples
 *
 */
import java.net.URL;
import java.sql.*;
import java.lang.*;

class DDL {

  public static void main (String argv[]) {

    if (argv.length == 0) {
      System.out.println("You must supply a URL to a JDBC data source.");
      System.out.println("");
      System.out.println("Example:");
      System.out.println("java DDL jdbc:odbc:DATA_SOURCE_NAME;" +
                         "UID=userid;PWD=password");
      System.exit(0);
    }

    String url   = argv[0];

    // the user might have passed in a username or password,
```

**Continued**

```
// so try to read those in, as well
//
String user, pwd;
if (argv.length > 1) {
  user = argv[1];
} else {
  user = "";
}
if (argv.length > 2) {
  pwd = argv[2];
} else {
  pwd = "";
}

try {

   // register all of the JDBC classes you might use
   // you can comment out or remove the ones you
   // are not using.
   //
   Class.forName("textFileDriver");            // the tinySQL textFile driver
   Class.forName("jdbc.odbc.JdbcOdbcDriver");  // JDBC-ODBC bridge
   Class.forName("imaginary.sql.iMsqlDriver"); // mSQL

   Connection con = DriverManager.getConnection(url, user, pwd);
   Statement stmt = con.createStatement();

   // The drops need to be included in these special
   // try...catch clauses. Since the tables might not
   // exist, an exception might be thrown that you
   // want to ignore.
   try {
     stmt.executeUpdate("DROP TABLE tree");
   } catch (Exception e) { }

   // create the tables
```

```
        stmt.executeUpdate("CREATE TABLE tree " +
                           "(name CHAR(80), tree_id INT, parent_id INT)");


    // insert some sample tree items
    // I don't feel like coding each and every
    // insert, so I'm putting it into a two-dimensional
    // array, and generating the INSERT statements from
    // that.
    //
    String data[][] = {
       {"Some sort of lobster-like creature",        "100", "0"},
       {"CEO",                                       "110", "100"},
       {"CFO",                                       "120", "100"},
       {"Regional managers",                         "130", "110"},
       {"Accounting manager",                        "140", "120"},
       {"Belligerent, drunken mimes",                "150", "130"},
       {"Grunts in the accounting department",       "160", "140"},
       {"The crazy guy who brought a gun in " +
"and threatened to blow everyone's head off", "170", "130"},
       {"The crazy guy's buddy",                     "180", "130"}
    };


    for (int i=0; i < data.length; i++) {
        String insert = "INSERT INTO tree " +
                        " (name, tree_id, parent_id) " +
                        " VALUES (" +
                        "\"" + data[i][0] + "\", " +
                              data[i][1] + ", " +
                              data[i][2] + ") ";

        stmt.executeUpdate(insert);
    }

    stmt.close();
    con.close();
    System.out.println("Tables were created successfully.");
```

**Continued**

```
    } catch (SQLException e) {

      while (e != null) {
        System.out.println("SQLState: " + e.getSQLState());
        System.out.println("Message:  " + e.getMessage());
        System.out.println("Vendor:   " + e.getErrorCode());
        e = e.getNextException();
        System.out.println("");
      }
    } catch (Exception e) {
      e.printStackTrace ();
    }
  }

}
```

# outline.java — Expanding the Tree

Once this data is stored in its self-referential form, it can take a bit of effort to expand it to a visually appealing, hierarchical form. However, the following program, `outline.java`, does just that. The algorithm by which this is accomplished is complicated, but not wholly beyond someone intelligent enough to have purchased or stolen this book.

Running this program is quite simple. Because it contains a static `main()` method at the end, it can run by itself, or it can be instantiated in another program. Once you've compiled it down to a .class file, you can run it by giving it the name of a URL and optionally, a username or password, as in:

```
java outline jdbc:tinySQL
```

or

```
java outline jdbc:odbc:MSSQL username password
```

The first thing the program needs to do is to import several java packages. Following this, a Connection and Statement object are declared as fields of the outline class:

```
/*
 * outline.java
 *
 * Displays data in a hierarchical outline format.
 *
 */

import java.net.URL;
import java.sql.*;
import java.lang.*;
import java.util.*;

class outline {

    // a JDBC connection, and a Statement object
    //
    Connection con;
    Statement stmt;
```

The constructor for this object merely passes the URL, username, and password to the connect() method:

```
/**
 *
 * Constructs a new outline object.
 * @param url a URL to  a valid JDBC data source.
 * @param user a username
 * @param pwd a password
 *
 */
public outline(String url, String user, String pwd) {

    // invoke the connect() method
    connect(url, user, pwd);
}
```

The `connect()` method attempts to get a JDBC connection, given the URL, username, and password. It is the responsibility of any program that attempts to instantiate an outline object to register any JDBC drivers with the JDBC driver manager. After the Connection is instantiated, a Statement object is retrieved with `getConnection()`:

```
/*
 *
 * make a JDBC connection.
 *
 */
public void connect (String url, String user, String pwd) {

   try {

       // ask the DriverManager to find
       // a suitable driver for this URL.
       //
       con = DriverManager.getConnection(url, user, pwd);

       // create a Statement object. This is the
       // gateway into the world of playing
       // with fun things like SQL statements
       // and results
       //
       stmt = con.createStatement();

   } catch (SQLException e) {

       // invoke SQLErr in case of SQL exceptions
       SQLErr(e);
   } catch (Exception e) {
     e.printStackTrace ();
   }
}
```

A `finalize()` method is included, in the hopes that it will be invoked when the outline object is destructed. It ensures that the Statement and Connection objects are closed:

```
/**
 *
 * close the statement and the connection
 *
 */
public void finalize() throws Throwable {

    try {

        stmt.close();
        con.close();

    } catch (SQLException e) {
        SQLErr(e);
    } catch (Exception e) {
        e.printStackTrace ();
    }
    super.finalize();

}
```

This class has been pretty simple up until now. The next method, `traverseTree()`, is a little complicated. It does all the work of converting the information contained in the table into a hierarchical format. It then displays each element of the tree (a node) using the `addNode()` method. The `addNode()` method can be subclassed to hook into a visual component, such as a tree widget.

The `traverseTree()` method must be invoked with four parameters. The first is the name of the tree table. The second is the name of the row ID column, and the third parameter is the name of the column that references the row ID of the parent row. The last parameter is the name of the column that serves as a label; this will be displayed as part of the tree.

```
/**
 *
 * traverse the tree, and invoke addNode() for each
 * node on the tree.
 * In order for this to work, this method
 * needs a few pieces of metadata.
 *
 * @param tbl the name of the table containing the tree
 * @param idcol the primary key of that table
 * @param parcol the self-referencing foreign key into the parent row.
 * @param lbl the name of the "label", or descriptive column in the table.
 *
 */
public void traverseTree(String tbl, String idcol,
                         String parcol, String lbl) {
```

To speed up subsequent operations, all of the rows in the table are cached into a Hashtable, called rs_cached. For each row, this Hashtable is keyed by the row's ID; it contains yet another Hashtable, which contains the Integer parent ID, and the String label for the column. So, for the second item as shown in the previous table would be keyed by 100, have a label value of "CEO", and a parent ID of 100. As this Hashtable is populated, the program looks for a row that has a parent ID of zero; this is the top-level element. If it is not found, an Exception is thrown:

```
try {

    // get all the rows from the table containing the
    // outline.
    //
    ResultSet rs = stmt.executeQuery(
                "SELECT " + parcol + ", " + lbl + ", " + idcol +
                " FROM " + tbl);

    int current = 0;
```

```
// move the result set into a Hashtable, which is
// keyed by the ID column.
//
Hashtable rs_cached = new Hashtable();
boolean wasTopLevelFound = false;

while (rs.next()) {

    // Create another Hashtable, which will
    // actually contain the label and parent
    // ID. This is the information that
    // gets stored in the rs_cached Hashtable.
    //
    Hashtable row = new Hashtable();

    // retrieve the parent id
    //
    int parent_id = rs.getInt(parcol);

    // put the parent ID into the row Hashtable
    // as an Integer object, and the label value
    // as a String object.
    //
    row.put(parcol, new Integer(parent_id));
    row.put(lbl,  rs.getString(lbl));

    // find the current ID, which is the key for
    // the rs_cached Hashtable.
    //
    int current_id = rs.getInt(idcol);

    // put the row into the Hashtable
    //
    rs_cached.put(new Integer(current_id), row);

    // find the top-level row; it will have a
```

**Continued**

```
        // parent ID of zero. You can only have one of
        // these in the table.
        //
        if (parent_id == 0) {

            // get the *one* row from the table which has
            // a parent column reference to zero. In order for
            // any of these tables to work, it needs to have
            // a top-level row that has no parent. This row
            // should have zero in its parcol.
            //
            current = current_id;
            wasTopLevelFound = true;

        }
    }

    if (!wasTopLevelFound) {
        throw new Exception("Could not locate a top-level row.");
    }
```

Now that the result set has been cached, the program must process each row. The level variable contains an integer value (starting at one) that keeps track of how deep in the tree we are.

```
    // begin processing the result set that was
    // cached. start out at level 1 (the top)
    //
    int level = 1;
```

Another Hashtable, elem, is used to keep track of all unprocessed tree rows. As each row is processed (starting with the top-level row), its children are inserted into elem.

```
        // elem is a Hashtable that contains all of
        // the nodes as this method traverses the tree.
        // the current value of the current row (the top-
```

```
// level item in this case) is used as the Hash
// key, and the value is its level in the tree.
//
// This Hashtable is used to keep a list of
// "to be processed" rows. At first, just the top-
// level item is in there. As we process each row,
// this program adds each row's children to the
// elem Hashtable, thus growing the list of "to
// be processed" rows.
//
Hashtable elem = new Hashtable();
elem.put(new Integer(current), new Integer(1));
```

Next, a while loop is started; the program will continue to loop until it runs out of levels to process. When the program encounters a level with no children and no more rows to process at that level, it decrements the level. If the program encounters a level with children, the level is incremented. This continues until all of the elements have been processed, at which time the level is equal to zero. The levelFound variable is used to flag whether any unprocessed rows were found at the current level.

```
// keep digging in the tree until
// nothing's left!
//
while ( level > 0 ) {

    boolean levelFound = false;
```

An enumeration of the keys in the elem Hashtable is used to check each element (the value is its level, the key is its ID); if one is found that has a value equal to the current level, then the variable current (the ID of the next record to process) is populated, and this loop is broken:

```
// search for an element in the
// "to be processed" hash which is
// at the current value of level
```

**Continued**

```
//
Enumeration keys = elem.keys();
while (keys.hasMoreElements()) {

  Integer hashkey = (Integer) keys.nextElement();
  int currLevel  = ((Integer) elem.get(hashkey)).intValue();


  // as soon as an element is found whose level
  // is equal to the one currently being processed,
  // grab its primary key (the hashkey), flag
  // levelfound, and break!

  if (currLevel == level) {
    current = hashkey.intValue(); levelFound = true; break;
  }
}
```

When the previous loop is broken with the break command, the levelFound flag is also set to true. If it was set to true, then the program must process that row. Otherwise, control of flow drops down to the statement where the level is decremented:

```
// if we managed to find an unprocessed element that
// has the same level as the one we're processing,
// then we can add it to the tree and see if it has
// any children.
//
// If we didn't find it, we should decrement level,
// and see if there are any elements one level up. We
// can keep doing this until we have tried all the
// levels (until level = 0).
//
if (levelFound) {
```

To process a row, its information must be retrieved from the rs_cached Hashtable. This is convenient, as we don't need to make any extra SQL calls against the database to get the parent ID and label of this row. After its label is stored into the String object label, the object is removed from the elem Hashtable (the hash of unprocessed rows):

```
// retrieve the row that has current as
// its primary key
//
Hashtable currow = ((Hashtable) rs_cached.get(new Integer(current)));
String label = (String) currow.get(lbl);


// remove this (now) processed item from
// the elem Hashtable
//
elem.remove(new Integer(current));
```

Now, the program is going to try to discover if the row we are processing (the one we just retrieved and deleted from elem) has any children. To do so, the program has to iterate over all the elements in the cached result set (rs_cached) and isolate any that have a parent ID equal to the ID of the row we just processed.

If any of these were isolated, they are added to the elem Hashtable. Remember, the elem Hashtable is keyed by the ID of that row, and it contains the level of that row. Because any children are, by definition, one level deeper that their parent (the row that is currently being processed), the level stored in elem is one greater than the current level (level + 1):

```
int children = 0;


// search rs_cached for any children of the row
// that was just processed. First, produce an
// Enumeration of keys in rs_cached, and process
// each of those.
//
Enumeration rskeys = rs_cached.keys();
while (rskeys.hasMoreElements()) {

  // get the current key
```

**Continued**

```
//
Integer currKey = (Integer) rskeys.nextElement();

// pull the cached row out of rs_cached.
//
Hashtable testRow = (Hashtable) rs_cached.get(currKey);

// get the parent ID from this row.
//
int parent_id = ((Integer) testRow.get(parcol)).intValue();

// is this row a child of the one that was processed
// earlier?
//
if (parent_id == current) {

    // add the children's levels to the elem
    // Hashtable, keying into their level,
    // which is equal to level + 1
    //
    elem.put(currKey, new Integer(level + 1));
    children++;

}
}
```

Having retrieved all the children of this row, the program is just about finished with it. It now remains to add the row to the tree via addNode():

```
// add the item thatwas just processed to the tree
//
addNode(level, children, label.trim());
```

Now, level can be incremented. When the while loop returns to the top, it will look for any row at the new level.

```
        // increment each level; this lets us visit the children
        // of this row, if we added any.
        //
        level++;


    } else {
```

Anytime the program doesn't find any rows at the current level, the level variable is decremented, and the process continues, one level up, until zero is reached:

```
        // no more rows at this level, go one up!
        //
        level--;
    }


    }

} catch (SQLException e) {
    SQLErr(e);
} catch (Exception e) {
    e.printStackTrace();
}
}
```

The `addNode()` method is pretty simple; it merely prints out the label of the current row. It adds two spaces of indentation per level, so you can see how the hierarchy is organized; lower levels are indented under their parent row. This is the method that should be subclassed to do sophisticated and groovy things with the outline:

```
/**
 *
 * Adds a node to the tree display. This method should be subclassed
 * if you want the node to be displayed in a widget.
 *
 * @param level the level within the tree (starts at 1)
```

**Continued**

```java
 * @param children the number of children
 * @param label the text of the item
 *
 */
void addNode (int level, int children, String label) {

  // create some indentation; two spaces for every
  // level works well...
  //
  String value = "";
  for (int j = 0; j < level; j++) {
    value += "  ";
  }
  value += label; // add the label to the padding

  // print out the value
  System.out.println(value);

}


/**
 *
 * mindless error handler that prints out state, message,
 * and vendor info for SQL errors.
 */
public void SQLErr(SQLException e) {
  while (e != null) {
    System.out.println("SQLState: " + e.getSQLState());
    System.out.println("Message:  " + e.getMessage());
    System.out.println("Vendor:   " + e.getErrorCode());
    e.printStackTrace();
    e = e.getNextException();
    System.out.println("");
  }
}
```

A `main()` method is supplied; this checks the argv[] array for a URL, username, and password, passing it to the `outline()` constructor. After it has done so, it calls `traverseTree()` with the name of the tree table and the names of the ID, parent ID, and label columns:

```
/*
 * A static main(), which instantiates this object with
 * some test data.
 */
public static void main (String argv[]) {

  try {

    // register all of the JDBC classes you might use
    // you can comment out or remove the ones you
    // are not using.
    //
    Class.forName("textFileDriver");             // the tinySQL textFile driver
    Class.forName("jdbc.odbc.JdbcOdbcDriver");   // JDBC-ODBC bridge
    Class.forName("imaginary.sql.iMsqlDriver");  // mSQL

  } catch (Exception e) {
    e.printStackTrace();
  }

  // require a parameter with a jdbc: URL, and complain
  // if it's not there.
  //
  if (argv.length == 0) {
    System.out.println("You must supply a URL to a JDBC data source.");
    System.out.println("");
    System.out.println("Example:");
    System.out.println("java DDL jdbc:odbc:DATA_SOURCE_NAME;" +
                "UID=userid;PWD=password");
    System.exit(0);
  }
```

**Continued**

```
// the user might have passed in a username or password,
// so try to read those in, as well
//
String user, pwd;
if (argv.length > 1) {
  user = argv[1];
} else {
  user = "";
}
if (argv.length > 2) {
  pwd = argv[2];
} else {
  pwd = "";
}


// create a new outline object,
// and invoke its traverseTree() method.
//
outline tr = new outline(argv[0], user, pwd);
tr.traverseTree("tree", "tree_id", "parent_id", "name");


  }

}
```

# outlineMlTree.java—Extending outline.java to Use a Visual Component

The Microline Component Toolkit (http://www.mlsoft.com/mct/mct.html) is a professional toolkit that adds four widgets to Java—a Grid, Tree, TabPanel, and a Progress widget. The outlineMlTree program is a simple subclass of outline that uses the MlTree widget to produce some really nice-looking displays of hierarchical data.

To use the toolkit, you will need to download it and install according to the instructions. The trial version allows you to work with a maximum of 105 rows in the Tree or Grid, which is sufficient for the example data.

In outlineMlTree.java, few things have changed. Notice that the mlsoft.mct.* package has been added to the import. Additionally, an MlTree has been added to the class:

```
/*
 *
 * outlineMlTree.java
 *
 * an extension of outline.class using the Microline
 * Component Toolkit tree component.
 *
 */

import mlsoft.mct.*;
import java.awt.*;

class outlineMlTree extends outline {

  MlTree tree;
```

The constructor for this class differs from its superclass in that it expects you to pass in a tree object, as well as the URL, username, and password. This makes it easy you to utilize the outlineMlTree along with other widgets; once you've instantiated the MlTree on your form, you can use outlineMlTree to add data to it.

```
/**
 *
 * Constructs a new outlineMlTree object.
 * @param url a URL to  a valid JDBC data source.
 * @param user a username
 * @param pwd a password
 * @param t an MlTree object
 *
 */
public outlineMlTree (String url, String user, String pwd, MlTree t) {
```

**Continued**

```
    super(url, user, pwd);
    tree = t;


}
```

Here's the subclassed version of addNode. The layoutFrozen attribute of the tree is set to true; this is required when you modify the tree. Then, the tree's addRow() method is called, along with the level, number of children, and label of the row. Once this is done, the layoutFrozen attribute is set to false.

```
/**
 *
 * addNode()
 *
 * This subclasses the addNode() method in outline.class to
 * use an MlTree
 *
 * @param level the level within the tree (starts at 1)
 * @param children the number of children
 * @param label the text of the item
 *
 */
void addNode (int level, int children, String label) {

    tree.setValue("layoutFrozen", true);
    tree.addRow(level, children > 0, label);
    tree.setValue("layoutFrozen", false);


}
```

The main() method is a little different from that in outline.java. The biggest difference is the addition of a Frame object, which holds the MlTree object. The Frame object is actually a subclass of Frame, which includes a handleEvent method to deal with being closed. An MlTree object is instantiated, and that is passed to the outlineMlTree constructor:

```java
/**
 *
 * instantiate the outline object with test data.
 *
 */
public static void main (String argv[]) {

  try {

    // register all of the JDBC classes you might use
    // you can comment out or remove the ones you
    // are not using.
    //
    Class.forName("textFileDriver");              // the tinySQL textFile driver
    Class.forName("jdbc.odbc.JdbcOdbcDriver");  // JDBC-ODBC bridge
    Class.forName("imaginary.sql.iMsqlDriver"); // mSQL

  } catch (Exception e) {
    e.printStackTrace();
  }

  if (argv.length == 0) {
    System.out.println("You must supply a URL to a JDBC data source.");
    System.out.println("");
    System.out.println("Example:");
    System.out.println("java DDL jdbc:odbc:DATA_SOURCE_NAME;" +
                       "UID=userid;PWD=password");
    System.exit(0);
  }

  // the user might have passed in a username or password,
  // so try to read those in, as well
  //
  String user, pwd;
  if (argv.length > 1) {
    user = argv[1];
```

**Continued**

```
    } else {
      user = "";
    }
    if (argv.length > 2) {
      pwd = argv[2];
    } else {
      pwd = "";
    }

    // create a myFrame object that knows how to close itself
    //
    myFrame f = new myFrame();
    f.setLayout(new BorderLayout());

    // create an MlTree object and add it to the frame
    //
    MlTree tree = new MlTree();
    f.add("Center", tree);

    // resize and show the frame
    //
    f.resize(400, 300);
    f.show();

    // instantiate the outlineMlTree object and traverse it
    //
    outlineMlTree tr = new outlineMlTree(argv[0], user, pwd, tree);
    tr.traverseTree("tree", "tree_id", "parent_id", "name");
  }
}
```

The myFrame.java program contains a simple extension to Frame that knows how to close itself:

```java
import java.awt.*;

public class myFrame extends Frame {

  /**
   * handleEvent
   *
   * Deal with things the user did...
   */
  public boolean handleEvent(Event event) {

    boolean event_handled = false;

    switch(event.id) {

      // in case they closed the window, then take
      // it as a sign that they want to quit
      case Event.WINDOW_DESTROY:
        System.exit(0);
        break;                 // hmmm...

      // just pass these on
      case Event.ACTION_EVENT:
      case Event.MOUSE_DOWN:
      case Event.MOUSE_UP:
      case Event.MOUSE_DRAG:
      case Event.KEY_PRESS:
      case Event.KEY_ACTION:
      case Event.KEY_RELEASE:
      case Event.KEY_ACTION_RELEASE:
      case Event.GOT_FOCUS:
      case Event.LOST_FOCUS:
      case Event.MOUSE_ENTER:
      case Event.MOUSE_EXIT:
      case Event.MOUSE_MOVE:
        return false;
```

**Continued**

```
      }
      if(event_handled) {
        return true;
      } else {
        return super.handleEvent(event);
      };
    }
}
```

And that's all there is to subclassing outline.java. Figure 5.1 shows the outlineMlTree in action. This widget can now be used with JDBC data sources to add a tree component to your forms and screens with very little hassle. You will merely need to use the `main()` method as a guideline for implementing the outlineMlTree.

# Grids

The Microline Component Toolkit also provides an excellent grid widget. The next program featured in this chapter will allow you to bind a table to a grid; when you update a value in the grid, the corresponding row in the table is updated. Because this class (jdbcMlGrid) extends the MlGrid object, you can use it in your Java applications and applets just as you would the MlGrid object.

The `main()` method supplied with this class uses the CardFile table that was introduced in Chapter 4. Figure 5.2 shows the jdbcMlGrid bound to the CardFile table. You can execute

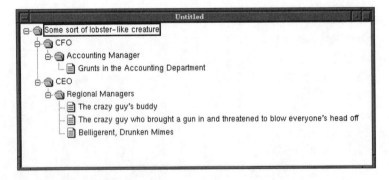

**FIGURE 5.1**  The outline MlTree in action.

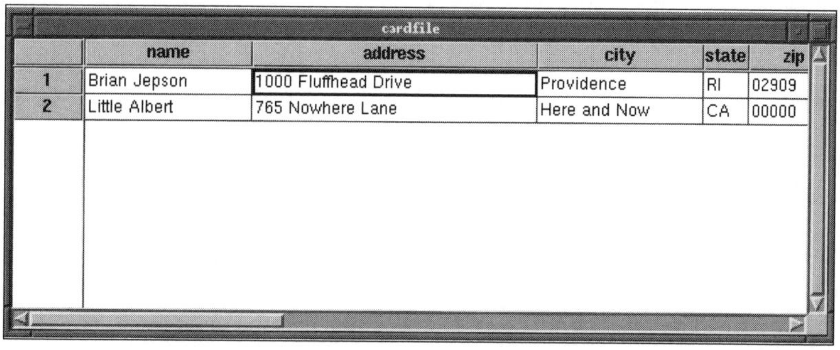


| | name | address | city | state | zip |
|---|---|---|---|---|---|
| 1 | Brian Jepson | 1000 Fluffhead Drive | Providence | RI | 02909 |
| 2 | Little Albert | 765 Nowhere Lane | Here and Now | CA | 00000 |

**FIGURE 5.2** A jdbc M1Grid showing the CardFile table.

the compiled jdbcMlGrid.class by passing it the name of a URL and, optionally, a username or password, as in:

```
java jdbcMlGrid jdbc:tinySQL
```

or

```
java jdbcMlGrid jdbc:odbc:MSSQL username password
```

The gridtree.java program contains a `main()` method that uses the tree table as sample data, which will let you edit the corporate hierarchy shown earlier in this chapter. After compiling it, you can run it the same way as jdbcMlGrid. Figure 5.3 shows gridtree in action.

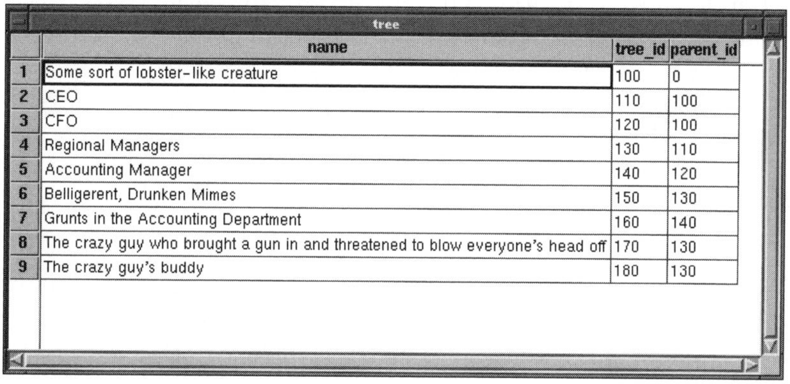


| | name | tree_id | parent_id |
|---|---|---|---|
| 1 | Some sort of lobster-like creature | 100 | 0 |
| 2 | CEO | 110 | 100 |
| 3 | CFO | 120 | 100 |
| 4 | Regional Managers | 130 | 110 |
| 5 | Accounting Manager | 140 | 120 |
| 6 | Belligerent, Drunken Mimes | 150 | 130 |
| 7 | Grunts in the Accounting Department | 160 | 140 |
| 8 | The crazy guy who brought a gun in and threatened to blow everyone's head off | 170 | 130 |
| 9 | The crazy guy's buddy | 180 | 130 |

**FIGURE 5.3** The gridtree program showing the corporate hierarchy.

Here's the jdbcMlGrid class:

```
/*
 *
 * jdbcMlGrid
 *
 * An extension of the MlGrid object that allows
 * in-place editing of a table.
 *
 */

import java.awt.*;
import mlsoft.mct.*;
import java.sql.*;
import java.util.*;

public class jdbcMlGrid extends MlGrid {
```

A few fields are declared in the class: the JDBC Connection and Statement object appear first. These are followed by the String objects table (the name of the table to which the jdbcMlGrid is bound), column_list (a comma-delimited list of columns to display), and pkey (the name of the primary key). Finally, pkey_col is an integer value that holds the column offset of the primary key column. This is the offset within the MlGrid, which starts at zero. JDBC column offsets with methods like `getString()` and `getInt()` start at one.

```
    // a JDBC connection, and a Statement object
    //
    Connection con;
    Statement stmt;

    String table, column_list, pkey;

    int pkey_col;
```

The jdbcMlGrid constructor invokes `connect()` to make the JDBC connection, and then it calls `prepareGrid()` to get the grid ready to have columns added to it. The `getData()` method then fills the columns with data and headers, and then `layout-Grid()` is called to make more cosmetic adjustments to the grid:

```
/**
 *
 * Constructs a new jdbcMlGrid object.
 * @param url a URL to a valid JDBC data source.
 * @param user a username
 * @param pwd a password
 * @param tbl the table to edit
 * @param cols a comma-delimited list of columns to view
 * @param pk the name of the primary key
 *
 */
public jdbcMlGrid(String url, String user, String pwd,
                  String tbl, String cols, String pk) {

    table       = tbl;
    column_list = cols;
    pkey        = pk;

    // invoke the connect() method
    //
    connect(url, user, pwd);

    // do some preliminary grid setup
    //
    prepareGrid();

    // retrieve the data
    //
    getData();

    // do some more grid setup
```

**Continued**

```
        //
        layoutGrid();

}
```

The `connect()` method simply attempts to make a JDBC connection and gets a Statement object. It is assumed that the application or applet that is using the grid has loaded the requisite drivers.

```
/*
 *
 * make a JDBC connection.
 *
 */
public void connect (String url, String user, String pwd) {

    try {

        // ask the DriverManager to find
        // a suitable driver for this URL.
        //
        con = DriverManager.getConnection(url, user, pwd);

        // create a statement object. This is the
        // gateway into the world of playing
        // with fun things like SQL statements
        // and results
        //
        stmt = con.createStatement();

    } catch (Exception e) {
        e.printStackTrace ();
    }
}
```

The prepareGrid() and layoutGrid() methods use an MlResources object to set the characteristics of the grid. Note that whenever you fool with the grid, the layout of the grid should be frozen by invoking setValue() with the parameters "layoutFrozen" and true. When you are done fooling with the grid, you should set the "layoutFrozen" value to false. See the MlGrid documentation and examples for a detailed explanation of programming with the MlGrid object.

```
public void prepareGrid () {



    MlResources res;
    Font boldFont;


    res = new MlResources();


    this.setValue("layoutFrozen", true);


    res.add("hsbDisplayPolicy", "DISPLAY_ALWAYS");
    res.add("vsbDisplayPolicy", "DISPLAY_ALWAYS");
    res.add("highlightRowMode", false);
    res.add("selectionPolicy", "SELECT_CELL");
    res.add("allowColumnResize", false);
    res.add("allowRowResize", false);
    res.add("shadowThickness", 1);
    this.setValues(res);


    res.clear();
    res.add("cellDefaults", true);
    res.add("cellEditable", true);
    res.add("cellAlignment", "ALIGNMENT_LEFT");
    res.add("cellBackground", "#ffffff");
    res.add("cellLeftBorderType", "BORDER_NONE");
    res.add("cellTopBorderType", "BORDER_NONE");
    this.setValues(res);


    this.setValue("layoutFrozen", false);
```

**Continued**

```
}

public void layoutGrid() {

  MlResources res;
  Font boldFont;

  boldFont = new Font("Helvetica", Font.BOLD, 12);
  res = new MlResources();

  this.setValue("layoutFrozen", true);

  res.clear();
  res.add("rowType", "ALL_TYPES");
  res.add("columnType", "HEADING");
  res.add("column", 0);
  res.add("cellAlignment", "ALIGNMENT_CENTER");
  res.add("cellBackground", "#c0c0c0");
  res.add("cellFont", boldFont);
  res.add("cellLeftBorderType", "BORDER_LINE");
  res.add("cellTopBorderType", "BORDER_LINE");
  this.setValues(res);

  res.clear();
  res.add("rowType", "HEADING");
  res.add("row", 0);
  res.add("cellAlignment", "ALIGNMENT_CENTER");
  res.add("cellBackground", "#c0c0c0");
  res.add("cellFont", boldFont);
  res.add("cellLeftBorderType", "BORDER_LINE");
  res.add("cellTopBorderType", "BORDER_LINE");
  this.setValues(res);

  this.setValue("layoutFrozen", false);

}
```

In the `getData()` method, all of the rows in column_list are retrieved and stored in the grid. Because it is simple to retrieve values from the grid, it's not necessary to maintain a separate data structure for the result set. If the program needs to look up a value, it can get it from the grid.

```
/**
 * getData()
 *
 */
public protected void getData() {

    ResultSet rs;

    try {

        this.setValue("layoutFrozen", true); // freeze the layout

        // retrieve all rows from the table.
        //
        rs = stmt.executeQuery("SELECT " + column_list + " FROM " + table);

        // get a ResultSetMetaData object
        //
        ResultSetMetaData meta = rs.getMetaData();

        // a resource object to manipulate the grid
        //
        MlResources res = new MlResources();

        Vector rows = new Vector(); // a Vector to contain each row

        int i;
        int rowcount = 0;
```

Before each row in the grid can be populated, it will be necessary to retrieve and store each row. A simple way of storing the result set's rows is to put each column in an array of String objects. Then, that array can be inserted into a Vector called rows:

```
// process the result set
//
while (rs.next()) {

    rowcount++;

    // create an array of columns; this will hold the
    // String objects corresponding to each column,
    // and will be inserted into the rows Vector.
    //
    String[] columns = new String[meta.getColumnCount()];

    // store the value of each column
    //
    for (i = 1; i <= meta.getColumnCount(); i++) {
        columns[i - 1] = rs.getString(i);
    }
    rows.addElement(columns);

}
```

Now that all of the rows have been retrieved, it's simple to get a count of rows, which is stored in the rowcount variable. The following code will add headers for both columns (horizontal) and rows (vertical), and it will also add rows and columns to the grid. The ResultSetMetaData object meta is used to get a count of columns:

```
// use the resource object to add heading rows, heading
// columns, and to set the number of columns and rows
// according to the number of columns and rows in the
// result set.
//
res.clear();
```

```
res.add("headingRows", 1);
res.add("headingColumns", 1);
res.add("columns", meta.getColumnCount());
res.add("rows", rowcount);
this.setValues(res);
```

The following code will loop over the number of columns in the result set, and it will use the ResultSetMetaData object to get each column name. Then, it sets each column header to the text of the column name. As it does so, it also determines a reasonable column width: the greater of the column's display width, as reported by getColumnDisplaySize(), or the width of the column name:

```
// loop for each column. Here, the column headers
// will be set to have the correct title and width.
//
for (i = 1; i <= meta.getColumnCount(); i++) {

    // get the column name
    //
    String col_name = meta.getColumnName(i);

    // set the string of the column header
    //
    this.setStrings(MlGrid.HEADING, 0, MlGrid.CONTENT, i - 1, col_name);

    // determine a suitable column width: the greater
    // of the column's display size or the size of
    // its column name.
    //
    int size = Math.max(meta.getColumnDisplaySize(i), col_name.length());

    // prepare the resource object to set the column width
    //
    res.clear();
    res.add("column", i - 1);
    res.add("columnWidth", size);
```

The primary key column is special, so its index is saved. The expression "i - 1" gives us the grid column offset, which starts at zero; this is different from the JDBC column offset, which starts at one. The primary key column is also made read-only because it cannot be changed; it must be preserved in order to perform updates.

```
// if this column is the primary key, make it non-editable,
// and store the index in the pkey_col field.
//
if (col_name.equals(pkey)) {
  res.add("cellEditable", false);
  pkey_col = i - 1;
}


this.setValues(res);


}
```

Now, the rows Vector comes into play. Each element is read in turn, and the array of String objects is retrieved. The index of each element corresponds to the grid columns, and each String object within the array can be used to populate the grid with values from the database.

```
// set each column value on a row by row basis
//
int j;
for (j = 0; j < rows.size(); j++) {

  // number each row
  //
  this.setStrings(MlGrid.CONTENT, j, MlGrid.HEADING, 0,
    Integer.toString(j + 1));

  // get the column array from the rows Vector
  //
  String[] columns = (String[]) rows.elementAt(j);

  // add each column's value to the grid
```

```
    //
    for (i = 0; i < columns.length; i++) {
      res.clear();
      res.add("column",    i);
      res.add("row",       j);
      res.add("cellString", columns[i]);
      this.setValues(res);
    }


  }

    this.setValue("layoutFrozen", false);


  } catch (SQLException e) {
    SQLErr(e);
  }
}
```

Here's a `handleEvents()` method. It subclasses the `handleEvents()` method in
MlGrid, so it's essential to pass any unhandled events up to the superclass. The handling of
MlGridEvent.EDIT_COMPLETE is special, though; it signifies that the user has finished edit-
ing a cell, and it means that it is time to send an update to the database.

```
/**
 * handleEvent
 *
 * Deal with things the user did...
 */
public boolean handleEvent(Event _event) {

  MlGridEvent event = null;

  boolean event_handled = false;
  switch(_event.id) {

    case MlGridEvent.EDIT_COMPLETE:
```

**Continued**

The MlGridEvent object has some extra attributes, so if it's determined that the event ID is an MlGrid-specific event, the Event object can be safely cast to an MlGridEvent object:

```
// if the user completed an edit,
// then cast the _event object to
// an MlGridEvent object
//
event = (MlGridEvent) _event;
```

Here's where things get simple; you need to retrieve only the name of the column that was changed, its value, and the value of the primary key for the row that's being edited:

```
// get the column name that was edited
//
String column_name = (String)
  getCellValue(MlGrid.HEADING, 0, MlGrid.CONTENT,
                  event.column, "cellString");

// get the column value
//
String column_val = (String)
  getCellValue(event.row, event.column, "cellString");

// get the value of this row's primary key
//
String pkey_val = (String)
  getCellValue(event.row, pkey_col, "cellString");
```

Armed with the column name, value, and primary key value, it's simple to construct an SQL UPDATE statement and send it off to the server:

```
// construct an SQL UPDATE statement
//
String update = "UPDATE " + table +
            " SET " + column_name + " = '" + column_val + "' " +
```

```
                        " WHERE " + pkey + " = " + pkey_val;

        // issue the UPDATE
        //
        try {
          stmt.executeUpdate(update);
        } catch (SQLException e) {
          SQLErr(e);
        }

        event_handled = true;
        break;

    }

    if(event_handled) {
      return true;
    } else {
      return super.handleEvent(_event);
    }
  }
}
```

Here's the `main()` method that instantiates the jdbcMlGrid object. If you were to imple-ment the jdbcMlGrid object in your own programs, you would probably want to use this as a guideline:

```
/**
 *
 * instantiate the jdbcMlGrid object with test data.
 *
 */
public static void main (String argv[]) {

  try {
```

**Continued**

```
    // register all of the JDBC classes you might use
    // you can comment out or remove the ones you
    // are not using.
    //
    Class.forName("textFileDriver");              // the tinySQL textFile driver
    Class.forName("jdbc.odbc.JdbcOdbcDriver");  // JDBC-ODBC bridge
    Class.forName("imaginary.sql.iMsqlDriver"); // mSQL

} catch (Exception e) {
  e.printStackTrace();
}


if (argv.length == 0) {
    System.out.println("You must supply a URL to a JDBC data source.");
    System.out.println("");
    System.out.println("Example:");
    System.out.println("java DDL jdbc:odbc:DATA_SOURCE_NAME;" +
                       "UID=userid;PWD=password");
  System.exit(0);
}


// the user might have passed in a username or password,
// so try to read those in, as well
//
String user, pwd;
if (argv.length > 1) {
  user = argv[1];
} else {
  user = "";
}
if (argv.length > 2) {
  pwd = argv[2];
} else {
  pwd = "";
}


// create a myFrame object that knows how to close itself
```

```
    //
    myFrame f = new myFrame();
    f.setLayout(new BorderLayout());

    // create an MlGrid object and add it to the frame
    //
    String column_list = "name, address, city, state, zip, country, phone, id";
    jdbcMlGrid grid =
      new jdbcMlGrid(argv[0], user, pwd, "rolodex", column_list, "id");

    f.add("Center", grid);
    f.setTitle("rolodex");

    // resize and show the frame
    //
    f.resize(400, 300);
    f.show();

  }

  /**
   *
   * mindless error handler that prints out state, message,
   * and vendor info for SQL errors.
   */
  public void SQLErr(SQLException e) {
    while (e != null) {
      System.out.println("SQLState: " + e.getSQLState());
      System.out.println("Message:  " + e.getMessage());
      System.out.println("Vendor:   " + e.getErrorCode());
      e.printStackTrace();
      e = e.getNextException();
      System.out.println("");
    }
  }
}
```

The jdbcMlGrid class can be used as a tool for modifying rows in your tables, and can form the basis of a widget that you might use in an applet or application. If you were to use it in a production environment, you might want to consider enhancing it in a couple of ways. For one, all updates are written when a column is changed, which can be somewhat inefficient. Further, there are no checks to ensure that another user has not changed the data. A useful improvement to this class would be to buffer the original data in another data structure, and send updates only when the data has changed. Also, the class could be modified to send updates only when the user has finished modifying an entire row, rather than each column. Finally, the values in the database could be checked against the original values; if anything was changed between the time that the user loaded the data and the time that the user modified it, it would indicate that another user or process had changed the data. In that case, the user could be warned. These features would be mandatory in a serious production environment. Nevertheless, the jdbcMlGrid is a useful starting point for such endeavors; I hope it will  prove useful and instructive.

# Chapter 6

# Inside the tinySQL Database Management System

You've already gotten some experience with tinySQL by using it with JDBC and by incorporating it into some example programs. From that perspective, however, tinySQL looks like any other SQL database. Well, almost any other SQL database. If you've tried to improvise on the examples in previous chapters, you've probably found some of the limitations of tinySQL.

This chapter will explore the internals of tinySQL. If this frightens you, you can safely skip this chapter. This chapter will be helpful, though not required, in understanding Chapter 7, which goes into the details of the tinySQL JDBC driver. Although this chapter touches on certain aspects of the tinySQL API, Chapter 7 covers the aspects of the tinySQL API needed for the JDBC driver.

Designing and coding tinySQL was an extremely enjoyable and educational experience for me. I remember it well; it was a couple of weeks before this book's deadline, and I was pretty behind. I was also pretty unhappy with the book's content; it was more of a survey of available APIs and products than a book that educates readers about Java database programming, as the title implies.

I set out to do something I've always wanted to do; I wrote a simple SQL engine. First, I had to learn about generating parsers and lexical analyzers. I picked up a copy of *lex and yacc* by John R. Levine, Tony Mason, and Doug Brown (O'Reilly and Associates). lex is a program that generates lexical analyzers, or scanners; a *scanner* reads an input stream and breaks it up into tokens. For example, the SQL statement "DELETE FROM tree WHERE name = 'CFO'" would be broken up into the tokens DELETE, table name, FROM,

WHERE, column name, comparison, and string value. The tokens table name, column name, comparison, and string value carry the associated value (tree, name, =, and 'CFO') with them for use by the parser. yacc is a program that generates parsers. A parser analyzes the tokens returned by the scanner and determines the meaning of the tokens according to a grammar. A grammar for a programming language such as SQL is a lot like one for English or any other language; certain combinations of tokens (words) are meaningful only in certain combinations and orderings, and some words mean different things in different contexts.

Fortunately, *lex and yacc* contains an example SQL grammar. Although both lex and yacc generate C code, they are similar to JavaLex (`http://www.cs.princeton.edu/~ejberk/ JavaLex/JavaLex.html`), a lexical analyzer generator for Java, and JavaCup (`http://www .cc.gatech.edu/gvu/people/Faculty/hudson/java_cup/home.html`), a parser generator for Java. The SQL grammar supported by tinySQL is much smaller than the example in *lex and yacc*, but it provides enough functionality to perform some simple queries.

I'm not going to go into great detail about grammars, parsers, and scanners here; the SQL engine is removed enough from the parser that it is quite comprehensible on its own. However, Appendix C provides a tutorial for JavaLex and JavaCup.

# The Two Tiers

The tinySQL engine is actually two-tiered in nature. tinySQL and tinySQLTable are both abstract classes. With the two of these, you get nothing but an engine that knows how to deal with the SQL statements coming from the parser and how to process them using the abstract methods in tinySQLTable. When you want to actually implement tinySQL, you need to subclass both of these classes. When you subclass tinySQL, you provide methods that deal with creating and dropping physical tables and instantiating a tinySQLTable object. When you subclass tinySQLTable, you provide methods that deal with getting data in and out of the physical table. The tinySQL JDBC driver is actually built on top of the textFile and textFileTable classes; these extend tinySQL to interact with flat text files in a tinySQL data directory.

The practical upshot of this approach is that tinySQL can be implemented to provide an SQL interface to non-SQL data sources. So, if you have data lying around somewhere (say, for instance, an ugly flat-file dump from some ancient mainframe), you can quickly subclass tinySQL to provide an SQL interface to that data. Chapter 8 will discuss some other potential subclasses of tinySQL. After I introduce tinySQL here, I will also explain the textFile and textFileTable classes.

# tinySQL.java

What follows is the rather lengthy listing of the tinySQL abstract class. At the top of each method, I will provide a high-level overview of what that method does and, wherever necessary, provide concrete illustrations of abstract concepts.

```
/*
 *
 * tinySQL.java
 *
 * A trivial implementation of SQL in an abstract class.
 * Plug it in to your favorite non-SQL data source, and
 * QUERY AWAY!
 *
 */
import java.util.*;
import java.lang.*;
import java.io.*;
```

The tinySQL class has a couple of fields worth mentioning. The first is the SQLStream InputStream. All of the SQL statements are read from here and are passed to the parser. The String sqlstatement is the string of the last SQL Statement read. The only time this is correctly populated is when the SQL is executed throw sqlexec(String s); when it is read from System.in via the sqlexec() method, it cannot be captured in this fashion.

```
public abstract class tinySQL {

    // This is the InputStream from which the parser reads.
    //
    InputStream SQLStream;

    // This is the last SQL Statement processed by sqlexec(String s).
    // Note that sqlexec() does *not* support this.
    //
    String sqlstatement = "";
```

The constructor for tinySQL does absolutely nothing except return a tinySQL object. All business is conducted through one of the sqlexec() methods.

```
/**
 *
 * Constructs a new tinySQL object.
 *
 */
public tinySQL() {


}
```

The sqlexec() methods return a tsResultSet, which contains the results of a single SQL statement. The sqlexec() method that takes no parameters sets the SQLStream to the System.in stream, reading SQL statements from standard input. The sqlexec() method that takes a String as its sole parameter converts that string into a StringBufferInputStream and sets the SQLStream to that stream, after casting it to InputStream:

```
/**
 *
 * Reads SQL statements from System.in() and returns a
 * tsResultSet for the last statement executed. This is
 * really only good for testing.
 *
 * @exception tinySQLException
 *
 */
public tsResultSet sqlexec() throws tinySQLException {

    SQLStream = (InputStream) System.in;
    System.err.println("Reading SQL Statements from STDIN...");
    return sql();

}

/**
 *
 * Processes the SQL Statement contained in s and returns
 * a tsResultSet.
```

```
 *
 * @param s String containing a SQL Statement
 * @exception tinySQLException
 *
 */
public tsResultSet sqlexec(String s) throws tinySQLException {

    sqlstatement = s;

    StringBufferInputStream st = new StringBufferInputStream(s);
    SQLStream = (InputStream) st;
    return sql();

}
```

The sql() method is invoked by the sqlexec() methods. This method instantiates a parser and makes it read SQL from the SQLStream. The parser makes a Vector available, which contains one Hashtable for each SQL statement in the batch. The sql() method iterates over each element in this Vector.

Each Hashtable contained within the Vector contains information that describes the SQL statement. The objects are keyed by a String object. The following table explains each of these:

| Key | Type | Description |
| --- | --- | --- |
| TYPE | String | The type of SQL Statement (UPDATE, DELETE, SELECT, INSERT, CREATE, DROP) |
| TABLE | String | For SQL statements that only affect one table, this is the name of the table. |
| COLUMNS | Vector | This Vector contains the name of every affected column as Strings. |
| WHERE | Vector | This Vector contains all of the WHERE clauses in the SQL statement. tinySQL does not support OR within a WHERE clause, so all of the WHERE clauses are expected to be ANDed together. That is, if any one of them fails, the whole WHERE clause does. |

| Key | Type | Description |
|-----|------|-------------|
| | | Each object in the WHERE Vector is an array of Strings, containing four elements: |
| | | Element 0: The type of operation |
| | | Element 1: The left hand of the expression |
| | | Element 2: The comparison (=, <>, etc.) |
| | | Element 3: The right hand of the expression |
| | | See TestResult() for more information on WHERE clauses in tinySQL. |
| TABLES | Vector | This is a Vector of tables for SQL statements (such as SELECT) which affect more than one table. |
| VALUES | Vector | This Vector contains String values which correspond to columns in the COLUMNS Vector. |
| COLUMN_DEF | Vector | The COLUMN_DEF Vector contains arrays of String which contain definitions for each column in the table. This is used exclusively by the CREATE action. The arrays have the following elements: |
| | | Element 1: Data type |
| | | Element 2: Column name |
| | | Element 3: Size |

```
/**
 *
 * Read SQL Statements from the SQLStream, and
 * return a result set for the last SQL Statement
 * executed.
 *
 * @exception tinySQLException
 *
 */
protected tsResultSet sql() throws tinySQLException {

    // the result set
    //
    tsResultSet rs = null;

    try {
```

```
// Instantiate a new parser object that reads from
// the SQLStream.
//
parser parse_obj = new parser(SQLStream);

// let the parser do its thing
//
parse_obj.parse();

// retrieve the action vector from the parser. As
// the parser parses the SQL Statement, it fills
// the action vector with information about each
// SQL Statement in the batch. This information
// takes the form of a Hashtable.
//
Vector actions = parse_obj.action_obj.getActions();


// each Hashtable corresponds to an SQL Statement. Although
// tinySQL does not return multiple result sets, it will
// nevertheless process each one in turn and return a
// result set for the last statement executed.
//
// Here, tinySQL processes each Hashtable in the actions Vector.
//
for (int i = 0; i < actions.size(); i++) {

  // get the Hashtable
  //
  Hashtable h = (Hashtable) actions.elementAt(i);


  //
  // SQL UPDATE
  //
  // If this statement is an UPDATE statement, then the
  // following components of the Hashtable are significant:
```

**Continued**

```
//
// String table_name - the name of the affected table
//
// Vector columns    - a list of columns to be updated
//
// Vector values     - a list of values with which to
//                       update the columns (both the columns
//                       and values must be in the same order)
//
// Vector where      - a list of WHERE clauses. tinySQL
//                       assumes AND, but support for OR
//                       will be added in later versions.
//
if ( ((String)h.get("TYPE")).equals("UPDATE") ) {

  String table_name = (String) h.get("TABLE");
  Vector columns     = (Vector) h.get("COLUMNS");
  Vector values      = (Vector) h.get("VALUES");
  Vector where       = (Vector) h.get("WHERE");


  UpdateStatement (table_name, columns, values, where);
  rs = new tsResultSet();


}


//
// SQL DELETE
//
// If this statement is a DELETE statement, then the
// following components of the Hashtable are significant:
//
// String table_name - the name of the affected table
//
// Vector where      - a list of WHERE clauses.
//
if ( ((String)h.get("TYPE")).equals("DELETE") ) {
```

```
    String table_name = (String) h.get("TABLE");
    Vector where       = (Vector) h.get("WHERE");


    DeleteStatement (table_name, where);
    rs = new tsResultSet();

}


//
// SQL SELECT
//
// If this statement is a SELECT statement, then the
// following components of the Hashtable are significant:
//
// Vector tbls    - a list of affected tables
//
// Vector columns - a list of columns to be retrieved
//
// Vector where   - a list of WHERE clauses.
//
if ( ((String)h.get("TYPE")).equals("SELECT") ) {

  Vector tbls    = (Vector) h.get("TABLES");
  Vector columns = (Vector) h.get("COLUMNS");
  Vector where   = (Vector) h.get("WHERE");


  rs = SelectStatement (tbls, columns, where);

}


//
// SQL INSERT
//
// If this statement is an INSERT statement, then the
// following components of the Hashtable are significant:
//
// String table_name - the name of the affected table
```

**Continued**

```
//
// Vector columns    - a list of columns to be updated
//
// Vector values     - a list of values with which to
//                         update the columns (both the columns
//                         and values must be in the same order)
//
if ( ((String)h.get("TYPE")).equals("INSERT") ) {

   String table_name = (String) h.get("TABLE");
   Vector columns = (Vector) h.get("COLUMNS");
   Vector values = (Vector) h.get("VALUES");

   InsertStatement (table_name, columns, values);
   rs = new tsResultSet();

}


//
// SQL CREATE TABLE
//
// If this statement is a CREATE TABLE statement, then the
// following components of the Hashtable are significant:
//
// String table_name - the name of the affected table
//
// Vector columns    - a list of columns to be created
//
//
if ( ((String)h.get("TYPE")).equals("CREATE") ) {

   String table_name = (String) h.get("TABLE");
   Vector columns = (Vector) h.get("COLUMN_DEF");

   CreateTable (table_name, columns);
   rs = new tsResultSet();
```

```
    }


    //
    // SQL DROP TABLE
    //
    // If this statement is a DROP TABLE statement, then the
    // following components of the Hashtable are significant:
    //
    // String table_name - the name of the affected table
    //
    //
    if ( ((String)h.get("TYPE")).equals("DROP_TABLE") ) {

      DropTable( (String) h.get("TABLE") );
      rs = new tsResultSet();
    }


  }


} catch (Exception e) {
  throw new tinySQLException(e.getMessage() + ": " + sqlstatement);
}

  return rs;
}
```

The SelectStatement() method is probably the most complicated of all methods in the class. What it does is quite simple, however. It retrieves every row from each table in the query, but it does so by creating a Cartesian product. This amounts to every possible combination of rows from each table. For example, assume that we have the following tables:

| Contacts | |
|---|---|
| **cn_name** | **cn_co_id_** |
| Cody Pomeroy | 100 |
| Will Hubbard | 120 |

| Sal Paradise | 100 |
|---|---|
| Carlo Marx | 130 |

Companies

| co_name | co_id |
|---|---|
| Amalgamated Magnets | 100 |
| Variegated Vanities | 120 |
| Soporific Slumbers | 130 |

If you were to issue the SQL SELECT statement (notice no WHERE clause) "SELECT * FROM companies, contacts", you would get the following result:

| cn_name | cn_co_id_ | co_name | co_id |
|---|---|---|---|
| Cody Pomeroy | 100 | Amalgamated Magnets | 100 |
| Will Hubbard | 120 | Amalgamated Magnets | 100 |
| Sal Paradise | 100 | Amalgamated Magnets | 100 |
| Carlo Marx | 130 | Amalgamated Magnets | 100 |
| Cody Pomeroy | 100 | Variegated Vanities | 120 |
| Will Hubbard | 120 | Variegated Vanities | 120 |
| Sal Paradise | 100 | Variegated Vanities | 120 |
| Carlo Marx | 130 | Variegated Vanities | 120 |
| Cody Pomeroy | 100 | Soporific Slumbers | 130 |
| Will Hubbard | 120 | Soporific Slumbers | 130 |
| Sal Paradise | 100 | Soporific Slumbers | 130 |
| Carlo Marx | 130 | Soporific Slumbers | 130 |

Because no join conditions are specified within the where clause, the default (and correct) response of any SQL engine is to match every row in each table with every row in every other table. Without a WHERE clause that joins each table to at least one other table, this can result in huge results (# rows in table 1 * # number of rows in table 2, etc.). In the previous example, 4 rows in the contact table and 3 in the company table gave rise to 12 in the result set. With real-world data in massive quantities, this could lead to enormous result sets.

One of tinySQL's major deficiencies is that it always constructs such a Cartesian product before eliminating rows from the result set. This is going to change in subsequent versions of tinySQL, since it is mainly intended as a learning tool. (As an example for this book, it was essential to produce a working version of the engine in as little time as possible. I will no doubt spend many a late night hacking on tinySQL after this book is finally put to bed.)

After tinySQL constructs this Cartesian product, it iterates over each row and passes the row and the WHERE clause vector to TestResult() method. If TestResult() returns false, then the row is not included in the final result set. If you were to issue the SQL SELECT statement "SELECT * FROM companies, contacts WHERE cn_co_id_ = co_id" then tinySQL would initially create the enormous Cartesian product, but eventually reduce it to the rows shown in the table below:

| cn_name | cn_co_id_ | co_name | co_id |
|---------|-----------|---------|-------|
| Cody Pomeroy | 100 | Amalgamated Magnets | 100 |
| Sal Paradise | 100 | Amalgamated Magnets | 100 |
| Will Hubbard | 120 | Variegated Vanities | 120 |
| Carlo Marx | 130 | Soporific Slumbers | 130 |

All of the other rows in the original Cartesian product would be eliminated, leaving only the rows shown above. When the SelectStatement() method has created the final result set, it is returned as a tsResultSet object.

```
/*
 *
 * Execute an SQL Select Statement
 *
 */
private tsResultSet SelectStatement (Vector t, Vector c, Vector w)
   throws tinySQLException {
```

**Continued**

```java
// this is a Hashtable of all tables participating
// in the Select
//
Hashtable tables = new Hashtable();

// instantiate a new tsResultSet
//
tsResultSet jrs = new tsResultSet();

// Some enumerations which will be used later
//
Enumeration col_keys, tbl_enum;

// for loop index
//
int i;

// instantiate a table object for each
// table in the list of tables
//
for (i = 0; i < t.size(); i++) {

    // the t Vector contains all the table names
    // in the SELECT. For each one of these, create
    // a new table
    //
    String table_name = (String) t.elementAt(i);
    tinySQLTable jtbl = getTable(table_name);

    // put each table object into the tables
    // Hashtable. They are keyed by name, so
    // they can be retrieved by name in
    // subsequent operations
    //
    tables.put( table_name, jtbl );
```

```
    jtbl.GoTop();


}


// the c_remove Vector is a list of columns to be removed
// from the c Vector. At present, this is only the '*' columns
// and they are only removed after they have been expanded.
//
// These need to be removed, since '*' is not a valid column
// name.
//
Vector c_remove = new Vector();


// This code iterates over each named column in the c
// Vector. If a column is found named '*', it is expanded
// to all columns in the query. Since this early version
// of tinySQL does not support table aliasing, it's probably
// best if the '*' is the only item in the column specification.
//
int c_size = c.size();
for(i = 0; i < c_size; i++) {

  // is this item a '*'?
  //
  if ( ((String) c.elementAt(i)).equals("*") ) {

    // get an enumeration of all tables
    //
    tbl_enum = tables.elements();

    // process each element in the enumeration
    //
    while (tbl_enum.hasMoreElements()) {

      // get the next table in the enumeration
```

**Continued**

```
        //
        tinySQLTable jtbl = (tinySQLTable) tbl_enum.nextElement();

        // retrieve an enumeration of columns for that table
        //
        col_keys = jtbl.column_info.keys();

        // process each column in the enumeration
        //
        while (col_keys.hasMoreElements()) {

          // add each column to the c Vector
          //
          String col_name = (String) col_keys.nextElement();
          c.addElement(col_name);
        }
      }

      // add the column that had the '*' to the
      // c_remove Vector
      //
      c_remove.addElement( new Integer(i) );
    }
  }

  // remove the '*' items from c
  //
  for (i = 0; i < c_remove.size(); i++) {
    c.removeElementAt( ((Integer) c_remove.elementAt(i)).intValue() );
  }

  // the columns Hashtable is keyed by table name. It contains
  // a Vector of columns just for that table.
  //
  Hashtable columns = new Hashtable();

  // process each element in the c Vector
```

```
//
for (i = 0; i < c.size(); i++) {

  // get the column name
  //
  String column = (String) c.elementAt(i);

  // find the table that "owns" this column
  //
  tinySQLTable jtbl = findTableForColumn(tables, column);

  // add this column to the list of columns
  // keyed by table name.
  //
  Vector cols;

  // is this table already represented in the hash
  // of columns? If it is, retrieve the Vector that
  // represents all the columns added for that table.
  // Otherwise, created a new Vector.
  //
  if (columns.containsKey(jtbl.table)) {
    cols = (Vector) columns.get(jtbl.table);
  } else {
    cols = new Vector();
  }

  // add this column to the cols Vector and put
  // it in the columns Hashtable, keyed by
  // table name.
  //
  cols.addElement(column);
  columns.put( jtbl.table, cols);

  // create a new tsColumn object and add it to the result
  // set's column field. This can be used for metadata
```

**Continued**

```
      // lookups.
      //
      tsColumn jsc = new tsColumn(column);
      jsc.type = jtbl.ColType(column);
      jsc.size = jtbl.ColSize(column);

      jrs.columns.addElement(jsc);

}


// the table scan here is an iterative tree expansion, similar to
// the algorithm shown in the outline example in Chapter 5.
//

// which table level are we on?
//
int level = 1;

// create a hashtable to enumerate the tables to
// be scanned
//
Hashtable tbl_list = new Hashtable();

// put the name of the first table into it
//
String current = (String) t.elementAt(0);
tbl_list.put( current, new Integer(1) );

// create a row object; this is added to the
// result set
//
tsRow record = new tsRow();

// the resultSet vector is a temporary holding
// pen for the result set; later on, data in the rows
// in this Vector are evaluated before being added
```

```
// to  the real result set. This is pretty
// inefficient; things would be better if WHERE
// clauses were evaluated as (or before) the initial
// result set is retrieved.
//
// Subsequent versions of tinySQL will optimize this
// quite a bit.
//
Vector resultSet = new Vector();

// keep retrieving rows until we run out of rows to
// process.
//
while ( level > 0 ) {

  boolean levelFound = false;

  // find an item within the tbl_list
  // which has the same level as the
  // one we're on.
  //
  Enumeration keys = tbl_list.keys();
  while (keys.hasMoreElements()) {

    // get the next element in the "to be processed"
    // Hashtable and find out its level, storing this
    // value in currLevel.
    //
    String hashkey = (String) keys.nextElement();
    int currLevel  = ((Integer) tbl_list.get(hashkey)).intValue();

    // as soon as an element is found whose level
    // is equal to the one currently being processed,
    // grab its primary key (the hashkey), flag
    // levelfound, and break!
    //
```

**Continued**

```
     if (currLevel == level) {
       current = hashkey; levelFound = true; break;
     }
   }
}


boolean eof = false;          // did we hit eof?
boolean haveRecord = false; // did we get a record or not?

// if a table was found at the current level, then we should
// try to get another row from it.
//
if (levelFound) {

  // get the current table
  //
  tinySQLTable jtbl = (tinySQLTable) tables.get(current);

  // skip to the next undeleted record; at some point,
  // this will run out of records, and found will be
  // false.
  //
  boolean found = false;

  while (jtbl.NextRecord()) {
    if (!jtbl.isDeleted()) {
      found = true;
      break;
    }
  }

  if (found) {

    // add each column for this table to
    // the record; record is a tsRow object that
    // is used to hold the values of the current
    // row. It represents every row in every table,
```

```
// and is not added to the result set Vector
// until we have read a row in the last table
// in the table list.
//
Enumeration cols = jtbl.column_info.keys();
while (cols.hasMoreElements()) {

  String column_name = (String) cols.nextElement();
  record.put(column_name, jtbl.GetCol(column_name));


}


// since we were just able to get a row, then
// we are not at the end of file
//
eof = false;

// If the table we are processing is not the last in
// the list, then we should increment level and loop
// to the top.
//
if (level < t.size()) {

  // increment level
  //
  level++;

  // add the next table in the list of tables to
  // the tbl_list, the Hashtable of "to be processed"
  // tables.
  //
  String next_tbl = (String) t.elementAt( level - 1);
  tbl_list.put( next_tbl, new Integer(level) );

} else {
```

**Continued**

```
                    // if the table that was just processed is the last in
                    // the list, then we have drilled down to the bottom;
                    // all columns have values, and we can add it to the
                    // result set. The next time through, the program
                    // will try to read another row at this level; if it's
                    // found, only columns for the table being read will
                    // be overwritten in the tsRow.
                    //
                    // Columns for the other table will be left alone, and
                    // another row will be added to the result set. Here
                    // is the essence of the Cartesian Product that is
                    // being built here.
                    //
                    haveRecord = true;


                }

            } else {

                // we didn't find any more records at this level.
                // Reset the record pointer to the top of the table,
                // and decrement level. We have hit end of file here.
                //
                level--;
                eof = true;
                jtbl.GoTop();


            }

        } else {

            // no tables were found at this level; back up a level
            // and see if there's any up there.
            //
            level--;

        }
```

```
      // if we got a record, then add it to the result set.
      //
      if (haveRecord) {
         resultSet.addElement( (tsRow) record.clone() );
      }


   }


   // filter the result set. The result set Vector just created is
   // a Cartesian Product, which represents all possible combinations
   // of rows in all tables. The TestResult method will evaluate the
   // WHERE clause for each row, and determine if it qualifies
   // to be included in the final result set.
   //
   for (int y = 0; y < resultSet.size(); y++) {

     tsRow rec =  (tsRow) resultSet.elementAt(y);

     if (TestResult(rec, w, tables)) {
       jrs.rows.addElement(rec);
     }

   }


   // close all the tables
   //
   tbl_enum = tables.elements();
   while (tbl_enum.hasMoreElements()) {
     ( (tinySQLTable) tbl_enum.nextElement() ).close();
   }

   // return a result set
   //
   return jrs;

}
```

The `TestResult()` method is used by the SELECT, UPDATE, and DELETE statements to determine which rows satisfy a given WHERE clause. The types of comparisons that tinySQL can make are somewhat limited; the left-hand side of the expression must always be a column, and it only understands the equals operator (=) and the not equals operator (<>). This will be significantly enhanced in later versions of tinySQL.

```
/*
 *
 * Evaluate a record based on a where clause Vector.
 * The WHERE clause Vector contains a four element
 * array of Strings:
 *
 * Element 0: The type of operation
 * Element 1: The left hand of the expression
 * Element 2: The comparison (=, <>, etc.)
 * Element 3: The right hand of the expression
 *
 */
private boolean TestResult (tsRow rec, Vector w, Hashtable tables)
   throws tinySQLException {

   // w is a Vector containing all of the WHERE clause arrays.
   // Because tinySQL does not support OR within WHERE clauses,
   // the processing of these is pretty simple. If one fails,
   // throw out the row.
   //
   for(int i = 0; i < w.size(); i++) {

      // get the WHERE clause info array
      //
      String[] info = (String[]) w.elementAt(i);

      String op         = info[0];
      String left       = info[1];
      String comparison = info[2];
      String right      = info[3];
```

```
// JOIN
//
// Simple column to column comparison
//
if (op.equals("JOIN")) {

  // get the datatype for each column
  //
  String ltype = findTableForColumn(tables, left).ColType(left);
  String rtype = findTableForColumn(tables, right).ColType(right);

  // if the types don't match, throw an Exception
  //
  if (!ltype.equals(rtype)) {
    throw new tinySQLException("Data type mismatch.");
  }

  // if it's a character comparison, reset the op to
  // STRING_COMPARE, and set the right-hand side of the
  // expression to the value of the right-hand column.
  // Another lame feature of tinySQL is that all
  // expressions must include at least one column, and
  // it must be on the left.
  //
  if (ltype.equals("CHAR")) {
    op = "STRING_COMPARE";
    right = (String) rec.get(info[3]);
    if (right == null) {
      throw new tinySQLException("Invalid column: " + info[3]);
    }
  }

  // if it's a character comparison, reset the op to
  // INT_COMPARE, and set the right-hand side of the
  // expression to the value of the right-hand column.
```

**Continued**

```
  //
  if (ltype.equals("NUMERIC")) {
    op = "INT_COMPARE";
    right = (String) rec.get(info[3]);
    if (right == null) {
      throw new tinySQLException("Invalid column: " +  info[3]);
    }
  }

}


// column to string comparison?
//
if (op.equals("STRING_COMPARE")) {

  // attempt to read the column value
  //
  String colval = (String) rec.get(left);
  if (colval == null) {
    throw new tinySQLException("Invalid column: " + left);
  }

  // if the comparison is =, then do a simple
  // startsWith comparison. That way, if the
  // column is "FOOBAR", it will match "FOO".
  //
  if (comparison.equals("=")) {
    if (!colval.startsWith(right)) {
      return false;
    }
  }

  // if it's <>, then throw it out for matching the
  // right-hand value.
  //
  if (comparison.equals("<>")) {
```

```
      if (colval.startsWith(right)) {
        return false;
      }
    }

  }


  // column to integer comparison?
  //
  if (op.equals("INT_COMPARE")) {

    long colval, rval;
    String colstr = null;

    // attempt to read the column value
    //
    colstr = (String) rec.get(left);
    if (colstr == null) {
      throw new tinySQLException("Invalid column: " + left);
    }

    // try to convert the column value and the
    // right-hand value to numeric
    //
    try {
      colval = Long.parseLong( colstr.trim() );
    } catch (Exception e) {
      throw new tinySQLException( e.getMessage() +
        ": Could not convert [" + colstr.trim() + "] to numeric.");
    }

    try {
      rval = Long.parseLong(right.trim());
    } catch (Exception e) {
      throw new tinySQLException( e.getMessage() +
        ": Could not convert [" + right.trim() + "] to numeric.");
```

**Continued**

```
        }


        // if the comparison is simply =, throw it out
        // if it doesn't match (!=)
        //
        if (comparison.equals("=")) {
          if (colval != rval) {
            return false;
          }
        }


        // if the comparison is simply <> throw it out
        // if it does match (==)
        //
        if (comparison.equals("<>")) {
          if (colval == rval) {
            return false;
          }
        }


      }


    }


    // if none of the comparisons failed, return true
    //
    return true;


  }
```

Because there will often be multiple tables and columns in an SQL statement, the
findTableForColumn() method comes in handy. Given a Hashtable keyed by table
names and containing tinySQLTable objects, and given a column name, this method will
make an attempt to find the table that the column belongs to. If it finds it, it will return the
tinySQLTable object. Otherwise, it throws a tinySQLException.

```
/**
 *
 * Given a column name, and a Hashtable containing tables,
 * try to find which table "owns" a given column.
 *
 */
private tinySQLTable findTableForColumn (Hashtable tables, String col_name)
  throws tinySQLException {

  tinySQLTable tbl;

  // process each table in the tables Hashtable
  //
  Enumeration enum = tables.elements();
  while (enum.hasMoreElements()) {

    // retrieve the tinySQLTable object
    //
    tbl = (tinySQLTable) enum.nextElement();

    // get the table's column info, and check to
    // see if it contains the column name in question.
    // if so, return the tinySQLTable object.
    //
    Hashtable column_info = tbl.column_info;

    if (column_info.containsKey(col_name)) {
      return tbl;
    }
  }

  // looks like we couldn't find the column, so throw an exception
  //
  throw new tinySQLException("Column " + col_name + " not found.");
}
```

The DeleteStatement() method processes every row in the table. For any row that satisfies the WHERE clause of the statement (or all rows if no WHERE clause was supplied), the row is deleted.

```
/*
 *
 * Delete rows that match a WHERE clause.
 *
 */
private void DeleteStatement (String table_name, Vector w)
   throws tinySQLException {

   // create the table
   //
   tinySQLTable jtbl = getTable(table_name);

   // put this table into the tables hash
   //
   Hashtable tables = new Hashtable();
   tables.put(table_name, jtbl);

   // process each row in the table
   //
   jtbl.GoTop();
   while (jtbl.NextRecord()) {

      // ignore deleted rows.
      //
      if (!jtbl.isDeleted()) {

         // create a new tsRow object and add each column
         // to it.
         //
         tsRow rec = new tsRow();

         // add each column for this table to
```

```
        // the tsRow object
        //
        Enumeration cols = jtbl.column_info.keys();
        while (cols.hasMoreElements()) {
          String column_name = (String) cols.nextElement();
          rec.put(column_name, jtbl.GetCol(column_name));
        }

        // invoke TestResult to see if the table matches
        // the WHERE clause(s) - if so, delete it.
        //
        if (TestResult(rec, w, tables)) {
          jtbl.DeleteRow();
        }
      }
    }
  jtbl.close();
}
```

The `UpdateStatement()` method can update specific columns with values. Unfortunately, the right-hand side of the `SET` clause must be a value and cannot include a column or an expression. This method must process each row in the table. For any row that satisfies the `WHERE` clause of the statement (or all rows if no `WHERE` clause was supplied), the row is updated with the supplied values.

```
/*
 *
 * Update rows that match a WHERE clause
 *
 */
private void UpdateStatement(String table_name, Vector c, Vector v, Vector w)
  throws tinySQLException {

  // create the table
  //
  tinySQLTable jtbl = getTable(table_name);
```

**Continued**

```java
// put this table into the tables hash
//
Hashtable tables = new Hashtable();
tables.put(table_name, jtbl);

// process each row in the table
//
jtbl.GoTop();
while (jtbl.NextRecord()) {

  // ignore deleted rows.
  //
  if (!jtbl.isDeleted()) {

    // create a new tsRow object and add each column
    // to it.
    //
    tsRow rec = new tsRow();

    // add each column for this table to
    // the tsRow object
    //
    Enumeration cols = jtbl.column_info.keys();
    while (cols.hasMoreElements()) {
      String column_name = (String) cols.nextElement();
      rec.put(column_name, jtbl.GetCol(column_name));
    }

    // invoke TestResult to see if the table matches
    // the WHERE clause(s) - if so, update it with the
    // columns and values Vectors.
    //
    if (TestResult(rec, w, tables)) {
      jtbl.UpdateCurrentRow(c, v);
    }
  }
}
```

```
   }
   jtbl.close();
}
```

The `InsertStatement()` method processes an `SQL INSERT`. First, it inserts a blank row and then updates the columns with the supplied values.

```
/*
 *
 * Issue an insert statement
 *
 */
private void InsertStatement (String table_name, Vector c, Vector v)
   throws tinySQLException {

   // create the tinySQLTable object
   //
   tinySQLTable jtbl = getTable(table_name);

   // insert a row, and update it with the c and v Vectors
   //
   jtbl.InsertRow();
   jtbl.UpdateCurrentRow(c, v);
   jtbl.close();

}
```

Here's where the abstract methods start appearing. The `CreateTable()` method, which is totally dependent on the underlying physical table, must be defined in any subclass of tinySQL. The same goes for `DropTable()`, which permanently removes a table.

```
/*
 *
 * Creates a table given a table_name, and a Vector of column
 * definitions.
 *
 * The column definitions are an array of Strings having the following
 * elements:
```

**Continued**

```
 *
 * Element 1: Data type
 * Element 2: Column name
 * Element 3: Size
 *
 */
abstract void CreateTable (String table_name, Vector v)
   throws IOException, tinySQLException;


/*
 *
 * Drops a table by name
 *
 */
abstract void DropTable (String table_name)
   throws tinySQLException;
```

This next abstract method is very critical to the tinySQL architecture. Because tinySQLTable is an abstract class, it cannot be directly instantiated. Nevertheless, the tinySQL class needs to use these objects all over the place. Because the tinySQLTable will be subclassed, it can be cast back to a tinySQLTable. When your subclass of tinySQL defines the `getTable()` method, it needs to instantiate the subclass of tinySQLTable. Once it has created the table, it can then cast it to tinySQLTable and return it. This allows tinySQL to use subclasses of tinySQLTable. If this is confusing, things will become a little more clear when the code for textFile.java and textFileTable.java is explained.

```
/*
 *
 * Create a tinySQLTable object by table name
 *
 */
abstract tinySQLTable getTable(String table_name) throws tinySQLException;

}
```

The tsColumn is a class that is used by tinySQL and tinySQLTable to store information about columns.

```
/*
 *
 * tsColumn - object to hold column metadata
 *
 */
class tsColumn {

  public String name = null;   // the column's name
  public String type = null;   // the column's type
  public int    size = 0;       // the column's size
  public String table = null; // the table which "owns" the column


  /**
   *
   * Constructs a tsColumn object.
   *
   * @param s the column name
   */
  tsColumn (String s) {
    name = s;
  }

}
```

A tsRow object is merely a Hashtable that is used to hold column values for a given row. These are added to the tsResultSet object, which holds each row in the result set.

```
/*
 *
 * tsRow - an extension to Hashtable to hold a given row.
 *
 */
class tsRow extends Hashtable {

  /**
   *
   * Given a column name, returns its value as a string.
```

**Continued**

```
 *
 * @param column the name of the column
 *
 */
public String columnAsString (String column) {
   return (String) get(column);
}


/**
 *
 * Given a tsColumn object, returns its value as a String.
 *
 * @param column the tsColumn object
 *
 */
public String columnAsString (tsColumn column) {
   return (String) get(column.name);
}

}
```

The tsResultSet has two Vectors as its fields. The first, rows, contains a tsRow for every row in the result set. The second, columns, contains a tsColumn for every column in the result set. This enables client applications to retrieve results and get information about the result set.

```
/*
 *
 * tsResultSet - object to hold query results
 *
 */
class tsResultSet {

   public Vector rows = new Vector();     // all of the rows
   public Vector columns = new Vector(); // all of the tsColumn objects

   /**
```

```
 *
 * Returns the number of columns in the result set.
 *
 */
public int numcols() {
  return columns.size();
}

/**
 *
 * Returns the number of rows in the result set.
 *
 */
public int size() {
  return rows.size();
}

/**
 *
 * Returns the tsRow at a given row offset (starts with zero).
 *
 * @param i the row offset/index
 *
 */
public tsRow rowAt(int i) {
  return (tsRow) rows.elementAt(i);
}

/**
 *
 * Returns the tsColumn at a given column offset (starts with zero).
 *
 * @param i the column offset/index
 *
 */
public tsColumn columnAtIndex (int i) {
```

**Continued**

```
        return (tsColumn) columns.elementAt(i);
}
```

Here's a method left over from when I was debugging tinySQL. It simply dumps out an entire result set to the console, which can be useful if you want to modify and examine the behavior of tinySQL and related classes.

```java
/**
 *
 * Debugging method to dump out the result set
 *
 */
public void PrintResultSet() {

  // print out column headers
  //
  StringBuffer header = new StringBuffer(" ");
  for (int k = 0; k < numcols(); k++) {

    tsColumn column = columnAtIndex(k);

    header.append(column.name);
    for (int f = 0; f < column.size - column.name.length(); f++) {
      header.append(' ');
    }
    header.append(' ');
  }
  System.out.println("");
  System.out.println(header);

  for (int i = 0; i < size(); i++) {

    StringBuffer printrow = new StringBuffer(" ");

    tsRow row = rowAt(i);

    for (int j = 0; j < numcols(); j++) {
```

```
             tsColumn column = columnAtIndex(j);
             String colval    = row.columnAsString(column);

             if (colval == null) {
               colval = "null";
             }
             int len = colval.length();

             printrow.append(colval);
             for (int f = 0; f < (column.size - len); f++) {
             printrow.append(' ');
             }
             printrow.append(' ');
           }
         System.err.println(printrow);
       }
     }

   }
```

# tinySQLException.java

The tinySQLException class provides a specialized Exception object that can be thrown by tinySQL and tinySQLTable. While it does not provide any extra features over the Exception object, its presence will ease customization and enhancement of tinySQL in the future.

```
/*
 *
 * tinySQLException.java
 *
 * An Exception that is thrown when a problem has occurred in tinySQL
 *
 */
public class tinySQLException extends Exception {
```

**Continued**

```
/**
 *
 * Constructs a new tinySQLException
 * @param message the exception's message
 *
 */
public tinySQLException(String message) {
    super(message);
}

/**
 *
 * Constructs a new tinySQLException with no message.
 *
 */
public tinySQLException() {
}

}
```

# tinySQLTable.java

The tinySQLTable class is a purely abstract class that provides all of the methods needed for table manipulation by tinySQL and its subclasses.

```
/*
 *
 * tinySQLTable - abstract class for physical table access under tinySQL
 *
 */
import java.util.*;
import java.lang.*;
import java.io.*;

public abstract class tinySQLTable {

    public String table; // the name of the table
```

```java
// Hashtable to contain info about columns in the table
//
public Hashtable column_info = new Hashtable();

/**
 *
 * Closes the table.
 *
 */
public abstract void close() throws tinySQLException;

/**
 *
 * Returns the size of a column.
 *
 * @param column name of the column.
 *
 */
public abstract int ColSize(String column);

/**
 *
 * Returns the datatype of a column.
 *
 * @param column name of the column.
 *
 */
public abstract String ColType(String column);

/**
 *
 * Updates the current row in the table.
 *
 * @param c Ordered Vector of column names
 * @param v Ordered Vector (must match order of c) of values
 *
```

**Continued**

```java
  */
public abstract void UpdateCurrentRow(Vector c, Vector v)
  throws tinySQLException;

/**
 *
 * Position the record pointer at the top of the table.
 *
 */
public abstract void GoTop() throws tinySQLException;

/**
 *
 * Advance the record pointer to the next record.
 *
 */
public abstract boolean NextRecord() throws tinySQLException;

/**
 *
 * Insert a blank row.
 *
 */
public abstract void InsertRow() throws tinySQLException;

/**
 *
 * Retrieve a column's string value from the current row.
 *
 * @param column the column name
 *
 */
public abstract String GetCol ( String column ) throws tinySQLException ;

/**
 *
 * Update a single column.
```

```
     *
     * @param column the column name
     * @param value the String value with which update the column
     *
     */
   public abstract void UpdateCol( String column, String value )
      throws tinySQLException;

   /**
     *
     * Delete the current row.
     *
     */
   public abstract void DeleteRow() throws tinySQLException;

   /**
     *
     * Is the current row deleted?
     *
     */
   public abstract boolean isDeleted() throws tinySQLException;

}
```

# textFile.java

While most of the table-specific methods are encapsulated in tinySQLTable and its subclasses, there are a few abstract methods in tinySQL that must be extended. textFile.java extends these and provides the beginnings of a tinySQL implementation. The textFileTable class will provide the rest.

```
/*
 *
 * textFile - an extension of tinySQL for text file access
 *
 */
import java.util.*;
```

**Continued**

```
import java.lang.*;
import java.io.*;


public class textFile extends tinySQL {
```

Because textFile works with flat files on your computer's file system, it needs someplace to store them. This defaults to a directory called .tinySQL in your home directory.

```
// the data directory where textFile stores its files
//
static String dataDir = System.getProperty("user.home") + "/.tinySQL";
```

The `CreateTable()` method will create the table specified by a Vector of column definition arrays. The table's definition is stored in a file that has the same name as the table, but has the extension .def. The table itself is created when you add rows and has the same name as the table's name, with no extension. Some database management systems, such as dBase or FoxPro, use an extension .DBF after the table name. Not so with textFile.

```
/**
 *
 * Creates a table given the name and a vector of
 * column definition arrays.
 * The column definition arrays have the following elements:
 *
 * Element 1: Data type
 * Element 2: Column name
 * Element 3: Size
 *
 * @param table_name the name of the table
 * @param v a Vector containing arrays of column definitions.
 * @see tinySQL#CreateTable
 *
 */
void CreateTable ( String table_name, Vector v )
   throws IOException, tinySQLException {

   // make the data directory, if it needs to be made
   //
   mkDataDirectory();
```

```
      // perform an implicit drop table.
      //
      DropTable(table_name);

      // create the table definition file
      //
      FileOutputStream fdef =
          new FileOutputStream( dataDir + "/" + table_name + ".def" );

      // open it as a DataOutputStream
      //
      DataOutputStream def = new DataOutputStream (fdef);

      // write out the column definition for the _DELETED column
      //
      def.writeBytes("CHAR|_DELETED|1\n");

      // write out the rest of the columns' definition. The
      // definition consists of datatype, column name, and
      // size delimited by a pipe symbol
      //
      for (int i = 0; i < v.size(); i++) {
          def.writeBytes( ((String[]) v.elementAt(i))[0] + "|");
          def.writeBytes( ((String[]) v.elementAt(i))[1] + "|");
          def.writeBytes( ((String[]) v.elementAt(i))[2] + "\n");
      }

      // flush the DataOutputStream and jiggle the handle
      //
      def.flush();

      // close the file
      //
      fdef.close();
}
```

Here is a very important part of this class—the getTable() method that is called by tinySQL and its subclasses. Regardless of what table it instantiates (in this case, a textFileTable), it needs to return a tinySQLTable. Because textFileTable is a subclass of tinySQLTable, this method needs only to cast it to a tinySQLTable before returning it.

```
/**
 *
 * Return a tinySQLTable object, given a table name.
 *
 * @param table_name
 * @see tinySQL#getTable
 *
 */
tinySQLTable getTable (String table_name) throws tinySQLException {
    return (tinySQLTable) new textFileTable (dataDir, table_name);
}
```

The `DropTable()` method completely deletes a table and its .def file by calling the `delFile()` method:

```
/**
 *
 * Drop a named table by deleting it and its associated
 * .def file.
 *
 * @param fname table name
 * @see tinySQL#DropTable
 *
 */
void DropTable (String fname) throws tinySQLException {

    try {

        delFile(fname);
        delFile(fname + ".def");

    } catch (Exception e) {
```

```
        throw new tinySQLException(e.getMessage());
    }


}
```

Although all of the abstract methods from tinySQL have now been defined, some of the methods here rely on certain routines, which follow. These are not called by tinySQL, but are nevertheless important. The first is mkDataDirectory(), which simply makes the data directory. If it fails, it throws an exception:

```
/*
 *
 * Make the data directory unless it already exists
 *
 */
void mkDataDirectory() throws NullPointerException {

  File dd = new File( dataDir );

  if (!dd.exists()) {
    dd.mkdir();
  }


}
```

The delFile() method deletes a file within the data directory. This is used by the DropTable() method:

```
/*
 *
 * Delete a file in the data directory
 *
 */
void delFile (String fname) throws NullPointerException, IOException {

  File f = new File( dataDir + "/" + fname );

  // only delete a file that exists
```

**Continued**

```
    //
    if (f.exists()) {

        // try the delete. If it fails, complain
        //
        if (!f.delete()) {
            throw new IOException("Could not delete file: " +
                        dataDir + "/" + fname + ".");
        }


    }


}
```

The static method `main()` is provided as a regression test. Once you have compiled textFile and textFileTable, you need only to issue the command:

```
java textFile
```

This automatically invokes `main()` and creates a table called test, inserts into it, and selects the value from it. If it finds the expected value and does not report an error, then it has been installed correctly.

```
/*
 * regression test
 */
public static void main(String argv[]) {
    textFile foo = new textFile();
    tsResultSet trs = null;
    try {
        trs = foo.sqlexec("CREATE TABLE test (name CHAR(10))");
        trs = foo.sqlexec("INSERT INTO test (name) VALUES('test')");
        trs = foo.sqlexec("SELECT name FROM test");
    } catch (Exception e) {
        e.printStackTrace();
    }

    tsRow row = trs.rowAt(0);
```

```
    tsColumn column = trs.columnAtIndex(0);
    String colval     = row.columnAsString(column);

    if (colval.startsWith("test")) {
      System.err.println("textFile driver installed correctly.");
    } else {
      System.err.println("Test was not successful :-(");
      System.err.println("Got \"" + colval + "\", expected \"test\"");
    }


  }
}
```

# textFileTable.java

The textFileTable class performs all of the dirty, disgusting work needed to manipulate the text files. It takes care of fun things like opening tables, writing single rows, and deleting rows. This should serve, along with textFile, as a roadmap for individuals wishing to implement tinySQL in other contexts.

```
/*
 *
 * Extension of tinySQLTable which manipulates text files.
 *
 */
import java.util.*;
import java.lang.*;
import java.io.*;

public class textFileTable extends tinySQLTable {
```

Here, the dataDir and RandomAccessFile fields are declared. These will be used by textFileTable as we go along. The record_number and record length fields are declared, along with some constants, which are used when retrieving components of column definitions from the column_info field, which is actually declared in the superclass, tinySQLTable.

```
// The data directory for tables
//
```

**Continued**

```
public String dataDir;

// the object I'll use to manipulate the table
//
RandomAccessFile ftbl;

// some constants that I don't actually use that much...
//
int COLUMN_SIZE = 0;
int COLUMN_TYPE = 1;
int COLUMN_POS  = 2;

long record_number = 0; // current record
long record_length;     // length of a record
```

The constructor for textFileTable requires the data directory and table name. It concatenates these two values to obtain a full path to the table. The table is then opened using a RandomAccessFile object. This will allow a great deal of flexibility in manipulating the table. After this is done, `readColumnInfo()` is invoked, which stores column metadata by column name in the column_info Hashtable.

```
/**
 *
 * Constructs a textFileTable. This is only called by getTable()
 * in textFile.java.
 *
 * @param dDir data directory
 * @param table_name the name of the table
 *
 */
textFileTable( String dDir, String table_name ) throws tinySQLException {

    dataDir = dDir;       // set the data directory
    table = table_name;   // set the table name

    // attempt to open the file in read/write mode
    //
    try {
```

```
      ftbl = new RandomAccessFile(dataDir + "/" + table_name, "rw");
   } catch (Exception e) {
      throw new tinySQLException("Could not open the file " + table + ".");
   }

   // read in the table definition
   //
   readColumnInfo();

}
```

The `close()` method needs to be defined; it takes care of closing the table.

```
/**
 *
 * close method. Try not to call this until you are sure
 * the object is about to go out of scope.
 *
 */
public void close() throws tinySQLException {

   try {
      ftbl.close();
   } catch (IOException e) {
      throw new tinySQLException(e.getMessage());
   }

}
```

The `ColSize()` method is used to find out the width of a column. It consults the column_info Hashtable to retrieve information about the column.

```
/**
 *
 * Returns the size of a column
 *
 * @param column name of the column
 * @see tinySQLTable#ColSize
```

**Continued**

```
    *
    */
   public int ColSize(String column) {

      // retrieve the column info array from the column_info Hashtable
      //
      String info[] = (String[]) column_info.get(column);

      // return its size
      //
      return Integer.parseInt( info[COLUMN_SIZE] );

   }
```

The ColType() method is used to find out the datatype of a column. It consults the column_info Hashtable to retrieve information about the column.

```
   /**
    *
    * Returns the datatype of a column.
    *
    * @param column name of the column.
    * @see tinySQLTable#ColType
    *
    */
   public String ColType(String column) {

      // retrieve the column info array from the column_info Hashtable
      //
      String info[] = (String[]) column_info.get(column);

      // return its datatype
      //
      return info[COLUMN_TYPE];

   }
```

`UpdateCurrentRow()` takes a Vector of columns and a Vector of values and uses these to update each column named in the column Vector (c) with the corresponding value in the values Vector (v).

```
/**
 *
 * Updates the current row in the table.
 *
 * @param c Ordered Vector of column names
 * @param v Ordered Vector (must match order of c) of values
 * @see tinySQLTable#UpdateCurrentRow
 *
 */
public void UpdateCurrentRow(Vector c, Vector v) throws tinySQLException {

    // the Vectors v and c are expected to have the
    // same number of elements. It is also expected
    // that the elements correspond to each other,
    // such that value 1 of Vector v corresponds to
    // column 1 of Vector c, and so forth.
    //
    for (int i = 0; i < v.size(); i++) {

        // get the column name and the value, and
        // invoke UpdateCol() to update it.
        //
        String column = (String) c.elementAt(i);
        String value =  (String) v.elementAt(i);
        UpdateCol(column, value);
    }


}
```

`GoTop()` is used to reset the record pointer to the top of the file. This is useful when you have exhausted some or all of the rows in a table and need to start from the top.

```
/**
 *
```

**Continued**

```
 * Position the record pointer at the top of the table.
 *
 * @see tinySQLTable#GoTop
 *
 */
public void GoTop() throws tinySQLException {

    try {
        ftbl.seek(0);
        record_number = 0;
    } catch (IOException e) {
        throw new tinySQLException(e.getMessage());
    }


}
```

`NextRecord()` is used to advance to the next record. Methods such as `Update CurrentRow()`, `UpdateCol()`, `DeleteCol()`, and `GetCol()` operate on the row that is advanced to by this method.

```
/**
 *
 * Advance the record pointer to the next record.
 *
 * @see tinySQLTable#NextRecord
 *
 */
public boolean NextRecord() throws tinySQLException {

    // if the record number is greater than zero,
    // advance the pointer. Otherwise, we're on the first
    // record, and it hasn't been visited before.
    //
    if (record_number > 0) {

        // try to make it to the next record. An IOException
        // indicates that we have hit the end of file.
```

```
    //
    try {
       ftbl.seek( ftbl.getFilePointer() + record_length + 1);
    } catch (IOException e) {
       return false;
    }


  }


  // increment the record pointer
  //
  record_number++;

  // check for end of file, just in case...
  //
  try {
    if (ftbl.getFilePointer() == ftbl.length()) {
       return false;
    }
  } catch (Exception e) {
    throw new tinySQLException(e.getMessage());
  }

  return true;

}
```

This method inserts a blank row into the table and positions the file pointer in such a
way that `DeleteRow()`, `UpdateCol()`, `UpdateCurrentRow()`, or `GetCol()` would
operate on the newly inserted row.

```
/**
 *
 * Insert a blank row.
 *
 * @see tinySQLTable#InsertRow()
 *
 */
```

**Continued**

```java
public void InsertRow() throws tinySQLException {

    try {

        // go to the end of the file
        //
        ftbl.seek( ftbl.length() );

        // write out the deleted indicator
        //
        ftbl.write('N');

        // write out a blank record
        //
        for (int i = 1; i < record_length; i++) {
            ftbl.write(' ');
        }
        ftbl.write('\n');

        // reposition at start of current record
        //
        ftbl.seek( ftbl.getFilePointer() - (record_length + 1) );

    } catch (Exception e) {
        throw new tinySQLException(e.getMessage());
    }

}
```

GetCol() retrieves the value of a named column as a String. It is up to programs that invoke this method to perform any necessary conversion.

```java
/**
 *
 * Retrieve a column's string value from the current row.
 *
 * @param column the column name
 * @see tinySQLTable#GetCol
```

```
 *
 */
public String GetCol(String column) throws tinySQLException {

  try {

    // get the column info
    //
    String info[] = (String[]) column_info.get(column);

    // retrieve datatype, size, and position within row
    //
    String datatype = info[COLUMN_TYPE];
    int size       = Integer.parseInt(info[COLUMN_SIZE]);
    int pos        = Integer.parseInt(info[COLUMN_POS]);

    // save the file pointer
    //
    long OldPosition = ftbl.getFilePointer();

    // read the whole line from this row.
    //
    String line = ftbl.readLine();

    // retrieve the column from the line we just read,
    // at offset pos, for length size
    //
    String result = line.substring(pos, pos + size);

    // restore the file pointer
    //
    ftbl.seek( OldPosition );

    // trim the result if it was numeric
    //
    if (datatype.equals("NUMERIC")) {
```

**Continued**

```
        return result.trim();
      } else {
        return result;
      }

    } catch (Exception e) {
      throw new tinySQLException(e.getMessage());
    }
  }
}
```

Given a column name, and a value, `UpdateCol()` will set the named column within the current row to the specified value.

```
/**
 *
 * Update a single column.
 *
 * @param column the column name
 * @param value the String value with which update the column
 * @see tinySQLTable#UpdateCol
 *
 */
public void UpdateCol( String column, String value ) throws tinySQLException {

  try {

    // read the column info
    //
    String info[] = (String[]) column_info.get(column);

    // retrieve datatype, size, and position within row
    //
    String datatype = info[COLUMN_TYPE];
    long size       = Long.parseLong(info[COLUMN_SIZE]);
    long pos        = Long.parseLong(info[COLUMN_POS]);

    // position the file pointer at the column
```

```
    // offset.
    //
    ftbl.seek( ftbl.getFilePointer() + pos );

    String writeval;

    if (value.length() > (int) size) {

      // truncate the value if it exceeds the width
      // of the column
      //
      writeval = value.substring(0, (int) size);

    } else {

      // add some padding to the end of the string
      //
      StringBuffer pad = new StringBuffer();
      for (int p = 0; p < ((int) size) - value.length(); p++) {
        pad.append(" ");
      }
      writeval = value + pad.toString();
    }

    // write out the column
    //
    ftbl.writeBytes(writeval);

    // rewind the file pointer
    //
    ftbl.seek( ftbl.getFilePointer() - (pos + (long) writeval.length()) );

  } catch (Exception e) {
    throw new tinySQLException(e.getMessage());
  }
}
```

DeleteRow() is implemented quite simply. Because every textFileTable has a
_DELETED field, it's only a matter of flipping its value to "Y" using UpdateCol(). Similarly, GetCol() is used by the isDeleted() method to determine if the current row is deleted.

```java
/**
 *
 * Delete the current row.
 *
 * @see tinySQLTable#DeleteRow
 *
 */
public void DeleteRow() throws tinySQLException {

  // this is real easy; just flip the value of the _DELETED column
  //
  UpdateCol("_DELETED", "Y");


}


/**
 *
 * Is the current row deleted?
 *
 * @see tinySQLTable#isDeleted()
 *
 */
public boolean isDeleted() throws tinySQLException {

  // this is real easy; just check the value of the _DELETED column
  //
  return (GetCol("_DELETED")).equals("Y");
}

// end methods implemented from tinySQLTable.java
// the rest of this stuff is internal methods
// for textFileTable
//
```

The `readColumnInfo()` method is invoked by the textFileTable constructor. It parses the contents of the .def file and stores information such as column datatype, size, and position within the column_info Hashtable.

```
/*
 *
 * Reads in a table definition and populates the column_info
 * Hashtable
 *
 */
void readColumnInfo() throws tinySQLException {

  try {

    // Open an FileInputStream to the .def (table
    // definition) file
    //
    FileInputStream fdef =
        new FileInputStream( dataDir + "/" + table + ".def" );

    // use a StreamTokenizer to break up the stream.
    //
    StreamTokenizer def = new StreamTokenizer (fdef);

    // set the | as a delimiter, and set everything between
    // 0 and z as word characters. Let it know that eol is
    // *not* significant, and that it should parse numbers.
    //
    def.whitespaceChars('|', '|');
    def.wordChars('0', 'z');
    def.eolIsSignificant(false);
    def.parseNumbers();

    // read each token from the tokenizer
    //
    while ( def.nextToken() != def.TT_EOF ) {

      // first token is the datatype
```

**Continued**

```
    //
    String datatype = def.sval;

    // get the next token; it's the column name
    //
    def.nextToken();
    String column   =  def.sval;

    // get the third token; it's the size of the column
    //
    def.nextToken();
    double size         =  def.nval;

    // create an info array
    //
    String[] info = new String[3];

    // store the datatype, the size, and the position
    // within the record (the record length *before*
    // we increment it with the size of this column
    //
    info[COLUMN_TYPE] = datatype;
    info[COLUMN_SIZE] = Double.toString(size);
    info[COLUMN_POS]  = Long.toString(record_length);

    // this is the start position of the next column
    //
    record_length += size;

    // store this info in the column_info hash,
    // keyed by column name.
    //
    column_info.put(column, info);

}
```

```
     fdef.close(); // close the file

  } catch (Exception e) {

    throw new tinySQLException(e.getMessage());

  }

 }

}
```

# The Chrome Plated textFile of Destiny

You've seen the guts and inner workings of the tinySQL engine. Although it's mainly intended as a learning tool, I plan to enhance it further as time goes on. Of course, you are welcome to hack on it yourself, especially if you think you can improve it or make it easier to use. This chapter has focused on the data retrieval engine aspect of tinySQL. For those of you interested in the parser and lexer, you can check out Appendix C, which explains JavaCup and JavaLex.

The next chapter details the tinySQL JDBC driver, which is based on George Reese's (http://www.imaginary.com/~borg/Java/java.html) mSQL JDBC driver. It explains the minimal work a developer will need to do in order to develop a JDBC driver, and it should be of interest to folks with this objective. In addition, it also describes a practical use of the tinySQL API, which is exposed via the textFile class.

# Chapter 7

# The tinySQL JDBC Driver

To have seen an SQL engine isn't everything; the next tier of understanding comes when you learn how to build a JDBC driver for it. This part isn't all that complex; it's really a matter of mapping the database API to JDBC's objects and methods. While some database servers and engines may have peculiarities that require more programming than others, a JDBC driver should sit quite nicely on top of most SQL data engines. The functionality required by a JDBC Compliant driver is present in many commercial database products.

JDBC's mission is to provide a standard API and conformance level for programming SQL databases in Java. The JDBC driver is the first layer that your applets or applications use to communicate with the database; the JDBC driver manager works in conjunction with whichever JDBC driver you are using to communicate with the underlying database product.

A JDBC driver must implement some or all of the JDBC interfaces. The abstract methods in these interfaces must be defined in the classes that implement the interfaces. The following table lists the JDBC interfaces and the function they serve:

| Interface | Description |
|---|---|
| java.sql.Driver | The class that creates Connection objects, after making a connection to a data source. |
| java.sql.Connection | A Connection represents a connection to a data source. Among other things, it provides methods to create Statement, PreparedStatement, and CallableStatement objects, which are used to execute SQL statements. |
| java.sql.Statement | This class provides methods to execute SQL statements. |
| java.sql.PreparedStatement | This class, which extends Statement, can be used to pre-compile an SQL statement into a stored procedure. It can take variable parameters, allowing you to efficiently execute the same SQL statement multiple times and with different parameters. |
| java.sql.CallableStatement | An extension of PreparedStatement that provides a means of retrieving result parameters from stored procedures. |
| java.sql.ResultSet | This class represents the results of an SQL statement or stored procedure executed on one of the Statement objects. |
| java.sql.ResultSetMetaData | This class will provide information about the columns in a result set, such as size, data type, etc. |
| java.sql.DatabaseMetaData | DatabaseMetaData provides information about the database and the objects it contains. |

# The tinySQL JDBC Driver

The tinySQL JDBC driver is based on George Reese's (borg@imaginary.com) *Imaginary mSQL JDBC driver*. George's JDBC driver was the first JDBC driver ever released; it appeared shortly after the first beta release of the JDBC spec. Like the Imaginary driver, the tinySQL driver implements only a subset of the functionality required by a JDBC Compliant driver. The most notable exception to a fully compliant driver are the PreparedStatement, the CallableStatement, and DatabaseMetaData classes. In both the tinySQL and Imaginary driver, attempting to retrieve either a PreparedStatement or CallableStatement throws exceptions, as these require support for stored procedures. Attempting to retrieve a DatabaseMetaData object will return in null. Nevertheless, enough of the JDBC functionality is implemented to allow you to perform queries and updates and also to make discoveries about the result sets.

# tinySQLDriver.java

tinySQLDriver.java implements java.sql.Driver and provides the method needed to make a Connection. It also provides a method to determine which types of URLs the driver accepts, as well as ones to get the driver's version and property information.

```
/*
 *
 * tinySQLDriver - the tinySQLDriver abstract class
 *
 * A lot of this code is based on or directly taken from
 * George Reese's (borg@imaginary.com) mSQL driver.
 *
 * So, it's probably safe to say:
 *
 * Portions of this code Copyright (c) 1996 George Reese
 *
 */
import java.sql.Connection;
import java.sql.DriverPropertyInfo;
import java.sql.SQLException;
import java.sql.Driver;
import java.util.Properties;

public abstract class tinySQLDriver implements java.sql.Driver {
```

The constructor for the driver doesn't do much at all; it's the `connect()` method that does most of the work.

```
  /**
   *
   * Constructs a new tinySQLDriver
   *
   */
  public tinySQLDriver() {
  }
```

The `connect()` method returns a Connection object which is used to execute statements. This method uses the `acceptsURL()` method to determine if the URL is appropriate to the driver. If so, it uses `getConnection()` to return the new Connection; otherwise, it returns null.

```
/**
 *
 * Check the syntax of the URL.
 * @see java.sql.Driver#connect
 * @param url the URL for the database in question
 * @param info the properties object
 * @return null if the URL should be ignored, or a new Connection
 *         object if the URL is a valid tinySQL URL
 *
 */
public Connection connect(String url, Properties info)
      throws SQLException {

  if( !acceptsURL(url) ) {
    return null;
  }


  // if it was a valid URL, return the new Connection
  //
  return getConnection(info.getProperty("user"), url, this);
}
```

The `acceptsURL()` method examines the URL to determine if it is one that can be handled by the driver:

```
/**
 *
 * Check to see if the URL is a tinySQL URL. It should start
 * with jdbc:tinySQL in order to qualify.
 *
 * @param url The URL of the database.
```

```
* @return True if this driver can connect to the given URL.
*
*/
public boolean acceptsURL(String url) throws SQLException {

  // make sure the length is at least 12
  // before bothering with the substring
  // comparison.
  //
  if( url.length() < 12 ) {
    return false;
  }

  // if everything after the jdbc: part is
  // tinySQL, then return true.
  //
  return url.substring(5,12).equals("tinySQL");

}
```

The getPropertyInfo() method can be used if it is desired to allow the driver to use a generic GUI tool to prompt the user for connection info. This is a little fancy, and since we're doing this driver on the cheap, it will simply return an empty array.

```
/**
 *
 * The getPropertyInfo method is intended to allow a generic GUI tool to
 * discover what properties it should prompt a human for in order to get
 * enough information to connect to a database.  Note that depending on
 * the values the human has supplied so far, additional values may become
 * necessary, so it may be necessary to iterate through several calls
 * to getPropertyInfo.
 *
 * @param url The URL of the database to connect to.
```

**Continued**

```
 * @param info A proposed list of tag/value pairs that will be sent on
 *           connect open.
 * @return An array of DriverPropertyInfo objects describing possible
 *           properties.  This array may be an empty array if no properties
 *           are required.
 *
 */
public DriverPropertyInfo[] getPropertyInfo(String url,
                       java.util.Properties info)
    throws SQLException {
  return new DriverPropertyInfo[0];
}
```

getMajorVersion() returns the major version number of the driver.

```
/**
 *
 * Gets the driver's major version number.
 * @see java.sql.Driver#getMajorVersion
 * @return the major version
 *
 */
public int getMajorVersion() {
  return 0;
}
```

getMinorVersion() returns the minor version number of the driver.

```
/**
 *
 * Gets the driver's minor version
 * @see java.sql.Driver#getMinorVersion
 * @return the minor version
 *
```

```
*/
public int getMinorVersion() {
   return 9;
}
```

The `jdbcCompliant()` method returns true if the driver is JDBC Compliant. tinySQL is pretty sub-compliant, so this returns false.

```
/**
 *
 * Report whether the Driver is a genuine JDBC COMPLIANT (tm) driver.
 * Unfortunately, the tinySQL is "sub-compliant" :-(
 *
 */
public boolean jdbcCompliant() {
   return false;
}
```

The `getConnection()` method is an abstract class that is used to return a tinySQLConnection object. The reason this is abstract is that tinySQL itself is abstract; even though the tinySQL driver defines a lot of the JDBC driver methods, each subclass of the tinySQL driver will need to define a few methods in order to function.

```
/**
 *
 * Abstract method to return a tinySQLConnection object, typically
 * a subclass of the abstract class tinySQLConnection.
 *
 */
public abstract tinySQLConnection getConnection
               (String user, String url, Driver d)
                               throws SQLException;

}
```

# textFileDriver.java

As you saw in the previous chapter, tinySQL is an abstract class that cannot be directly instantiated. As a result, in order for a tinySQLDriver to actually exist, it must be a subclass of the previous class. Here's the extension of tinySQLDriver that implements the needed functionality, including a static method to register the class with the JDBC DriverManager when the class is loaded:

```
/*
 *
 * textFile/tinySQL JDBC driver
 *
 * A lot of this code is based on or directly taken from
 * George Reese's (borg@imaginary.com) mSQL driver.
 *
 * So, it's probably safe to say:
 *
 * Portions of this code Copyright (c) 1996 George Reese
 */

import java.sql.Connection;
import java.sql.DriverPropertyInfo;
import java.sql.SQLException;
import java.sql.Driver;
import java.util.Properties;

public class textFileDriver extends tinySQLDriver {
```

This funky little static method causes a new textFileDriver to be registered with the JDBC driver manager as soon as the class is loaded.

```
/*
 *
 * Instantiate a new textFileDriver(), registering it with
 * the JDBC DriverManager.
 *
```

```
    */
   static {
     try {
       java.sql.DriverManager.registerDriver(new textFileDriver());
     } catch (Exception e) {
       e.printStackTrace();
     }
   }
```

The constructor simply makes a call to its superclass constructor:

```
   /**
    *
    * Constructs a new textFileDriver
    *
    */
   public textFileDriver() {
     super();
   }
```

The `getConnection()` method is subclassed here, which creates and returns a new textFileConnection object.

```
   /**
    *
    * returns a new textFileConnection object, which is cast
    * to a tinySQLConnection object.
    *
    * @exception SQLException when an error occurs
    * @param user the username - currently unused
    * @param url the url to the data source
    * @param d the Driver object.
    *
```

**Continued**

```
    */
    public tinySQLConnection getConnection
                (String user, String url, Driver d)
                throws SQLException {

      return (tinySQLConnection) new textFileConnection(user, url, d);
    }


  }
```

# tinySQLConnection.java

The tinySQLConnection object provides methods to create each of the Statement objects
(only the Statement object is supported by tinySQL), and set some properties of the
Connection. Because some of the standard properties are not supported by tinySQL, the
corresponding methods do nothing. The executetinySQL() and get_tinySQL() are
used by this and other classes to interact with the tinySQL object, and they are not part of
the JDBC Connection interface.

```
/*
 *

 * tinySQLConnection - a Connection object for the tinySQL JDBC Driver.
 *

 * Note that since the tinySQL class is abstract, this class needs to
 * be abstract, as well. It's only in such manifestations of tinySQL
 * as textFile that the tinySQLConnection can reach its true potential.
 *

 * A lot of this code is based on or directly taken from
 * George Reese's (borg@imaginary.com) mSQL driver.
 *

 * So, it's probably safe to say:
 *

 * Portions of this code Copyright (c) 1996 George Reese
 *
```

```
*/
import java.sql.CallableStatement;
import java.sql.DatabaseMetaData;
import java.sql.Driver;
import java.sql.PreparedStatement;
import java.sql.SQLException;
import java.sql.SQLWarning;
import java.sql.Statement;

public abstract class tinySQLConnection implements java.sql.Connection {

  /**
   *
   * The tinySQL object
   *
   */
  private tinySQL tsql = null;

  /**
   *
   * The JDBC driver
   *
   */
  private Driver driver;

  /**
   *
   * The URL to the datasource
   *
   */
  private String url;

  /**
   *
```

**Continued**

```
      * The user name - currently unused

      *

      */

     private String user;


     /**

      *

      * the catalog - it's not used by tinySQL

      *

      */

     private String catalog;


     /**

      *

      * Transaction isolation level - it's not used by tinySQL

      *

      */

     private int isolation;
```

The constructor takes care of assigning the user, url, and drivers to the appropriate fields of this object, and then instantiates a new tinySQL object.

```
     /**

      *

      * Constructs a new JDBC Connection for a tinySQL database

      *

      * @exception SQLException in case of an error

      * @param user the user name - currently unused

      * @param u the URL used to connect to the datasource

      * @param d the Driver that instantiated this connection

      *

      */

     public tinySQLConnection(String user, String u, Driver d)

          throws SQLException {


       this.url    = u;
```

```
    this.user   = user;
    this.driver = d;

    // call get_tinySQL() to return a new tinySQL object.
    // get_tinySQL() is an abstract method that allows
    // subclasses of tinySQL, such as textFile, to be used
    // as JDBC datasources
    //
    tsql = get_tinySQL();

}
```

`createStatement()` **creates and returns a Statement object.**

```
/**
 *
 * Create and return a tinySQLStatement.
 * @see java.sql.Connection#createStatement
 * @exception SQLException thrown in case of error
 *
 */
public Statement createStatement() throws SQLException {
    return new tinySQLStatement(this);
}
```

`prepareStatement()` **would like to create and return a PreparedStatement object, but since such things are not supported by tinySQL, it throws an exception.**

```
/**
 *
 * Create and return a PreparedStatement. tinySQL doesn't support
 * these, so it always throws an exception.
 *
 * @see java.sql.Connection#prepareStatement
 * @param sql the SQL Statement
 * @exception SQLException gets thrown if you even look at this method
```

**Continued**

```
     *
     */
    public PreparedStatement prepareStatement(String sql)
          throws SQLException {
        throw new SQLException("tinySQL does not support prepared statements.");
    }
```

prepareCall() would like to create and return a CallableStatement object, but since such things are not supported by tinySQL, it throws an exception.

```
    /**
     *
     * Create and return a CallableStatement. tinySQL does not support
     * stored procs, so this automatically throws an exception.
     *
     * @see java.sql.Connection#prepareCall
     * @param sql the SQL Statement
     * @exception SQLException gets thrown always
     *
     */
    public CallableStatement prepareCall(String sql)
          throws SQLException {
        throw new SQLException("tinySQL does not support stored procedures.");
    }
```

The nativeCall() method is supposed to take care of converting escaped ODBC SQL to tinySQL syntax. This functionality is not provided yet, so it simply returns the original SQL.

```
    /**
     *
     * Converts escaped SQL to tinySQL syntax. This is not supported yet,
     * but some level of it will be meaningful, when tinySQL begins to
     * support scalar functions. For now, it just returns the original SQL.
     *
     * @see java.sql.Connection#nativeSQL
     * @param sql the SQL statement
```

```
 * @return just what you gave it
 *
 */
public String nativeSQL(String sql) throws SQLException {
  return sql;
}
```

The `setAutoCommit()` method should put the driver into autocommit mode. This is unsupported.

```
/**
 *
 * Sets autocommit mode - tinySQL has no support for transactions,
 * so this does nothing.
 * @see java.sql.Connection#setAutoCommit
 * @param b this does nothing
 *
 */
public void setAutoCommit(boolean b) throws SQLException {
}
```

The `commit()` method is used to commit any uncommitted transactions on this connection. This is not supported, but since everything is implicitly committed under tinySQL, it does not throw an exception.

```
/**
 *
 * Commits a transaction. Since all SQL statements are implicitly
 * committed, it's saved to preserve the illusion, and when this
 * method is invoked, it does not throw an exception.
 * @see java.sql.Connection#commit
 *
 */
public void commit() throws SQLException {
}
```

**Continued**

The `rollback()` method is used to roll back any uncommitted transactions on this connection. This is not supported; since everything is implicitly committed under tinySQL, it is never possible to roll anything back, so this throws an exception.

```
/**
 *
 * Rolls back a transaction. tinySQL does not support transactions,
 * so this throws an exception.
 * @see java.sql.Connection#rollback
 * @exception SQLException gets thrown automatically
 *
 */
public void rollback() throws SQLException {
    throw new SQLException("tinySQL does not support rollbacks.");
}
```

The `close()` method closes a Connection object. This has no meaning to tinySQL.

```
/**
 *
 * Close a Connection object. Does nothing, really.
 * @see java.sql.Connection#close
 * @exception SQLException is never thrown
 *
 */
public void close() throws SQLException {
}
```

The `isClosed()` method tells whether or not a Connection is closed.

```
/**
 *
 * Returns the status of the Connection.
 * @see java.sql.Connection#isClosed
 * @exception SQLException is never thrown
 * @return true if the connection is closed, false otherwise
```

```
  *
  */
public boolean isClosed() throws SQLException {
  return (tsql == null);
}
```

The `getMetaData()` method is used to return a DatabaseMetaData object, which is currently unsupported by the driver.

```
/**
  *
  * This method would like to retrieve some DatabaseMetaData, but it
  * is presently unsupported.
  * @see java.sql.Connection#getMetData
  * @exception SQLException is never thrown
  * @return a DatabaseMetaData object - someday
  *
  */
public DatabaseMetaData getMetaData() throws SQLException {
  return null;
}
```

Since tinySQL does not have a read-only mode, and since allowing a program to assume that the database is in such a state, the `setReadOnly()` method throws an exception.

```
/**
  * Puts the database in read-only mode... not! This throws an
  * exception whenever it is called. tinySQL does not support
  * a read-only mode, and it might be dangerous to let a program
  * think it's in that mode.
  * @see java.sql.Connection#setReadOnly
  * @param b meaningless
  */
public void setReadOnly(boolean b) throws SQLException {
  throw new SQLException("tinySQL does not have a read-only mode.");
}
```

The `isReadOnly` method returns whether or not the database is in read-only mode. This always returns false.

```
/**
 *
 * Returns true if the database is in read-only mode. It always
 * returns false.
 * @see java.sql.Connection#isReadOnly
 * @return the false will be with you... always
 *
 */
public boolean isReadOnly() throws SQLException {
  return false;
}
```

The `setCatalog()` method sets the current catalog, or database. Since tinySQL does not support multiple databases, this doesn't do anything.

```
/**
 *
 * Sets the current catalog within the database. This is not
 * supported by tinySQL, but we'll set the catalog String anyway.
 * @see java.sql.Connection#setCatalog
 * @param str the catalog
 *
 */
public void setCatalog(String str) throws SQLException {
  catalog = str;
}
```

The `getCatalog()` method returns the current catalog.

```
/**
 *
 * Returns the current catalog. This has no significance in tinySQL
 * @see java.sql.Connection#getCatalog
```

```
 * @return the catalog name
 *
 */
public String getCatalog() throws SQLException {
  return catalog;
}
```

The setTransactionIsolation() method should set the database server into a
different transaction isolation level. This would affect the types of locks that certain update
and retrieval functions acquire, but since tinySQL does not support such features, this
remains unimplemented.

```
/**
 *
 * Sets the transaction isolation level, which has no meaning in tinySQL.
 * We'll set the isolation level value anyhow, just to keep it happy.
 * @see java.sql.Connection#setTransactionIsolation
 * @param x the isolation level
 *
 */
public void setTransactionIsolation(int x)
      throws SQLException {
  isolation = x;
}
```

The getTransactionIsolation() method returns the current transaction isolation
level.

```
/**
 *
 * Returns the isolation level. This is not significant for tinySQL
 * @see java.sql.Connection#getTransactionIsolation
 * @return the transaction isolation level
 *
 */
public int getTransactionIsolation() throws SQLException {
```

**Continued**

```
   return isolation;
}
```

`disableAutoClose()` **turns off autoclosing of connections and result sets, but is not implemented by tinySQL.**

```
/**
 *
 * Disables autoclosing of connections and result sets. This is
 * not supported by tinySQL.
 * @see java.sql.Connection#disableAutoClose
 *
 */
public void disableAutoClose() throws SQLException {
}
```

**The** `getWarnings()` **method should return any warnings associated with the current connection. However, this is not supported by tinySQL.**

```
/**
 *
 * Returns a chain of warnings for the current connection; this
 * is not supported by tinySQL.
 * @see java.sql.Connection#getWarnings
 * @return the chain of warnings for this connection
 *
 */
public SQLWarning getWarnings() throws SQLException {
   return null;
}
```

`clearWarnings()` **should clear the warning chain, but tinySQL does not have one.**

```
/**
 *
 * Clears the non-existent warning chain.
```

```
 * @see java.sql.Connection#clearWarnings
 *
 */
public void clearWarnings() throws SQLException {
}
```

executetinySQL() is a method that is used to execute an SQL string. It is used by the Statement objects to execute SQL.

```
/**
 *
 * Execute a tinySQL Statement
 * @param sql the statement to be executed
 * @return tsResultSet containing the results of the SQL statement
 *
 */
public tsResultSet executetinySQL(String sql) throws SQLException {

  // the result set
  //
  tsResultSet result;

  // try to execute the SQL
  //
  try {
    result = tsql.sqlexec(sql);
  } catch( tinySQLException e ) {
    throw new SQLException("Exception: " + e.getMessage());
  }

  return result;

}
```

The get_tinySQL() method is needed to create a tinySQL object. The Connection uses this object to get at the tinySQL engine. This is an abstract method that needs to be defined by classes such as textFileConnection.

```
/**
 *
 * creates a new tinySQL object and returns it. Well, not really,
 * since tinySQL is an abstract class. When you subclass tinySQLConnection,
 * you will need to include this method and return some subclass
 * of tinySQL.
 *
 */
public abstract tinySQL get_tinySQL();
}
```

## textFileConnection.java

Like the tinySQLDriver class, the tinySQLConnection class is an abstract class. In order for you to work with it, it must be extended to support a subclass of tinySQL. This is the last of the JDBC classes that need to be subclassed in such a way; the remaining three use generic tinySQL methods, so they are complete as is.

```
/*
 *
 * Connection class for the textFile/tinySQL
 * JDBC driver
 *
 * A lot of this code is based on or directly taken from
 * George Reese's (borg@imaginary.com) mSQL driver.
 *
 * So, it's probably safe to say:
 *
 * Portions of this code Copyright (c) 1996 George Reese
 *
 */

import java.sql.CallableStatement;
import java.sql.DatabaseMetaData;
import java.sql.Driver;
import java.sql.PreparedStatement;
```

```
import java.sql.SQLException;
import java.sql.SQLWarning;
import java.sql.Statement;


public class textFileConnection extends tinySQLConnection {
```

Here's the constructor for textFileConnection; it merely calls its superclass constructor.

```
/**
 *
 * Constructs a new JDBC Connection object.
 *
 * @exception SQLException in case of an error
 * @param user the user name - not currently used
 * @param u the url to the data source
 * @param d the Driver object
 *
 */
public textFileConnection(String user, String u, Driver d)
        throws SQLException {
   super(user, u, d);
}
```

Here, the `get_tinySQL()` method is fleshed out to create a new textFile object.

```
/**
 *
 * Returns a new textFile object that is cast to a tinySQL
 * object.
 *
 */
public tinySQL get_tinySQL() {
    return (tinySQL) new textFile();
}

}
```

# tinySQLStatement.java

This class provides the methods that are needed to execute SQL statements and process their results. Unlike the PreparedStatement and CallableStatement class, no support is included for precompiling SQL statements or working with stored procedure parameters.

```java
/**
 *
 * Statement object for the tinySQL driver
 *
 * A lot of this code is based on or directly taken from
 * George Reese's (borg@imaginary.com) mSQL driver.
 *
 * So, it's probably safe to say:
 *
 * Portions of this code Copyright (c) 1996 George Reese
 *
 */

import java.sql.SQLException;
import java.sql.SQLWarning;
import java.sql.ResultSet;

public class tinySQLStatement implements java.sql.Statement {

    /**
     *
     * A connection object to execute queries and... stuff
     *
     */
    private tinySQLConnection connection;

    /**
     *
     * A result set returned from this query
     *
```

```
    */
    private tinySQLResultSet result;

    /**
     *
     * The max field size for tinySQL
     * This can be pretty big, before things start to break.
     *
     */
    private int max_field_size = 0;

    /**
     *
     * The max rows supported by tinySQL
     * I can't think of any limits, right now, but I'm sure some
     * will crop up...
     *
     */
    private int max_rows = 65536;

    /**
     *
     * The number of seconds the driver will allow for a SQL statement to
     * execute before giving up.  The default is to wait forever (0).
     *
     */
    private int timeout = 0;
```

Here's the constructor for the tinySQLStatement object. Note that it requires a Connection object as a parameter; the Connection object contains all the methods needed to execute SQL, so it is quite essential to this class.

```
    /**
     *
     * Constructs a new tinySQLStatement object.
     * @param conn the tinySQLConnection object
```

**Continued**

```
 *
 */
public tinySQLStatement(tinySQLConnection conn) {

  connection = conn;

}
```

The `executeQuery()` method executes an SQL statement and returns a ResultSet object.

```
/**
 *
 * Execute an SQL statement and return a result set.
 * @see java.sql.Statement#executeQuery
 * @exception SQLException raised for any errors
 * @param sql the SQL statement string
 * @return the result set from the query
 *
 */
public ResultSet executeQuery(String sql)
     throws SQLException {

  // tinySQL supports only one result set at a time, so
  // don't let them get another one, just in case it's
  // hanging out.
  //
  result = null;

  // create a new tinySQLResultSet with the tsResultSet
  // returned from connection.executetinySQL()
  //
  return new tinySQLResultSet(connection.executetinySQL(sql));

}
```

This method, `executeUpdate()`, executes an SQL statement, but doesn't return a result set. This can be useful for statements such as UPDATE, INSERT, DELETE, and CREATE TABLE. One of the drawbacks of this version of the tinySQL driver is that it is not possible to get a count of affected rows with `getUpdateCount()` from such operations, since it is not supported in the current incarnation of tinySQL.

```
/**
 *
 * Execute an update, insert, delete, create table, etc. This can
 * be anything that doesn't return rows.
 * @see java.sql.Statement#executeUpdate
 * @exception java.sql.SQLException thrown when an error occurs executing
 * the SQL
 * @return 0 - tinySQL does not support row count returns, yet
 */
public int executeUpdate(String sql) throws SQLException {

    connection.executetinySQL(sql);
    return 0;

}
```

The `execute()` method is used to execute some SQL and return true or false depending on its success. The result set can be retrieved with `getResultSet()`.

```
/**
 *
 * Executes some SQL and returns true or false, depending on
 * the success. The result set is stored in result and can
 * be retrieved with getResultSet();
 * @see java.sql.Statement#execute
 * @exception SQLException raised for any errors
 * @param sql the SQL to be executed
 * @return true if there is a result set available
```

**Continued**

```
*/
public boolean execute(String sql) throws SQLException {

  // a result set object
  //
  tsResultSet r;

  // execute the query
  //
  r = connection.executetinySQL(sql);

  // check for a null result set. If it wasn't null,
  // use it to create a tinySQLResultSet and return whether or
  // not it is null (not null returns true).
  //
  if( r == null ) {
    result = null;
  } else {
    result = new tinySQLResultSet(r);
  }
  return (result != null);

}
```

This method, `close()`, will close any open result sets. This feature is not used by tinySQL.

```
/**
 *
 * Close any result sets. This is not used by tinySQL.
 * @see java.sql.Statement#close
 *
 */
public void close() throws SQLException {
}
```

`getResultSet()` will return the last result set created by `execute()`.

```
/**
 *
 * Returns the last result set
 * @see java.sql.Statement#getResultSet
 * @return null if no result set is available, otherwise a result set
 *
 */
public ResultSet getResultSet() throws SQLException {

  ResultSet r;

  r = result;     // save the existing result set
  result = null; // null out the existing result set
  return r;       // return the previously extant result set
}
```

The `getUpdateCount()` method returns the number of rows that were affected by the last operation. This is unsupported by tinySQL.

```
/**
 *
 * Return the row count of the last operation. tinySQL does not support
 * this, so it returns -1
 * @see java.sql.Statement#getUpdateCount
 * @return -1
 */
public int getUpdateCount() throws SQLException {
  return -1;
}
```

The `getMoreResults()` method will indicate whether or not there are any pending result sets.

```
/**
 *
```

**Continued**

```
* This returns true if there are any pending result sets. This
* should be true only after invoking execute()
* @see java.sql.Statement#getMoreResults
* @return true if rows are to be gotten
*
*/
public boolean getMoreResults() throws SQLException {

  return (result != null);

}
```

The `getMaxFieldSize()` method will return the maximum field size that should be returned in a result set.

```
/**
 *
 * Get the maximum field size to return in a result set.
 * @see java.sql.Statement#getMaxFieldSize
 * @return the value of max field size
 *
 */
public int getMaxFieldSize() throws SQLException {
  return max_field_size;
}
```

The `setMaxFieldSize()` method sets the maximum field size that can be returned in a result set.

```
/**
 *
 * set the max field size.
 * @see java.sql.Statement#setMaxFieldSize
 * @param max the maximum field size
 *
 */
```

```
public void setMaxFieldSize(int max) throws SQLException {
  max_field_size = max;
}
```

The getMaxRows() method will return the maximum number of rows that should be returned in a result set.

```
/**
 *
 * Get the maximum row count that can be returned by a result set.
 * @see java.sql.Statement#getMaxRows
 * @return the maximum rows
 *
 */
public int getMaxRows() throws SQLException {
  return max_rows;
}
```

The setMaxRows() method will set the maximum number of rows that can be returned from a result set.

```
/**
 *
 * Get the maximum row count that can be returned by a result set.
 * @see java.sql.Statement.setMaxRows
 * @param max the max rows
 *
 */
public void setMaxRows(int max) throws SQLException {
  max_rows = max;
}
```

This method, setEscapeProcessing(), will turn the escape substitution on. Although this is unsupported by this driver, this would normally be used to convert ODBC SQL to vendor-specific SQL.

```
/**
 *
 * If escape scanning is on (the default) the driver will do
 * escape substitution before sending the SQL to the database.
 * @see java.sql.Statement#setEscapeProcessing
 * @param enable this does nothing right now
 *
 */
public void setEscapeProcessing(boolean enable)
      throws SQLException {
  throw new SQLException("The tinySQL Driver doesn't " +
                          "support escape processing.");
}
```

The `getQueryTimeout()` method will return the query timeout in seconds.

```
/**
 *
 * Discover the query timeout.
 * @see java.sql.Statement#getQueryTimeout
 * @see setQueryTimeout
 * @return the timeout value for this statement
 *
 */
public int getQueryTimeout() throws SQLException {
  return timeout;
}
```

The `setQueryTimeout()` method allows you to set the query timeout in seconds. This is ignored by tinySQL.

```
/**
 *
 * Set the query timeout.
 * @see java.sql.Statement#setQueryTimeout
```

```
 * @see getQueryTimeout
 * @param x the new query timeout value
 *
 */
public void setQueryTimeout(int x) throws SQLException {
   timeout = x;
}
```

The `cancel()` method allows another thread to cancel a running statement.

```
/**
 *
 * This can be used by another thread to cancel a statement. This
 * doesn't matter for tinySQL, as far as I can tell.
 * @see java.sql.Statement#cancel
 *
 */
public void cancel() {
}
```

The `getWarnings()` method should return any warnings associated with the current connection. However, this is not supported by tinySQL.

```
/**
 *
 * Get the warning chain associated with this Statement
 * @see java.sql.Statement#getWarnings
 * @return the chain of warnings
 *
 */
public final SQLWarning getWarnings() throws SQLException {
   return null;
}
```

`clearWarnings()` should clear the warning chain, but tinySQL does not have one.

```
/**
 *
 * Clear the warning chain associated with this Statement
 * @see java.sql.Statement#clearWarnings
 *
 */
public void clearWarnings() throws SQLException {
}
```

setCursorName() should set the cursor the this Statement/Connection, but it is unsupported by tinySQL.

```
/**
 *
 * Sets the cursor name for this connection. Currently unsupported.
 *
 */
public void setCursorName(String unused) throws SQLException {
    throw new SQLException("tinySQL does not support cursors.");
}
}
```

# tinySQLResultSet.java

This is the big one; the ResultSet class provides all the functionality needed to manipulate the results of queries you execute on a Statement object. Many methods are provided for retrieving column data. Regardless of the SQL data types, column data can be retrieved as a variety of Java objects and datatypes, provided that a legal conversion is specified. Columns can be retrieved by name or column offset. JDBC columns are numbered starting at one, while tinySQL columns are numbered starting at zero. This doesn't cause too many programming adjustments, though they are noted as necessary in the code.

```
/*
 *
 * The tinySQLResultSet class for the tinySQL JDBC Driver
```

```
*
* A lot of this code is based on or directly taken from
* George Reese's (borg@imaginary.com) mSQL driver.
*
* So, it's probably safe to say:
*
* Portions of this code Copyright (c) 1996 George Reese
*
*/

import java.sql.Date;
import java.sql.Bignum;
import java.sql.ResultSet;
import java.sql.ResultSetMetaData;
import java.sql.SQLException;
import java.sql.SQLWarning;
import java.sql.Time;
import java.sql.Timestamp;
import java.sql.Types;
import java.util.Hashtable;

public class tinySQLResultSet implements java.sql.ResultSet {

  /**
   *
   * The tsResultSet
   *
   */
  private tsResultSet result;

  /**
   *
   * A tsRow object to hold the current row
   *
   */
  private tsRow current_row;
```

**Continued**

```
/**
 *
 * The index of the current row
 *
 */
private int current_row_index = 0;

/**
 *
 * The meta data for this result set.
 *
 */
private tinySQLResultSetMetaData meta;

/**
 *
 * A Hashtable that maps column names to columns
 *
 */
private Hashtable column_map = null;
```

Here's the constructor, which requires a tinySQLResultSet as its parameter.

```
/**
 *
 * Given a tsResultSet, this will construct a new tinySQLResultSet
 * @param res the tsResultSet from a query
 *
 */
public tinySQLResultSet(tsResultSet res) {
  result = res;
}
```

The `next()` method is used to advance to the next row in the result set. Any columns retrieved after this will read from the next row.

```java
/**
 *
 * Advance to the next row in the result set.
 * @see java.sql.ResultSet#next
 * @exception SQLException thrown in case of error
 * @return true if there are any more rows to process, otherwise false.
 *
 */
public synchronized boolean next() throws SQLException {

  try {

    // automatically return false if the
    // result set is empty
    //
    if( result.size() < 1 ) {
      return false;
    }

    // return false if the index of the current row
    // is equal to the size of the result set
    //
    if( current_row_index == result.size() ) {
      return false;
    }

    // increment the current row index
    //
    current_row_index++;

    // retrieve the row at the current_row_index and store
```

**Continued**

```
    // it in the current_row field.
    //
    current_row = result.rowAt(current_row_index - 1);
    return true;

  } catch( Exception e ) {
    throw new SQLException(e.getMessage());
  }

}
```

The close() method closes a result set, but this is not meaningful to tinySQL.

```
/**
 *
 * Provides a method to close a ResultSet
 *
 * @see java.sql.ResultSet#close
 *
 */
public void close() throws SQLException {
}
```

If tinySQL were to support SQL nulls, the wasNull() method would tell you if the last column read was null.

```
/**
 *
 * Returns whether or not the last column read was null.
 * tinySQL doesn't have nulls, so this is inconsequential...
 * @see java.sql.ResultSet#wasNull
 * @return true if the column was null, false otherwise
 *
 */
public boolean wasNull() throws SQLException {
```

```
      return false;
   }
```

The next sixteen methods are concerned with retrieving values from the result set by
column index.

```
/**
 *
 * Gets the value of a column (by index) as a String.
 * @see java.sql.ResultSet#getString
 * @exception SQLException thrown for bogus column index
 * @param column the column index
 * @return the column's String value
 *
 */
public String getString(int column) throws SQLException {

   // retrieve the column at the specified index. tinySQL
   // has a column offset of zero, while JDBC uses one.
   // Because of this, I need to subtract one from the
   // index to get the tinySQL index.
   //
   tsColumn col = result.columnAtIndex(column-1);

   // return the column's value
   //
   return current_row.columnAsString(col);

}

/**
 *
 * Get the value of a column in the current row as a Java byte.
 *
 * @param columnIndex the first column is 1, the second is 2, ...
 * @return the column value
```

**Continued**

```
   *
   */
  public byte getByte(int column) throws SQLException {

    // get the column as a string
    //
    String str = getString(column);

    // if it's a blank string, return 0,
    // otherwise, cast the first character
    // in the string to byte and return it.
    //
    if( str.equals("") ) {
      return 0;
    } else {
      return (byte)str.charAt(0);
    }

  }


  /**
   *
   * Get the value of a column in the current row as boolean
   * @see java.sql.ResultSet#getBoolean
   * @exception SQLException Harum Scarum's coming down fast, Clay...
   * @param column the column index
   * @return false for "", null, or "0"; true otherwise
   */
  public boolean getBoolean(int column) throws SQLException {

    try {

      // get the column as a string
      //
      String str = getString(column);
```

```
      // a blank string is false
      //
      if( str.equals("") ) return false;

      // a zero is false
      //
      if( str.equals("0") ) return false;

      // nothing is true... everything is permitted
      //
      return true;

   } catch( Exception e ) {
     throw new SQLException(e.getMessage());
   }
}

/**
 *
 * Get the value of a column in the current row as a short.
 * @see java.sql.ResultSet#getShort
 * @exception SQLException D'ohh!
 * @param column the column being retrieved
 * @return the column as a short
 *
 */
public short getShort(int column) throws SQLException {

  // get the column as a string
  //
  String str = getString(column);

  // if it's null, return 0
  //
```

**Continued**

```java
   if( str == null ) return 0;

   // try to convert it to an integer, and cast it to short
   //
   try {
     return (short)(Integer.valueOf(str).intValue());
   } catch( NumberFormatException e ) {
     throw new SQLException(e.getMessage());
   }

}

/**
 *
 * Retrieve a column from the current row as an int
 * @see java.sql.ResultSet#getInt
 * @exception SQLException bad things... the wind began to howl...
 * @param column the column being retrieved
 * @return the column as an integer
 *
 */
public int getInt(int column) throws SQLException {

   // get the column as a string
   //
   String str = getString(column);

   // if it's null, return 0
   //
   if( str == null ) return 0;

   // try to convert this string to integer
   //
   try {
     return Integer.valueOf(str).intValue();
```

```java
    } catch( NumberFormatException e ) {
      throw new SQLException(e.getMessage());
    }

}


/**
 *
 * Get the value of a column in the current row as a long
 * @see java.sql.ResultSet#getLong
 * @exception SQLException in case of an error
 * @param column the column being retrieved
 * @return the column as a long
 *
 */
public long getLong(int column) throws SQLException {

  // get the column as a string
  //
  String str = getString(column);

  // it it's null, return 0
  if( str == null ) return 0;

  // try to convert the String to a long
  //
  try {
    return Long.valueOf(str).longValue();
  } catch( NumberFormatException e ) {
    throw new SQLException(e.getMessage());
  }

}

/**
```

**Continued**

```
    *
    * Return a column as a float.
    * @see java.sql.ResultSet#getFloat
    * @exception SQLException in case of error
    * @param column the column being retrieved
    * @return the column as a float
    *
    */
public float getFloat(int column) throws SQLException {

    // get the column as a string
    //
    String str = getString(column);

    // if it's null, assume zero
    //
    if( str == null ) return 0;

    // try to perform the conversion
    //
    try {
        return Float.valueOf(str).floatValue();
    } catch( NumberFormatException e ) {
        throw new SQLException(e.getMessage());
    }

}

/**
 *
 * Return a column as a double
 * @see java.sql.ResultSet#getDouble
 * @exception SQLException in case of error
 * @param column the column being retrieved
 * @return the column as a double
```

```
  *
  */
public double getDouble(int column) throws SQLException {

   // get the column as a string
   //
   String str = getString(column);

   // if it's null, return zero
   //
   if( str == null ) return 0;

   // attempt the conversion
   //
   try {
     return Double.valueOf(str).doubleValue();
   } catch( NumberFormatException e ) {
     throw new SQLException(e.getMessage());
   }

}

/**
 *
 * Return a column as a Bignum object
 * @see java.sql.ResultSet#getBignum
 * @exception SQLException in case of a problem
 * @param column the column being retrieved
 * @param scale the number of digits to the right of the decimal
 * @return the column as a Bignum
 *
 */
public Bignum getBignum(int column, int scale)
     throws SQLException {
```

**Continued**

```java
    // get the column as a string
    //
    String str = getString(column);

    // return null as zero, otherwise use the string
    //
    if( str == null ) {
      return new Bignum(0, scale);
    } else {
      return new Bignum(str, scale);
    }

  }


/**
 *
 * Get the value of a column in the current row as a Java byte array.
 * @see java.sql.ResultSet#getBytes
 * @exception SQLException thrown in case of trouble
 * @param column the column being retrieved
 * @return a byte array that is the value of the column
 *
 */
public byte[] getBytes(int column) throws SQLException {

  // get the column as a string
  //
  String str = getString(column);

  byte b[];

  // return null if the string is null
  //
  if( str == null ) return null;
```

```
   // populate a byte array with values from
   // the string
   //
  b = new byte[str.length() + 10];
  str.getBytes(0, str.length(), b, 0);
  return b;

}


/**
 *
 * Get the value of a column in the current row as a java.sql.Date object.
 * @see java.sqlResultSet#getDate
 * @exception SQLException thrown in case of error
 * @param column the column being retrieved
 * @return the java.sql.Date object for the column
 *
 */
public java.sql.Date getDate(int column)
     throws SQLException {

  // get the column as a string
  //
  String str = getString(column);

  // return null if the string is null
  //
  if( str == null ) return null;

  // try to use the string to instantiate a java.util.Date object,
  // then use that object to instantiate a java.sql.Date object.
  //
  try {
```

**Continued**

```
      java.util.Date d;
      d = new java.util.Date(str);
      return new java.sql.Date(d.getYear(), d.getMonth(), d.getDate());


    } catch( Exception e ) {
      throw new SQLException("Date format error: " + e.getMessage());
    }


}


/**
 *
 * Get the value of a column in the current row as a java.sql.Time object.
 *
 * @see java.sql.ResultSet#getTime
 * @exception SQLException thrown in the event of troubles
 * @param column the column being retrieved
 * @return the column as a java.sql.Time object
 *
 */
public java.sql.Time getTime(int column)
      throws SQLException {

  // get the column as a string
  //
  String str = getString(column);

  // if the string is null, return null
  //
  if( str == null ) return null;

  // try to use the string to instantiate a java.util.Date object,
  // then use that object to instantiate a java.sql.Time object.
  //
  try {
```

```java
      java.util.Date d;

      d = new java.util.Date(str);
      return new java.sql.Time(d.getHours(), d.getMinutes(), d.getSeconds());

    } catch( Exception e ) {
      throw new SQLException("Data format error: " + e.getMessage());
    }
}


/**
 * Get the value of a column in the current row as a java.sql.Timestamp
 * @see java.sql.ResultSet#getTimestamp
 * @exception SQLException thrown in the event of troubles
 * @param column the column being retrieved
 * @return the column as a java.sql.Timestamp object
 */
public java.sql.Timestamp getTimestamp(int column)
      throws SQLException {

  // get the column as a string
  //
  String str = getString(column);

  // if the string is null, return null
  //
  if( str == null ) return null;

  // try to use the string to instantiate a java.util.Date object,
  // then use that object to instantiate a java.sql.Timestamp object.
  //
  try {

    java.util.Date d = new java.util.Date(str);
```

**Continued**

```
                return new java.sql.Timestamp(d.getYear(), d.getMonth(), d.getDate(),
                                        d.getHours(), d.getMinutes(),
                                        d.getSeconds(), 0);


    } catch( Exception e ) {
        throw new SQLException("Data format error: " + e.getMessage());
    }


}


/**
 *
 * This is not currently supported.
 *
 */
public java.io.InputStream getAsciiStream(int column)
        throws SQLException {
    return null;
}


/**
 *
 * This is not currently supported.
 *
 */
public java.io.InputStream getUnicodeStream(int column)
        throws SQLException {
    return null;
}


/**
 *
 * This is not currently supported.
 *
 */
```

```
public java.io.InputStream getBinaryStream(int column)
     throws SQLException {
  return null;
}
```

This is used to get the name of the cursor for this result set, but is unimplemented.

```
/**
 *
 * Get the name of the cursor corresponding to this result set.
 * This has no meaning to tinySQL
 * @see java.sql.ResultSet#getCursorName
 * @return ""
 *
 */
public String getCursorName() throws SQLException {
  return "";
}
```

The getMetaData() method is used to retrieve a ResultSetMetaData object for this result set.

```
/**
 *
 * Returns a ResultSetMetaData object for this result set
 * @see java.sql.ResultSet#getMetaData
 * @exception SQLException thrown on error getting metadata
 * @return ResultSetMetaData object containing result set info
 *
 */
public ResultSetMetaData getMetaData()
     throws SQLException {

  // if we didn't instantiate a metadata object, then
  // do so. Since it's a field of this object, and
```

**Continued**

```
          // not private to this method, it will stay around
          // between calls to this method.
          //
          if( meta == null ) {
            meta = new tinySQLResultSetMetaData(result);
          }


          // return the ResultSetMetaData object
          //
          return meta;
        }
```

The next three methods are used to retrieve column values as objects, given a column index.

```
/**
 *
 * Retrieves data as objects
 * @see java.sql.ResultSet#getObject
 * @exception SQLException in the event of an error
 * @param column the column desired
 * @param type the SQL data type of the field
 * @scale precision for Bignum
 * @return the column specified as an Object
 *
 */
public Object getObject(int column, int type, int scale)
      throws SQLException {

    switch(type) {
    case Types.BIT:
      return new Boolean(getBoolean(column));

    case Types.TINYINT:
      return new Character((char)getInt(column));
```

```
case Types.SMALLINT:
  return new Integer(getShort(column));

case Types.INTEGER:
  return new Integer(getInt(column));

case Types.BIGINT:
  return new Long(getLong(column));

case Types.FLOAT:
  return new Float(getFloat(column));

case Types.REAL:
  return new Float(getFloat(column));

case Types.DOUBLE:
  return new Double(getDouble(column));

case Types.BIGNUM:
  return getBignum(column, scale);

case Types.DECIMAL:
  return getNumeric(column, scale);

case Types.CHAR:
  return getString(column);

case Types.VARCHAR:
  return getString(column);

case Types.LONGVARCHAR:
  return getString(column);

case Types.DATE:
  return getDate(column);
```

**Continued**

```
    case Types.TIME:
      return getTime(column);

    case Types.TIMESTAMP:
      return getTimestamp(column);

    case Types.BINARY:
      return getBytes(column);

    case Types.VARBINARY:
      return getBytes(column);

    case Types.LONGVARBINARY:
      return getBytes(column);

    default:
      return null;
    }
}

/**
 *
 * Same as above, except with a default scale to 0.
 *
 */
public Object getObject(int column, int type)
      throws SQLException {
   return getObject(column, type, 0);
}

/**
 *
 * Same as above, except using the column's default SQL type.
 *
 */
```

```
public Object getObject(int column) throws SQLException {
  ResultSetMetaData meta = getMetaData();
  int type = meta.getColumnType(column);

  return getObject(column, type);
}
```

The next nineteen or so methods are used to return a value from the result set by column name.

```
/**
 *
 * Return the String value of a column given its name, rather than
 * its index.
 * @see java.sql.ResultSet#getString
 * @param name the name of the column desired
 * @return the value of the column as a String
 *
 */
public String getString(String name) throws SQLException {

  return getString(findColumn(name));

}


/**
 *
 * Returns the column as a byte based on column name
 *
 */
public byte getByte(String columnName) throws SQLException {

  return getByte(findColumn(columnName));

}
```

**Continued**

```java
/**
 *
 * Get the value of a boolean column in the current row
 * @param columnName is the SQL name of the column
 * @return the column value; if isNull the value is false
 *
 */
public boolean getBoolean(String columnName) throws SQLException {

    return getBoolean(findColumn(columnName));

}


/**
 *
 * Get the value of a short by column name
 * @param columnName is the SQL name of the column
 * @return the column value; if isNull the value is 0
 *
 */
public short getShort(String columnName) throws SQLException {

    return getShort(findColumn(columnName));

}


/**
 *
 * Get the integer value of a column by name
 * @param columnName is the SQL name of the column
 * @return the column value; if isNull the value is 0
 *
 */
public int getInt(String columnName) throws SQLException {
```

```
    return getInt(findColumn(columnName));

}

/**
 *
 * Get the long value of a column by name
 * @param columnName is the SQL name of the column
 * @return the column value; if isNull the value is 0
 *
 */
public long getLong(String columnName) throws SQLException {

    return getLong(findColumn(columnName));

}

/**
 *
 * Get the float value of a column by name
 * @param columnName is the SQL name of the column
 * @return the column value; if isNull the value is 0
 *
 */
public float getFloat(String columnName) throws SQLException {

    return getFloat(findColumn(columnName));

}

/**
 *
 * Get the double value of a named column
 * @param columnName is the SQL name of the column
```

**Continued**

```
 * @return the column value; if isNull the value is 0
 *
 */
public double getDouble(String columnName) throws SQLException {

  return getDouble(findColumn(columnName));

}


/**
 *
 * Get the value of a named column as a Bignum object
 * @param columnName is the SQL name of the column
 * @return the column value; if isNull the value is null
 *
 */
public Bignum getBignum(String columnName, int scale) throws SQLException {

  return getBignum(findColumn(columnName), scale);

}


/**
 *
 * Get the value of a named column as a byte array
 * @param columnName is the SQL name of the column
 * @return the column value; if isNull the value is null
 *
 */
public byte[] getBytes(String columnName) throws SQLException {

  return getBytes(findColumn(columnName));

}
```

```
/**
 *
 * Get a named column as a java.sql.Date
 * @param columnName is the SQL name of the column
 * @return the column value; if isNull the value is null
 *
 */
public java.sql.Date getDate(String columnName) throws SQLException {

    return getDate(findColumn(columnName));

}


/**
 *
 * Get a named column as a java.sql.Time
 * @param columnName is the SQL name of the column
 * @return the column value; if isNull the value is null
 *
 */
public java.sql.Time getTime(String columnName) throws SQLException {

    return getTime(findColumn(columnName));

}


/**
 *
 * Get a named column as a java.sql.Time
 * @param columnName is the SQL name of the column
 * @return the column value; if isNull the value is null
 *
 */
public java.sql.Timestamp getTimestamp(String columnName)
```

**Continued**

```
      throws SQLException {

  return getTimestamp(findColumn(columnName));

}


/**
 *
 * This is unsupported, but we'll try to call the corresponding
 * call by column index.
 *
 */
public java.io.InputStream getAsciiStream(String columnName)
      throws SQLException {

  return getAsciiStream(findColumn(columnName));

}


/**
 *
 * This is unsupported, but we'll try to call the corresponding
 * call by column index.
 *
 */
public java.io.InputStream getUnicodeStream(String columnName)
      throws SQLException {

  return getUnicodeStream(findColumn(columnName));

}


/**
 *
 * This is unsupported, but we'll try to call the corresponding
```

```
 * call by column index.
 *
 */
public java.io.InputStream getBinaryStream(String columnName)
     throws SQLException {

  return getBinaryStream(findColumn(columnName));

}

/**
 *
 * Get the value of a named column as an object
 * @param columnName the SQL column name
 * @param sqlType SQL type code defined by java.sql.Types
 * @return the parameter as an Object
 *
 */
public Object getObject(String columnName, int sqlType, int scale)
     throws SQLException {

  return getObject(findColumn(columnName), sqlType, scale);

}

/**
 *
 * Same as above, except defaulting scale to 0.
 *
 */
public Object getObject(String columnName, int type)
     throws SQLException {

  return getObject(findColumn(columnName), type, 0);
```

**Continued**

```
}

/**
 *
 * Same as above, except returning the default SQL type
 *
 */
public Object getObject(String columnName) throws SQLException {
    return getObject(findColumn(columnName));
}
```

The `findColumn()` method is a nifty method that was originally in the mSQL JDBC driver by George Reese. It takes a column name as an argument and finds the column number for it. It creates a map of this information in a Hashtable, so only the first call to this method incurs overead; each subsequent call is quite fast. This should be in every JDBC driver, and probably will be...

```
/**
 *
 * Given a column name, this method returns the column number for that
 * name.  Column name to number mappings are kept inside a Hashtable.
 * Applications that do not need the overhead of this calculation are
 * not penalized because  the mapping occurs only on the first attempt to
 * access a column number by name.
 * @exception java.sql.SQLException thrown if a bad name is passed
 * @param name the name of the column desired
 * @return the column number, 1 being the first column
 *
 */
public int findColumn(String name) throws SQLException {

    Integer num;

    // does the column map exist?
    //
```

```
  if( column_map == null ) {

    int i, maxi;

    // create a Hashtable that expects to hold
    // enough objects for all the columns in the
    // result set.
    //
    column_map = new Hashtable(maxi = result.numcols());

    // add each column by name, with an Integer index
    //
    for(i=0; i<maxi; i++) {
      tsColumn tsc = result.columnAtIndex(i);
      column_map.put(tsc.name, new Integer(i));
    }
  }

  // one way or another, we've got a column_map; either it
  // already existed, or the above code created it.
  //

  // look up the column name in the map, and find its
  // index (the Integer object)
  //
  num = (Integer)column_map.get(name);
  if( num == null ) {
    throw new SQLException("Invalid column name: " + name);
  }

  // return the column index as an int
  //
  return num.intValue() + 1;


}
```

The `getWarnings()` method should return any warnings associated with the result set. However, this is not supported by tinySQL.

```
/**
 *
 * Return the warning chain. This is currently unsupported.
 * @see java.sql.Statement#getWarnings
 * @return the chain of warnings
 *
 */
public SQLWarning getWarnings() throws SQLException {
    return null;
}
```

`clearWarnings()` should clear the warning chain, but tinySQL does not have one.

```
/**
 *
 * Clear the chain of warnings. This does nothing because the
 * warning chain is not used by tinySQL
 * @see java.sql.Statement#clearWarnings
 *
 */
public void clearWarnings() throws SQLException {
}

}
```

# tinySQLResultSetMetaData.java

Now here's a long filename. The tinySQLResultSetMetaData object is instantiated by the `getMetaData()` method in the ResultSet class. A ResultSetMetaData object provides you with access to information about the ResultSet. I expect that most programmers will not need to make metadata discoveries; most people will be coding either using stored procedures (for servers such as Sybase or Oracle) or regular SQL statements (tinySQL, mSQL, single-tier ODBC drivers). In these cases, information about column data is known in advance.

However, when developing generic tools or query-by-example programs, it is not always known what SQL will be executed, so you may need to make some inquiries as to the data types, column sizes, and number of columns in a ResultSet. It is for such purposes, the exceptional cases, that the ResultSetMetaData interface was included in JDBC. As the JDBC 1.0 spec states in section 2.7, "We would like to make sure that the common cases are simple, and that the uncommon cases are doable."

```
/**
 * This is the tinySQL Result Set Meta Data class.
 *
 * A lot of this code is based on or directly taken from
 * George Reese's (borg@imaginary.com) mSQL driver.
 *
 * So, it's probably safe to say:
 *
 * Portions of this code Copyright (c) 1996 George Reese
 *
 */

import java.sql.SQLException;
import java.sql.Types;

public class tinySQLResultSetMetaData implements java.sql.ResultSetMetaData {

  /**
   *
   * The result set.
   *
   */
  private tsResultSet tsql;
```

Here's the constructor for the tinySQLResultSet.

```
/**
 *
```

**Continued**

```
 * Constructs a tinySQLResultSet; requires a tsResultSet object
 * @param result the tsResultSet object
 *
 */
public tinySQLResultSetMetaData(tsResultSet result) {
  tsql = result;
}
```

The `getColumnCount()` method is used to return the number of columns in the result set.

```
/**
 *
 * Returns the number of columns in this result set.
 * @see java.sqlResultSetMetaData#getColumnCount
 * @return number of columns
 *
 */
public int getColumnCount() throws SQLException {
  return tsql.numcols();
}
```

This will tell you whether or not the column (specified by an integer index) is an autoincrement or identity column. tinySQL does not support such columns, so this will always return false.

```
/**
 *
 * Is the column an autoincrement (identity, counter) column?
 * @see java.sql.ResultSetMetaData#isAutoIncrement
 * @return false - tinySQL does not support autoincrement columns
 *
 */
public boolean isAutoIncrement(int column) throws SQLException {
  return false;
}
```

This method, `isCaseSensitive()`, will tell you whether or not case is significant in column names.

```
/**
 *
 * Is case significant in column names?
 * @see java.sql.ResultSetMetaData#isCaseSensitive
 * @return true
 *
 */
public boolean isCaseSensitive(int column) throws SQLException {
   return true;
}
```

The `isSearchable()` method tells you whether or not the column can be used in a WHERE clause. This is true for all columns in tinySQL.

```
/**
 *
 * Can the column be used in a WHERE clause?
 * @see java.sql.ResultSetMetaData#isSearchable
 * @return
 *
 */
public boolean isSearchable(int column) throws SQLException {
   return true;
}
```

`isCurrency()` will tell you whether or not a column is some sort of currency column. tinySQL doesn't have these, so it always returns false.

```
/**
 *
 * Is the column some sort of currency?
 * @see java.sql.ResultSetMetaData#isCurrency
 * @return tinySQL doesn't have such things, so it's false
```

**Continued**

```
    *
    */
public boolean isCurrency(int column) throws SQLException {
  return false;
}
```

The isNullable() method will tell you whether or not the given column accepts SQL nulls. tinySQL does not support SQL nulls, so this will return false.

```
/**
  *
  * Determines if the column in question is nullable. tinySQL
  * does not yet support nulls.
  * @see java.sql.ResultSetMetaData#isNullable
  * @return columnNoNulls, columnNullable, or columnNullableUnknown
  *
  */
public int isNullable(int column) throws SQLException{
  return columnNoNulls;
}
```

You can pass a column index to isSigned() to find out whether an integer column is signed.

```
/**
  *
  * All tinySQL integers are signed, so this returns true.
  * @see java.sql.ResultSetMetaData#isSigned
  * @return true
  *
  */
public boolean isSigned(int column) throws SQLException {
  return true;
}
```

The `getColumnDisplaySize()` method returns the width in characters of the column.

```
/**
 *
 * Gives the display size for this column.
 * @see java.sql.ResultSetMetaData#getColumnDisplaySize
 *
 */
public int getColumnDisplaySize(int column) throws SQLException {

    // get a column object. Remember, tinySQL uses a column
    // offset of zero, but JDBC columns start numbering at one.
    // That's why there's a -1 in the columnAtIndex invocation.
    //
    tsColumn col = tsql.columnAtIndex(column-1);
    return col.size;

}
```

The `getColumnLabel()` method returns the verbose name of a column, which is the same as its real name.

```
/**
 *
 * This returns the column name in the form table_name.column_name.
 * @see java.sql.ResultSetMetaData#getColumnLabel
 * @param column the column whose label is wanted
 * @return the fully qualified column name
 *
 */
public String getColumnLabel(int column)
     throws SQLException {

  // get the column, return its table and name, separated by a '.'
```

**Continued**

```
    //
    tsColumn col = tsql.columnAtIndex(column-1);
    return (col.table + "." + col.name);
}
```

The `getColumnName()` method returns the name of a column.

```
/**
 * The name of a given column
 * @see java.sql.ResultSetMetaData#getColumnName
 * @param column the column whose name is wanted
 * @return the name of the requested column
 */
public String getColumnName(int column)
     throws SQLException {

   // get the column and return its name
   //
   tsColumn col = tsql.columnAtIndex(column-1);
   return col.name;
}
```

The `getSchemaName()` method would return the schema or owner or a column, but this does not apply to tinySQL.

```
/**
 *
 * What's the column's schema? This is not applicable to tinySQL,
 * so it returns an empty string.
 *
 */
public String getSchemaName(int column)
     throws SQLException {
  return "";
}
```

The `getPrecision()` method will return the column's precision, but tinySQL does not support this.

```
/**
 *
 * What's the column's precision? This is also not supported by
 * tinySQL.
 *
 */
public int getPrecision(int column)
     throws SQLException {
   throw new SQLException("tinySQL does not support precision.");
}
```

The `getScale()` method will return the number of digits right of the decimal point, but tinySQL does not support this.

```
/**
 *
 * What's a column's number of digits to right of decimal? Yet
 * another fine feature *not* supported by tinySQL.
 *
 */
public int getScale(int column) throws SQLException {
   throw new SQLException("tinySQL does not support scale.");
}
```

The `getTableName()` method will return the name of the table to which a column belongs.

```
/**
 *
 * Gives the name of the table to which this column belongs.
 * @see java.sql.ResultSetMetaData#getTableName
 * @param column the column of the field this information is needed for
```

**Continued**

```
            * @return the table name
            *
            */
            public String getTableName(int column)
                 throws SQLException {

                 // retrieve the column info and return the table name
                 //
                 tsColumn col = tsql.columnAtIndex(column-1);
                 return col.table;
            }
```

The getCatalog() method will return the name of the catalog or database to which a column belongs, but this is not supported by tinySQL.

```
            /**
             *
             * Return the column's table catalog name. Not supported by tinySQL
             *
             */
            public String getCatalogName(int column)
                 throws SQLException {
               throw new SQLException("tinySQL does not support catalogues.");
            }
```

getColumnType() returns the JDBC type of the column.

```
            /**
             *
             * Gives the column type using the types in java.sql.Types.
             * @see java.sqlTypes
             * @see java.sql.ResultSetMetaData#getColumnType
             * @exception SQLException thrown for any number of reasons
             * @param column the column type information is needed on
             * @return the type as listed in java.sql.Types
```

```
 *
 */
public int getColumnType(int column) throws SQLException {

  // get the column info object
  //
  tsColumn col = tsql.columnAtIndex(column-1);

  // report on either of these two types
  //
  if (col.type.equals("CHAR")) {
    return Types.CHAR;
  }
  if (col.type.equals("NUMERIC")) {
    return Types.INTEGER;
  }

  throw new SQLException("Unknown data type.");
}
```

getColumnTypeName() returns the column's datatype as a String.

```
/**
 *
 * Gives the column type as a string.
 * @see java.sql.ResultSetMetaData#getColumnTypeName
 * @exception SQLException thrown at you
 * @param column the column for which the type name is wanted
 * @return the name of the column type
 *
 */
public String getColumnTypeName(int column)
     throws SQLException {

  // just call getColumnType, and report on what it said
```

**Continued**

```
//
switch(getColumnType(column)) {

case Types.INTEGER:
  return "INT";


case Types.CHAR:
  return "CHAR";


default:
  return "NULL";
  }
}
```

Although this method has no meaning to tinySQL, isReadOnly() would tell you whether or not a column is read only.

```
/**
 *
 * Is the column definitely not writable? This has no meaning
 * in tinySQL
 *
 */
public boolean isReadOnly(int column) throws SQLException {
  return false;
}
```

isWritable() would tell you whether or not a column *should* be writable, but it is not supported by tinySQL.

```
/**
 *
 * Is the column potentially writable? This has no meaning
 * in tinySQL
 *
```

```
  */
  public boolean isWritable(int column) throws SQLException {
    return true;
  }
```

isWritable() would tell you whether or not a column *is* writable, but this feature is
not supported by tinySQL.

```
/**
 *
 * Is the column definitely writable? This has no meaning
 * in tinySQL
 *
 */
public boolean isDefinitelyWritable(int column) throws SQLException {
    return true;
  }

}
```

# testTextFile.java

The following program tests the installation of the tinySQL/textFile JDBC driver. To use and
test the driver, you will need to have set your CLASSPATH as described in Chapter 3.

```
/*
 *
 * Test the textFileDriver
 *
 */

import java.net.URL;
import java.sql.*;
```

**Continued**

```java
class testTextFile {


    public static void main(String argv[]) {


        // Uncomment the next line to get noisy messages
        // during the test
        //
        // java.sql.DriverManager.setLogStream(System.out);


        try {


            // load the driver
            //
            Class.forName("textFileDriver");

            // the url to the tinySQL data source
            //
            String url = "jdbc:tinySQL";

            // get the connection
            //
            Connection con = DriverManager.getConnection(url, "", "");

            // create a statement, create a table, populate
            // it, and query it
            //
            Statement stmt = con.createStatement();
            stmt.executeUpdate("CREATE TABLE test (name CHAR(10))");
            stmt.executeUpdate("INSERT INTO test (name) VALUES('test')");


            ResultSet rs = stmt.executeQuery("SELECT name FROM test");
```

```
    // fetch the row
    //
    rs.next();

    // get the column, and see if it matches our expectations
    //
    String colval = rs.getString(1);
    if (colval.startsWith("test")) {
      System.err.println("textFile JDBC driver installed correctly.");
    } else {
      System.err.println("Test was not successful :-(");
      System.err.println("Got \"" + colval + "\", expected \"test\"");
    }

    stmt.close();
    con.close();
  } catch( Exception e ) {
    System.out.println(e.getMessage());
    e.printStackTrace();
  }

  }
}
```

# That's It for the Other One

As you can see, a JDBC Driver includes quite a bit of code. Nevertheless, much of this code involves mapping a database product's API to the standard JDBC CLI. The fact that JDBC is based on ODBC makes your life easier, if you ever want to develop a JDBC driver because ODBC has become such a standard, most vendors have considered ODBC when developing their product, and many provide an ODBC driver as well. If it's possible to develop an ODBC driver for a product, it should be even easier to develop a JDBC driver for it. I hope this chapter has made the inner workings of the JDBC driver a little more comprehensible. With a tool such as JDBC, which is inherently "black boxish," it is often easy to imagine that what lies within the tool is incredibly complex.

# Chapter 8

# Extending tinySQL

Because tinySQL follows a two-tier design, it is very easy to implement tinySQL "drivers" to other data sources. You've already seen textFile, which provides a tinySQL implementation for simple text file manipulation. Given that the SQL processing is very much separated from the layer that processes physical file access, you need only define methods for file access to implement tinySQL.

This chapter will examine a very simple read/only interface to DBF (dBase, FoxPro, etc.) files. It is based on Pratap Pereira's Xbase.pm module, which is a Perl module that provides read-only access to DBF files. Xbase.pm is available from the CPAN multiplexer at:

```
http://www.perl.com/CPAN/modules/by-module/Xbase
```

## dbfFile—A read/only Interface to DBF Files

As with the textFile class, it is necessary to subclass tinySQL. Like the textFile class, a variable called dataDir is used to determine the working directory where the DBF tables reside. There are also three abstract methods in tinySQL that must be implemented. Two of these, CreateTable() and DropTable(), are kind of no-brainers because dbfFile provides read-only access to files. The third method, getTable(), will instantiate and return a dbfFileTable object, which is used to retrieve data from the table.

We introduce a new constructor to this class; one that takes a data directory as an argument. Another difference between dbfFile and textFile is that textFile declares the dataDir variable as a static variable, which means that for every instance of textFile within a given application, each one must use the same data directory. This innovation within dbfFile makes it easy to work with multiple instances of the class with their own data directories but, unfortunately, does not allow for joins across each instance. Therefore, you can join data only from tables that are in the same data directory.

At the end of this class, the main method is defined, which will create a dbfFile object, using the current directory(".") , and retrieves data from the PEOPLE.DBF table. The PEOPLE.DBF table is included along with the example code for this chapter; you should ensure that you run this example in the same directory as the examples and the PEOPLE.DBF file.

```java
/*
 *
 * dbfFile - an extension of tinySQL for dbf file access
 *
 */
import java.util.*;
import java.lang.*;
import java.io.*;

public class dbfFile extends tinySQL {

    public String dataDir = System.getProperty("user.home") + "/.tinySQL";

    /**
     *
     * Constructs a new dbfFile object
     *
     */
    public dbfFile() {

        super();

    }

    /**
```

```
   *
   * Constructs a new dbfFile object
   *
   * @param d directory with which to override the default data directory
   *
   */
  public dbfFile( String d ) {

    super();
    dataDir = d;

  }

  /**
   *
   * The DBF File class provides read-only access to DBF
   * files, so this baby should throw an exception.
   *
   */
  void CreateTable ( String table_name, Vector v )
    throws IOException, tinySQLException {

    throw new tinySQLException("The dbfFile engine is read-only");

  }

  /**
   *
   * Return a tinySQLTable object, given a table name.
   *
   * @param table_name
   * @see tinySQL#getTable
   *
   */
  tinySQLTable getTable (String table_name) throws tinySQLException {
```

**Continued**

```java
        return (tinySQLTable) new dbfFileTable (dataDir, table_name);
    }

    /**
     *
     * The DBF File class provides read-only access to DBF
     * files, so this baby should throw an exception.
     *
     * @param fname table name
     * @see tinySQL#DropTable
     *
     */
    void DropTable (String fname) throws tinySQLException {

        throw new tinySQLException("The dbfFile engine is read-only");

    }

    /*
     * regression test
     */
    public static void main(String argv[]) {

        dbfFile foo = new dbfFile(".");
        tsResultSet trs = null;

        try {
            trs = foo.sqlexec("SELECT * FROM PEOPLE");
        } catch (Exception e) {
            e.printStackTrace();
        }

        trs.PrintResultSet();

    }
}
```

# dbfFileTable—The Implementation
# of the tinySQLTable

The dbfFileTable class provides an implementation of the methods defined in tinySQLTable. One of the major differences between the files used by textFileTable and the .DBF files is that the .DBF files store their column definitions within the same file as the table. Further, the .DBF file includes information such as the number of rows in the table.

This class also includes an extension of tsColumn, which provides a position variable. The position variable is the character at which the column starts within each row. This always starts at one because, like textFileTable, the deleted column is always the first column (position zero) in each row. Instead of using a Vector of String objects to store in the column_info hash, a dbfCol object is used.

While textFileTable uses "Y" to indicated that a row is deleted and "N" to indicate that it is not, the DBF file leaves the column blank for records that have not been deleted and uses an asterisk ("*") to indicate that the record is deleted.

```
/*
 *
 * Extension of tinySQLTable that manipulates dbf files.
 *
 */
import java.util.*;
import java.lang.*;
import java.io.*;

public class dbfFileTable extends tinySQLTable {

    // the full path to the file
    //
    String fullpath;

    // the file type (dbase, fox, etc) and the file update date values
    //
    short file_type, file_update_year, file_update_month, file_update_day;

    // number of records in the table
```

**Continued**

```
   //
   double file_numrecs;

   // data start position, and length of the data
   //
   int file_datap, file_datalength;

   // number of columns
   //
   int num_fields;

   // the object I'll use to manipulate the table
   //
   RandomAccessFile ftbl;

   // current record
   //
   long record_number = 0; // current record

   // end of file flag
   //
   boolean eof = false;

   /**
    *
    * Constructs a dbfFileTable. This is called only by getTable()
    * in dbfFile.java.
    *\
    * @param dDir data directory
    * @param table_name the name of the table
    *
    */
   dbfFileTable( String dDir, String table_name ) throws tinySQLException {

      // the full path to the file
      //
```

```
    fullpath = dDir + "/" + table_name;

    // strip the name out of the path
    //
    table     = new File(table_name).getName();

    // ensure that the full path includes the
    // .DBF suffix
    //
    if (! fullpath.toUpperCase().endsWith(".DBF") ) {
      fullpath = fullpath + ".DBF";
    }

    // Open the DBF file
    //
    open_dbf();

  }

  /**
   *
   * close method. Try not to call this until you are sure
   * the object is about to go out of scope.
   *
   */
  public void close() throws tinySQLException {

    try {
      ftbl.close();
    } catch (IOException e) {
      throw new tinySQLException(e.getMessage());
    }

  }

  /**
```

**Continued**

```
     *
     * Returns the size of a column
     *
     * @param column name of the column
     * @see tinySQLTable#ColSize
     *
     */
    public int ColSize(String col_name) {

        // retrieve the column object from the column_info Hashtable
        //
        dbfCol column = (dbfCol) column_info.get(col_name);

        // return its size
        //
        return column.size;

    }

    /**
     *
     * Returns the datatype of a column.
     *
     * @param column name of the column.
     * @see tinySQLTable#ColType
     *
     */
    public String ColType(String col_name) {

        // retrieve the column object from the column_info Hashtable
        //
        dbfCol column = (dbfCol) column_info.get(col_name);

        // return its type
        //
        return column.type;
```

```
}

/**
 *
 * Updates the current row in the table. This fails because
 * dbfFileTable operates in read-only mode.
 *
 * @param c Ordered Vector of column names
 * @param v Ordered Vector (must match order of c) of values
 * @see tinySQLTable#UpdateCurrentRow
 *
 */
public void UpdateCurrentRow(Vector c, Vector v) throws tinySQLException {

   throw new tinySQLException("dbfFileTable operates in read/only mode.");
}

/**
 *
 * Position the record pointer at the top of the table.
 *
 * @see tinySQLTable#GoTop
 *
 */
public void GoTop() throws tinySQLException {

   record_number = 0;
   eof           = false;

}

/**
 *
 * Advance the record pointer to the next record.
 *
```

**Continued**

```
 * @see tinySQLTable#NextRecord
 *
 */
public boolean NextRecord() throws tinySQLException {

  if (record_number < file_numrecs) {
    record_number++;
    eof = false;
    return true;
  } else {
    eof = true;
    return false;
  }

}

/**
 *
 * Insert a blank row.
 *
 * @see tinySQLTable#InsertRow()
 *
 */
public void InsertRow() throws tinySQLException {

  throw new tinySQLException("dbfFileTable operates in read-only mode.");

}

/**
 *
 * Retrieve a column's string value from the current row.
 *
 * @param column the column name
 * @see tinySQLTable#GetCol
 *
```

```
*/
public String GetCol(String col_name) throws tinySQLException {

   try {

      // retrieve the dbfCol object that corresponds
      // to this column.
      //
      dbfCol column = (dbfCol) column_info.get(col_name);

      // seek the starting offset of the current record,
      // as indicated by record_number
      //
      ftbl.seek( file_datap + (record_number - 1) * file_datalength);

      // fully read a byte array out to the length of
      // the record.
      //
      byte[] b = new byte[file_datalength];
      ftbl.readFully(b);

      // make it into a String
      //
      String result = new String(b, 0);

      // if it's the pseudo column _DELETED, return
      // the first character in it
      //
      if (col_name.equals("_DELETED")) {
        return result.substring(0, 1);
      }

      // for all other columns, return the substring that begins at
      // the column's position within the record and continues
      // for the column's size.
      //
```

```java
        return result.substring(column.position, column.position + column.size);


    } catch (Exception e) {
      e.printStackTrace();
      throw new tinySQLException(e.getMessage());
    }
  }


/**
 *
 * Update a single column.
 *
 * @param column the column name
 * @param value the String value with which to update the column
 * @see tinySQLTable#UpdateCol
 *
 */
public void UpdateCol( String column, String value ) throws tinySQLException {

    throw new tinySQLException("dbfFileTable operates in read/only mode.");

}


/**
 *
 * Delete the current row.
 *
 * @see tinySQLTable#DeleteRow
 *
 */
public void DeleteRow() throws tinySQLException {

    throw new tinySQLException("dbfFileTable operates in read/only mode.");

}
```

```java
/**
 *
 * Is the current row deleted?
 *
 * @see tinySQLTable#isDeleted()
 *
 */
public boolean isDeleted() throws tinySQLException {

   // this is really easy; just check the value of the _DELETED column
   //
   return (GetCol("_DELETED")).equals("*");
}

// end methods implemented from tinySQLTable.java
// the rest of this stuff is private methods
// for dbfFileTable
//

/*
 *
 * opens a DBF file. This is based on Pratap Pereira's
 * Xbase.pm perl module
 *
 */
private void open_dbf() throws tinySQLException {

   try {

      // open the file
      //
      ftbl = new RandomAccessFile(fullpath, "r");

      // position the record pointer at 0
      //
```

**Continued**

```
ftbl.seek(0);

// read the file type
//
file_type          = fixByte(ftbl.readByte());

// get the last update date
//
file_update_year  = fixByte(ftbl.readByte());
file_update_month = fixByte(ftbl.readByte());
file_update_day   = fixByte(ftbl.readByte());

// a byte array to hold little-endian long data
//
byte[] b = new byte[4];

// read that baby in...
//
ftbl.readFully(b);

// convert the byte array into a long (really a double)
//
file_numrecs       =  vax_to_long(b);

// a byte array to hold little-endian short data
//
b = new byte[2];

// get the data position (where it starts in the file)
//
ftbl.readFully(b);
file_datap         = vax_to_short(b);

// find out the length of the data portion
//
ftbl.readFully(b);
```

```
    file_datalength    = vax_to_short(b);


    // calculate the number of fields
    //
    num_fields = (int) (file_datap - 33)/32;


    // skip the next 20 bytes - looks like this is not needed...
    //ftbl.skipBytes(20);


    // read in the column data
    //
    int i;
    int locn = 0; // offset of the current column


    // process each field
    //
    for (i = 1; i <= num_fields; i++) {

      // seek the position of the field definition data.
      // This information appears after the first 32-byte
      // table information, and lives in 32-byte chunks.
      //
      ftbl.seek( (i - 1) * 32 + 32 );


      // get the column name into a byte array
      //
      b = new byte[10];
      ftbl.readFully(b);


      // convert the byte array to a String
      //
      String col_name = (new String(b, 0)).trim();


      // read in the column type
      //
      char c[] = new char[1];
```

**Continued**

```
    c[0] = ftbl.readChar();
    String ftyp = new String(c);

    // skip 4 bytes
    //
    ftbl.skipBytes(4);

    // get field length and precision
    //
    short flen = fixByte(ftbl.readByte());
    short fdec = fixByte(ftbl.readByte());

    // set the field position to the current
    // value of locn
    //
    int fpos  = locn;

    // increment locn by the length of this field.
    //
    locn += flen;

    // create a new dbfCol object and assign it the
    // attributes of the current field
    //
    dbfCol column   = new dbfCol(col_name);
    column.type     = new String(c);
    column.size     = flen;
    column.position = fpos + 1;
    column.table    = table;

    // now, why don't we do it this way in
    // textFileTable.java???
    //
    column_info.put(col_name, column);

}
```

```
    } catch (Exception e) {

      e.printStackTrace();
      throw new tinySQLException(e.getMessage());

    }
  }


/**
 *
 * Converts a little-endian 4-byte array to a long,
 * represented as a double, since long is signed.
 *
 * I don't know why Java doesn't supply this. It could
 * be that it's there somewhere, but I looked and couldn't
 * find it.
 *
 */
public static double vax_to_long(byte[] b) {
  return fixByte(b[0]) + ( fixByte(b[1]) * 256) +
         ( fixByte(b[2]) * (256^2)) + ( fixByte(b[3]) * (256^3));
}


/**
 *
 * Converts a little-endian 4-byte array to a short,
 * represented as an int, since short is signed.
 *
 * I don't know why Java doesn't supply this. It could
 * be that it's there somewhere, but I looked and couldn't
 * find it.
 *
 */
public static int vax_to_short(byte[] b) {
  return (int) ( fixByte(b[0]) + ( fixByte(b[1]) * 256));
}
```

**Continued**

```
    /*
     *
     * bytes are signed; let's fix them...
     *
     */
    public static short fixByte (byte b) {

      if (b < 0) {
        return (short) ( b + 256);
      }
      return b;
    }


}

/*
 *
 * extend tsColumn to hold the column's position, as well as all the
 * other groovy characteristics of a column.
 *
 */
class dbfCol extends tsColumn {

  int position = 0;
  public dbfCol(String c) {
     super(c);
  }
}
```

# dbfFileDriver—The JDBC Driver for This Bad Boy

The dbfFile and dbfFileTable classes can be used in the same fashion as the textFile classes. The following classes define the dbfFile JDBC driver. In order to avoid confusion when loading drivers, the dbfFiledriver class looks for URLs of the form jdbc:dbfFile rather than jdbc:tinySQL. This way, you can have both drivers available, and the JDBC driver manager can distinguish between them.

```
/*
 *
 * dbfFile/tinySQL JDBC driver
 *
 * A lot of this code is based on or directly taken from
 * George Reese's (borg@imaginary.com) mSQL driver.
 *
 * So, it's probably safe to say:
 *
 * Portions of this code Copyright (c) 1996 George Reese
 */

import java.sql.Connection;
import java.sql.DriverPropertyInfo;
import java.sql.SQLException;
import java.sql.Driver;
import java.util.Properties;

public class dbfFileDriver extends tinySQLDriver {

  /*
   *
   * Instantiate a new dbfFileDriver(), registering it with
   * the JDBC DriverManager.
   *
   */
  static {
    try {
      java.sql.DriverManager.registerDriver(new dbfFileDriver());
    } catch (Exception e) {
      e.printStackTrace();
    }
  }
```

**Continued**

```
/**
 *
 * Constructs a new dbfFileDriver
 *
 */
public dbfFileDriver() {
  super();
}

/**
 *
 * returns a new dbfFileConnection object, which is cast
 * to a tinySQLConnection object.
 *
 * @exception SQLException when an error occurs
 * @param user the username - currently unused
 * @param url the url to the data source
 * @param d the Driver object.
 *
 */
public tinySQLConnection getConnection
                  (String user, String url, Driver d)
                    throws SQLException {

  return (tinySQLConnection) new dbfFileConnection(user, url, d);
}

/**
 *
 * Check to see if the URL is a dbfFile URL. It should start
 * with jdbc:dbfFile in order to qualify.
 *
 * @param url The URL of the database.
 * @return True if this driver can connect to the given URL.
 *
```

```
    */
    public boolean acceptsURL(String url) throws SQLException {

        // make sure the length is at least 12
        // before bothering with the substring
        // comparison.
        //
        if( url.length() < 12 ) {
          return false;
        }

        // if everything after the jdbc: part is
        // dbfFile, then return true.
        //
        return url.substring(5,12).equals("dbfFile");

    }

}
```

# dbfFileConnection—The JDBC Connection Object for dbfFile

The dbfFileConnection object includes the ability to parse out a data directory path within the URL, so you could use a URL such as jdbc:dbfFile:`/home/bjepson/.data` instead of the default (`~/.tinySQL`). Other than this, the dbfFileConnection class is little different from textFileConnection.

```
/*
 *
 * Connection class for the dbfFile/tinySQL
 * JDBC driver
 *
 * A lot of this code is based on or directly taken from
 * George Reese's (borg@imaginary.com) mSQL driver.
 *
```

**Continued**

```
 * So, it's probably safe to say:
 *
 * Portions of this code Copyright (c) 1996 George Reese
 *
 */

import java.sql.CallableStatement;
import java.sql.DatabaseMetaData;
import java.sql.Driver;
import java.sql.PreparedStatement;
import java.sql.SQLException;
import java.sql.SQLWarning;
import java.sql.Statement;

public class dbfFileConnection extends tinySQLConnection {

  /**
   *
   * Constructs a new JDBC Connection object.
   *
   * @exception SQLException in case of an error
   * @param user the username - not currently used
   * @param u the url to the data source
   * @param d the Driver object
   *
   */
  public dbfFileConnection(String user, String u, Driver d)
        throws SQLException {
    super(user, u, d);
  }

  /**
   *
   * Returns a new dbfFile object that is cast to a tinySQL
   * object.
   *
```

```
    */
   public tinySQL get_tinySQL() {

      // if there's a data directory, it will
      // be everything after the jdbc:dbfFile:
      //
      if (url.length() > 13) {
        String dataDir = url.substring(13);
        return (tinySQL) new dbfFile(dataDir);
      }

      // if there was no data directory specified in the
      // url, then just use the default constructor
      //
      return (tinySQL) new dbfFile();

   }

}
```

# A Test Program for dbfFileDriver

The following program will test the dbfFileDriver by using a URL that includes the current directory as the data directory. It should be executed in the same directory as the chapter examples, since a .DBF file, PEOPLE.DBF, is included.

```
/*
 *
 * Test the dbfFileDriver
 *
 */

import java.net.URL;
import java.sql.*;

class testDbfFile {
```

**Continued**

```
public static void main(String argv[]) {


    // Uncomment the next line to get noisy messages
    // during the test
    //
    // java.sql.DriverManager.setLogStream(System.out);

    try {

        // load the driver
        //
        Class.forName("dbfFileDriver");

        // the url to the tinySQL data source
        //
        String url = "jdbc:dbfFile:.";

        // get the connection
        //
        Connection con = DriverManager.getConnection(url, "", "");

        // create a statement and execute a query
        //
        Statement stmt = con.createStatement();

        ResultSet rs = stmt.executeQuery("SELECT LAST_NAME FROM people");

        // fetch each row
        //
        while (rs.next()) {

            // get the column, and see if it matches our expectations
            //
            String colval = rs.getString(1);
```

```
        System.err.println("LAST_NAME = " + colval);

    }


    stmt.close();
    con.close();

} catch( Exception e ) {
    System.out.println(e.getMessage());
    e.printStackTrace();
}


}

}
```

# Conclusion

You've seen how tinySQL can be easily extended to support different data sources. There's really no limit to what can be done, and as tinySQL matures, it will gain speed and stability, complementing its extensibility. Any non-SQL data source can theoretically be manipulated with SQL, be it a POP or NNTP server, or even a freaky data feed from some dinosaur system.

# .mSQL and MsqlJava

mSQL is a lightweight (and cheap!) SQL engine, written by David Hughes (Bambi@Hughes.com.au), that supports a subset of ANSI SQL. It should compile out of the box on most Unix-compatible operating systems, and also under the not-so-Unix-compatible Win32 operating system. mSQL can be built on OS/2 as well.

mSQL was one of the first database products to be supported by a Java API. A shareware product, mSQL is very inexpensive (at the time of this writing, it is $225 Australian, which is approximately $170 U.S. dollars). It also includes the source code, which encourages people to develop tools that work with mSQL. One of the people who developed such a tool is Darryl Collins (darryl@minmet.uq.oz.au). Darryl is responsible for bringing MsqlJava to us. MsqlJava is a Java API for mSQL that allows Java developers to connect their applications and applets to mSQL data sources.

Many Web developers feel that mSQL is an excellent choice for Internet database development. Because of the application's open nature, quality, and low price, mSQL has become extremely popular. Further, using a free operating system such as Linux, you can get an Internet database server up and running for only a little more than the cost of the hardware and your Internet connection. This chapter will introduce you to mSQL, and show you how to develop simple Java applets that communicate with mSQL.

# Getting mSQL

mSQL is available by anonymous ftp from:

```
ftp://bond.edu.au/pub/Minerva/msql
```

You should retrieve the most recent version and extract the source. Note that the "1.0.14" portion of the filename shown below is the version number; this is the version that was current as of this writing. Because mSQL is frequently updated and improved, there may be a more recent version with a much higher number. The Contrib/ subdirectory contains precompiled versions for Win32 and OS/2.

I usually extract the release into /usr/src and leave it around because I am a packrat. You can extract the source with the command:

```
gunzip -c msql-1.0.14.tar.gz | tar xvf -
```

This causes gunzip to decompress the archive to stdout, and it is then piped to tar, which extracts it (x) verbosely (v) from stdin (f -). Remember, one process's (gunzip) stdout is another process's (tar) stdin! The tar file contacts the top-level directory so when you extract it, a directory called msql-1.0.14 is created. You should now 'cd' into it.

# Building and Installing mSQL

To build mSQL, you should be logged in as root. To start things off, issue a:

```
make target
```

This sets up the source tree for your target architecture. Once it has been run, you can 'cd' into the directory containing the target source. In many cases, you will have only one target. The name of the target directory is derived from your operating system and hardware, which comes from uname -s (operating system), uname -r (operating system revision), and uname -m (hardware platform). On my machine, the mSQL target is in:

```
/usr/src/msql-1.0.14/targets/Linux-1.3.20-i586/
```

But it will certainly vary greatly, depending on your OS and hardware. Once you have changed your working directory to the target directory, you should run the setup shell script with:

```
./setup
```

The ./ ensures that you don't mistakenly run another setup script, located somewhere else in your path. This script will ask you a few questions. It is usually safe to go with the defaults:

```
bjepson:/usr/src/msql-1.0.14/targets/Linux-1.3.20-i586# ./setup

Starting build of mSQL.


Interactive configuration section

        Note : Any prompt below that asks for a directory requires an
               absolute pathname.  A relative pathname such as ../foo
               or symbolic paths such as ~user/msql will not work


        Top of install tree ? [/usr/local/Minerva]
        Will this installation be running as root ? [y]
        Directory for pid file ? [/var/adm]



Automatic configuration section

checking for gcc
        setting CC to gcc
checking for return type of signal handlers
        defining RETSIGTYPE to be void
checking for ranlib
        setting RANLIB to ranlib
checking for bison
        setting YACC to bison -y
checking for strdup
        defining HAVE_STRDUP
checking for rindex
        defining HAVE_RINDEX
checking for bcopy
        defining HAVE_BCOPY
checking for getdtablesize
        defining HAVE_GETDTABLESIZE
checking for strsignal
```

```
              defining HAVE_STRSIGNAL
checking for ftruncate
              defining HAVE_FTRUNCATE
checking for -lsocket
checking for -lnsl
checking for -lgen
checking for -lx
checking for sys/sockio.h
checking how to run the C preprocessor
              setting CPP to gcc -E
checking for sys/dir.h
              defining HAVE_SYS_DIR_H
checking for dirent.h
              defining HAVE_DIRENT_H
checking for netinet/in_systm.h
              defining HAVE_NETINET_IN_SYSTM_H
checking for select.h
checking for sys/select.h
checking for sys/un.h
              defining HAVE_SYS_UN_H
creating config.status
creating site.mm
creating makegen/makegen.cf
creating common/config.h
common/config.h is unchanged

checking your directory stuff.  Using dirent.h and struct dirent
checking mmap().  Your mmap() is fine.
checking for u_int.  You're fine.

Ready to build mSQL.

You may wish to check "common/site.h" although the defaults should be fine. When
you're ready, type "make all" to build the software.

bjepson:/usr/src/msql-1.0.14/targets/Linux-1.3.20-i586#
```

You should now issue a `make all`, followed by a `make install`. This will install the binaries in the top of the install tree, as specified when you ran `./setup`.

The top of the install tree, which is usually `/usr/local/Minerva`, contains a file called msql.acl.sample. It's a sample access control file, which controls who has access to which database. You should create a file named `msql.acl` and put the following lines in it:

```
database=sample
read=*
write=*
```

This gives anyone in the world read and write access to a database, called `sample`, which you haven't created yet. You will naturally want to customize `msql.acl` to restrict access, but this should work fine for the examples in this chapter. See the `msql.acl` `.sample` file and the mSQL documentation for more information on access control files.

# Starting mSQL

To start mSQL, you should execute the msql daemon, with:

```
/usr/local/Minerva/bin/msqld &
```

This will start it in the background. It can also be added to your /etc/rc.d/rc.local (or whatever your machine's startup script is), with a line like:

```
echo "Running msql..."
/usr/local/Minerva/bin/msqld &
```

# Paying for mSQL

If you use mSQL, you should definitely send some money to David Hughes. David put a lot of work into it, and he continues to do so, releasing new versions frequently and responding to bug reports. That's it. I'm not going to preach.

# Command-line Tools

mSQL comes with a number of command-line tools that are used to manage databases and tables.

## msqladmin—A Tool for Managing Your Server

msqladmin can be used to create or drop (destroy) databases, shut down the server, or reload the access control file (`/usr/local/Minerva/msql.acl`) when it has changed. It's best to restrict the execution of this program to the root user or a privileged group because it is quite powerful.

**Databases** Databases are containers that can hold tables. In some relational database packages, the terms "database" and "table" are used synonymously, but in mSQL, a database refers to a collection of tables. The databases are merely directories under `/usr/local/Minerva/msqldb`, and the tables are files in these directories.

To create a database, simply invoke msqladmin with the Create command and the name of the database you wish to create:

```
msqladmin create sample
```

This will create a database named "sample."

## msql—Issuing Queries and Creating Tables Interactively

Once you have created the sample database, you can run some tests to see if mSQL was installed correctly. The msql source directory (`src/msql` under wherever you put the source code) contains a test script called `sample.msql`. After you change the directory to the mSQL source directory, you can test it out on your sample database with this command:

```
/usr/local/Minerva/bin/msql sample < sample.msql
```

Some of the commands in this test script are expected to generate errors. You may view the sample.msql file to get an idea of what to expect. In addition to running SQL scripts from the command line, you can also enter SQL commands directly into msql, by not redirecting a script into msql and simply letting it read from standard input.

# Getting and Installing MsqlJava

MsqlJava can be downloaded from:

```
http://www.minmet.uq.oz.au/msqljava
```

Because both Java and mSQL are in a constant state of change, you should frequently check this site for any new changes. The simplest way to install MsqlJava is to simply place the supporting `.class` files in the same directory with the Java applet or application you are building. This way, the classes will be immediately accessible to your Java program. You should ensure that your CLASSPATH specifies the 'current working directory' (specified by '.') , as in:

```
Unix, Bourne shell (/bin/sh):

export CLASSPATH=/usr/local/classes:.

Win32, Command Prompt (CMD.EXE or COMMAND.COM):

set CLASSPATH=c:\classes;.
```

Alternatively, you can put the files in another directory that is in your CLASSPATH. The only drawback is that the files must also be in your users' CLASSPATH. Further, if you are distributing your programs as applets, you have no control over what the user has installed in his or her CLASSPATH, and you are much better off keeping the `.class` files in the same directory as the `.class` files that comprise your program.

# Testing the Installation

Once you have installed MsqlJava, you can try out this sample program:

```java
/**
 * sample - a sample MsqlJava client.
 *
 * @author Brian Jepson
 * @author Copyright 1996, John Wiley and Sons
 *
 */
public class sample {

  /**
   * main() - the main method
   *
   * @param argv[0] name of mSQL host (default == localhost)
   *
   */
  public static void main(String argv[]) {

    // instantiate an Msql object...

    Msql msql = new Msql();
```

**Continued**

```
// a hostname can be specified on the command line

String host;
if (argv.length > 0) {

  host = argv[0];

} else {

  // if no hostname was specified, use localhost

  host = "localhost";
}

try {

    // make a connection to the specified host,
    // and select the sample database

    msql.Connect(host);
    msql.SelectDB("sample");

    // if the "sample_table" already exists, drop it
    // we can determine if the table exists by iterating
    // over the output of ListTables()

    String[] tables = msql.ListTables();
    for (int i = 0; i < tables.length; i++) {
      if (tables[i].equals("sample_table")) {
        msql.Query("drop table sample_table");
      }
    }

    // create the "sample_table" table
```

```
msql.Query("create table sample_table (name char(15))");

// insert a few values into it

msql.Query("insert into sample_table (name) values ('Brian')");
msql.Query("insert into sample_table (name) values ('Chris')");
msql.Query("insert into sample_table (name) values ('David')");
msql.Query("insert into sample_table (name) values ('Michael')");
msql.Query("insert into sample_table (name) values ('Nathan')");
msql.Query("insert into sample_table (name) values ('Ron')");

// retrieve all of the rows from it

MsqlResult result = msql.Query("select name from sample_table");

// fetch each row from the results, and print out
// the first column. FetchRow returns an array of
// strings, which positionally correspond to the
// columns in the result set.

String row[];
while(( row = result.FetchRow()) != null) {
  System.out.println("[" + row[0] + "]");
}

}

// print a stack trace if we catch an exception

catch(MsqlException e ) {
  e.printStackTrace();
}

}

}
```

**Continued**

# The Msql Class

The example shown in the preceding pages makes use of many of the methods that you'll need to develop MsqlJava applications and applets.

## Instantiating and Initializing an Object

To get started, you naturally will need to instantiate an Msql object. This object is defined in Msql.java. It can be invoked without any parameters, like so:

```
Msql msql = new Msql();
```

You can include the name of the host as a String parameter, as in:

```
Msql msql = new Msql("localhost");
```

If you don't include the name of the host as a parameter, you must call the Connect method before performing any queries:

```
msql.Connect("localhost");
```

In the earlier program example, I examine the argv[] array for the name of the host. This is the only parameter that the sample.java program looks for. If it's not found, I default the name of the host to "localhost."

## Working with Tables and Issuing Queries

To issue any queries, you will first need to select a database that contains tables that you can query. The SelectDB() method allows you to do this:

```
msql.SelectDB("sample");
```

Once you have selected a database, you may start querying the tables contained therein. You can populate an array of Strings with the names of all tables in the database by using the ListTables() method:

```
String[] tables = msql.ListTables();
```

The Query() method will return an MsqlResult object, which can be used to get at the results of the query:

```
MsqlResult result = msql.Query("select name from sample_table");
```

To retrieve each row from the query, you will need to call the FetchRow() method of the MsqlResult object. The FetchRow() method will return an array of String objects until there are no more rows. After it runs out of rows to return, it returns null:

```
String row[];
while(( row = result.FetchRow()) != null) {
    System.out.println("[" + row[0] + "]");
}
```

The array returned by FetchRow() consists of one element for each column. If you issued the query

```
MsqlResult result = msql.Query("select name, id, age from my_table");
```

then the results of

```
row = result.FetchRow();
```

would consist of three elements, beginning at index zero. `row[0]` would hold the value of `my_table.name`, `row[1]` would contain the value of `my_table.id`, and `row[2]` would contain the value of `my_table.age`.

# CardFile.java—A Slightly More Complex Java Application

CardFile is a Java application that allows you to maintain a simple mailing list. It provides add, edit, and delete functionality. Additionally, you can navigate through the table using a Next and Previous button. To have this application work, you will need to have created a database called "sample," as described in the earlier section titled "Database." Then, you should run the following script through the `msql` utility:

```
#
# create a simple cardfile file

# just in case it already exists, drop the table. If it doesn't
# exist, this will produce an error...
#
drop table cardfile
\g

create table cardfile
    (name    char(20),
     address char(35),
```

```
city      char(20),
state     char(2),
zip       char(11),
country char(25),
phone     char(20),
id        char(4) primary key)
\g
```

The first thing CardFile needs to do is import the various Java packages that will be used by this application:

```
import java.awt.*;
import java.lang.*;
import java.util.*;
```

This application is encapsulated by the CardFile class. It extends Frame, so it is possible to add visual interface components to it, such as buttons and textfields. A new Msql object is instantiated and declared. Also, many of the class-wide objects are declared, as well.

```
public class CardFile extends Frame {

    // instantiate a new Msql object

    Msql msql = new Msql();

    // the TextField objects for each column

    TextField txt_name, txt_address, txt_city, txt_state,
              txt_zip, txt_country, txt_phone, txt_id;

    String formstate; // indicates whether we are adding or editing

    // String    name, address, city, state, zip, country, phone;

    // a layout manager for the Frame
```

```
GridBagLayout layoutmangler = new GridBagLayout();

// each of the buttons and a Panel to hold them

Button next, previous, quit, save, newrow, edit, cancel, delete;
Panel actionbuttons;

// the Vector holds the primary key (customer ID) for
// each row in the table. currentRow holds the index
// of the one we are currently viewing

int currentRow = 0;
Vector cardfileKeys = new Vector();

// this hash is used to map column names to the
// corresponding objects (the TextFields)

Hashtable columnmap = new Hashtable();
```

The CardFile() constructor performs some initialization steps, such as adding all of the interface components to the CardFile, under the control of a GridBagLayout disconcertingly known as layoutmangler. The constructor for Frame is implicitly invoked here.

The AddToFrame() method, which is defined later, is used to add each object to the frame, and each object is associated with a column within the columnmap Hashtable. This enables you to perform lookups by column name later on, when you want to find the corresponding interface object. The actionbuttons are created within a Panel, which is centered within the GridBagLayout.

Finally, the Msql.Connect() method is called to log in to the database server, and the Msql.SelectDB() method is invoked to set the current database to "sample." Once this is done, getKeys() is called to populate the cardfileKeys Vector with all of the primary key values in the table. The primary key "ID" is used to uniquely identify each record. This means that there cannot be more than one record with the same value in "ID." The cardfileKeys Vector enables the CardFile object to keep track of all the rows in the table without loading in all of the columns for each row. Later on, you will see a simple SQL statement that will retrieve all of the columns, using the value of "ID," as stored in the cardfileKeys

Vector. The integer variable `currentRow` holds the index of the `cardfileKeys` element that contains the ID value for the current row that the user is looking at or editing.

After `getKeys()` is invoked, the `getRow()` method is used to display the first row, which starts out at zero (the elements in a Vector start at zero, so the first element is element number zero).

```java
// the default constructor

public CardFile() {

    // set the layout for the frame
    this.setLayout(layoutmangler);

    // this is the offset within the GridBagLayout. If
    // I want the next object on a different line, I
    // postincrement. If not, I don't.
    int i = 0;

    // the name field
    //
    // first, I add an anonymous text label to the Frame using
    // the AddToFrame method. Note that it uses column 0, and
    // row i (currently zero). I don't want the textfield
    // to appear on a different row, so I don't postincrement i.

    AddToFrame(new Label("Name:"), 0, i);

    // now, I instantiate txt_name. This is a textfield with 20
    // spaces. Then, I add it to the frame and insert a reference
    // to it in the columnmap, keyed by 'name', which is the name
    // of the column in the CardFile table

    txt_name = new TextField(20);
    txt_name.setEditable(false);
    AddToFrame(txt_name, 1, i++);
```

```
columnmap.put("name", txt_name);

// the rest of the fields. Everything is pretty much the same as above.
//
// the address field

AddToFrame(new Label("Address:"), 0, i);
txt_address = new TextField(35);
txt_address.setEditable(false);
AddToFrame(txt_address, 1, i++);
columnmap.put("address", txt_address);

// the city field
// don't postincrement i, so state will show up
// on the same row.

AddToFrame(new Label("City:"), 0, i);
txt_city = new TextField(20);
txt_city.setEditable(false);
AddToFrame(txt_city, 1, i);
columnmap.put("city", txt_city);

// the state field

AddToFrame(new Label("State:"), 2, i);
txt_state = new TextField(2);
txt_state.setEditable(false);
AddToFrame(txt_state, 3, i++);
columnmap.put("state", txt_state);

// the zip field

AddToFrame(new Label("Zip:"), 0, i);
txt_zip = new TextField(11);
txt_zip.setEditable(false);
AddToFrame(txt_zip, 1, i++);
```

**Continued**

```
columnmap.put("zip", txt_zip);

// the country field

AddToFrame(new Label("Country:"), 0, i);
txt_country = new TextField(25);
txt_country.setEditable(false);
AddToFrame(txt_country, 1, i++);
columnmap.put("country", txt_country);

// the phone field

AddToFrame(new Label("Phone:"), 0, i);
txt_phone = new TextField(20);
txt_phone.setEditable(false);
AddToFrame(txt_phone, 1, i++);
columnmap.put("phone", txt_phone);

// the ID field.

AddToFrame(new Label("Id:"), 0, i);
txt_id = new TextField(4);
txt_id.setEditable(false);
AddToFrame(txt_id, 1, i++);
columnmap.put("id", txt_id);

// create the button panel and give it a new FlowLayout

actionbuttons = new Panel();
actionbuttons.setLayout(new FlowLayout(FlowLayout.CENTER, 5, 5));

// The constraints for the button panel are a little
// more complex than the constraints for the labels
// and textfields, so we'll set it up here and add
// the actionbuttons panel
```

```
GridBagConstraints c = new GridBagConstraints();
c.gridwidth = 3; c.gridheight = 1;
c.fill = GridBagConstraints.NONE;
c.anchor = GridBagConstraints.CENTER;
c.weightx = 0.0; c.weighty = 0.0;
c.gridx = 0; c.gridy = i;
((GridBagLayout)this.getLayout()).setConstraints(actionbuttons, c);
this.add(actionbuttons);

// instantiate and add each of the buttons

previous = new Button("Previous");
actionbuttons.add(previous);


next = new Button("Next");
actionbuttons.add(next);


quit = new Button("Quit");
actionbuttons.add(quit);


newrow = new Button("New");
actionbuttons.add(newrow);


edit = new Button("Edit");
actionbuttons.add(edit);


delete = new Button("Delete");
actionbuttons.add(delete);


// save and cancel are disabled until the user
// is adding or editing.

save = new Button("Save");
actionbuttons.add(save);
save.disable();
```

**Continued**

```
    cancel = new Button("Cancel");
    actionbuttons.add(cancel);
    cancel.disable();

    // connect to the localhost and use the database
    // named 'sample'

    try {
      msql.Connect("localhost");
      msql.SelectDB("sample");
    }
    catch(MsqlException e ) {
      e.printStackTrace();
    }

    // call getKeys() to populate cardfileKeys with unique identifiers
    // for all the keys in the table

    getKeys();

    // call getRow() to display the first row in the table.
    // this should be the element in cardfileKeys at index
    // currentRow, which starts out at zero.

    getRow();

    // pack the Frame and show it.
    pack();
    show();

  }
```

The getKeys() method issues an SQL Select statement to retrieve the ID column for each row in the table. After removing all of the elements in the cardfileKeys Vector, each ID is added to the Vector using the addElement() method. The row[] array, as returned by FetchRow(), contains one element for each column in the current row.

Because there's only one column (ID) in the result set, that value can be accessed with the expression `row[]`.

```
/**
 * getKeys()
 *
 * This populates the cardfileKeys Vector with unique identifiers
 * for all of the rows in the cardfile table. This lets us buffer
 * all of the rows, without storing the values for each column.
 * As a result, we only have to worry about dirty data if someone
 * changes a key, which of course, you would *never* do...
 *
 * now, if someone else deletes or inserts a row, that's a
 * different problem. Handling that is an exercise left to
 * the reader...
 */
public protected void getKeys() {

    try {

        // delete all the elements in cardfileKeys

        cardfileKeys.removeAllElements();

        // execute a query to get the ID column for each of the
        // rows. Then, process each row and add the ID column
        // to cardfileKeys

        MsqlResult    result = msql.Query("select id from cardfile");
        String row[];
        while(( row = result.FetchRow()) != null){
cardfileKeys.addElement(row[0]);
        }

    }
    catch (MsqlException e) {
```

**Continued**

```
      e.printStackTrace();
   }
}
```

The `clearForm()` method simply calls the `setText()` method of each TextField, blanking out each one. This is useful when adding a new record.

```java
/**
 * clearForm()
 *
 * Clear all of the input fields
 *
 */
public protected void clearForm () {

    // blank the name field
    txt_name.setText("");

    // blank the address field
    txt_address.setText("");

    // blank the city field
    txt_city.setText("");

    // blank the state field
    txt_state.setText("");

    // blank the zip field
    txt_zip.setText("");

    // blank the country field
    txt_country.setText("");

    // blank the phone field
    txt_phone.setText("");
```

```
   // blank the id field

   txt_id.setText("");


}
```

The `AddToFrame()` method is a simple way of invoking `GridBagConstraints()`; it makes it possible to lay out each component using only the x and y coordinates:

```
/**
 * AddToFrame()
 *
 * A convenient method to wrap the living hell
 * that is GridBagConstraints()
 *
 */
public protected void AddToFrame (Component item, int x, int y) {

   // some sane layout defaults.

   GridBagConstraints c = new GridBagConstraints();
   c.gridwidth = 1; c.gridheight = 1;
   c.fill = GridBagConstraints.NONE;
   c.anchor = GridBagConstraints.NORTHWEST;
   c.weightx = 0.0; c.weighty = 0.0;

   // set the grid coordinates

   c.gridx = x; c.gridy = y;

   // set the constraints, and add the item to the layout

   ((GridBagLayout)this.getLayout()).setConstraints(item, c);
   this.add(item);


}
```

The `save()` method constructs an SQL insert statement that inserts a new record into the cardfile table. This is called only when the user presses the Save button after editing a new record. It is assumed that the value supplied for the ID is unique, otherwise it may throw an exception.

After the insert is issued using the `Msql.Query()` method, the new record's ID is added to the `cardfileKeys` Vector, and the index of the new ID is stored to `currentRow`. After this is done, `getRow()` is invoked to retrieve the record from the form. This provides an extra level of confirmation; if the data appears okay after you press the Save button, then it means the insert was performed correctly.

```java
/**
 *
 * save()
 *
 * Save the record we are editing to the table
 *
 */
public protected void save() {

    // construct an INSERT statement, with values for each
    // column, including ID. Teaching this system to auto-
    // increment ID in a multiuser environment is an exercise
    // left up to the reader.
    //
    // Assuming, of course, that bambi hasn't released a version
    // of mSQL that supports this natively :-)

    String sql = "insert into cardfile " +
                 "     (name, address, city, state, zip, country, phone, id)" +
                 "     values ( " +
                        "'" + txt_name.getText() + "', " +
                        "'" + txt_address.getText() + "', " +
                        "'" + txt_city.getText() + "', " +
                        "'" + txt_state.getText() + "', " +
                        "'" + txt_zip.getText() + "', " +
                        "'" + txt_country.getText() + "', " +
```

```
                              "'" + txt_phone.getText() + "', " +
                              "'" + txt_id.getText() + "' " +
                ")";

    try {

        // if the query doesn't throw an exception, we can add the newly
        // created ID to the cardfileKeys Vector and set the currentRow
        // to the element that points to the new record

        MsqlResult    result = msql.Query(sql);
        cardfileKeys.addElement(txt_id.getText());
        currentRow = cardfileKeys.indexOf(txt_id.getText());

        // call getRow() to refresh the form. This really shouldn't
        // be necessary, but it lets us know that the record was
        // saved correctly. Or not, as the case may be :-)

        getRow();

    }
    catch(MsqlException e ) {
        e.printStackTrace();
    }

}
```

The update() method will build an SQL update statement; this updates the currently selected row, setting every value except the primary key, which should never change. This method is invoked when the user presses Save while editing a record.

The update statement is passed through the Msql.Query() method, and then getRow() is called, to verify that the data was saved correctly.

```
/**
 *
 * update()
```

**Continued**

```
 *
 * Send an update to the mSQL server.
 *
 */
public protected void update() {

    // construct an update string for each of the columns
    // except for the ID. This is used as the criteria
    // for the update, so we probably don't want to
    // update it...

    String sql = "update cardfile " +
                 " set name    = '" + txt_name.getText() + "', " +
                 "     address = '" + txt_address.getText() + "', " +
                 "     city    = '" + txt_city.getText() + "', " +
                 "     state   = '" + txt_state.getText() + "', " +
                 "     zip     = '" + txt_zip.getText() + "', " +
                 "     country = '" + txt_country.getText() + "', " +
                 "     phone   = '" + txt_phone.getText() + "' " +
                 " where id = '" + txt_id.getText() + "'";
    try {

        // send the query

        MsqlResult    result = msql.Query(sql);

        // call getRow() to refresh the form. This really shouldn't
        // be necessary, but it lets us know what the update did.

        getRow();
    }
    catch(MsqlException e ) {
        e.printStackTrace();
    }

}
```

The `handleEvent()` method is implicitly invoked when a user action, such as clicking a button, occurs.

```
/**
 * handleEvent
 *
 * Deal with things the user did...
 */
public boolean handleEvent(Event event) {

  switch(event.id) {

  // deal with action buttons

  case Event.ACTION_EVENT:

    // if the next button was pushed, then I want to
    // increment currentRow. But, if that would push
    // it out past cardfileKeys.size(), I will just
    // wrap around to the beginning (zero).

    if (event.target == next) {
      if (currentRow + 1 == cardfileKeys.size()) {
        currentRow = 0;
      } else {
        currentRow++;
      }

      // call getRow() to update the form
      getRow();

    }

    // if the user pushed the previous button, then
    // I want to decrement currentRow. If currentRow is
    // already zero, then decrementing further would
```

**Continued**

```
    // probably throw some evil exception, so I'll
    // set it to cardfileKeys.size() - 1, which is the
    // index of the last element.

    if (event.target == previous) {
      if (currentRow == 0) {
        currentRow = cardfileKeys.size() - 1;
      } else {
        currentRow--;
      }

      // call getRow() to update the form
      getRow();

    }


    // if the user pressed delete, then call the
    // delRow() method.

    if (event.target == delete) {
      delRow();
    }

    // if the user pressed quit, then let's get out of here!

    if (event.target == quit) {
      System.exit(0);
    }


    // if the user wants to edit the current row,
    // then set the formstate as appropriate, and
    // call the setEdit() method.

    if (event.target == edit) {
      formstate = "edit";
      setEdit();
```

```
}

// in case the user presses the new button, I
// want to 1) clear the form, 2) set the formstate
// to "new", 3) let them modify the ID field, and
// 4) call setEdit()

if (event.target == newrow) {
  clearForm();
  formstate = "new";
  txt_id.setEditable(true);

  setEdit();
}

// in case the user hits the Save button, I need
// to distinguish between "new" and "edit" mode,
// so I know whether to call save() or update().
// Also, I need
if (event.target == save) {
  if (formstate.equals("new")) {
    save();
    txt_id.setEditable(false); // make the id field uneditable
  }
  if (formstate.equals("edit")) {
    update();
  }

  // set the formstate to "browse", and call setBrowse()
  formstate = "browse";
  setBrowse();
}

// if the user pressed Cancel, return the formstate to browse

if (event.target == cancel) {
```

**Continued**

```java
        // if it was new, make sure that they can't edit the
        // ID field...

        if (formstate.equals("new")) {
          txt_id.setEditable(false);
        }


        // return the formstate to browse, call getRow()
        // to retrieve the row they were looking at
        // before editing or adding, and call setBrowse()

        formstate = "browse";
        getRow();
        setBrowse();
      }


    break;

  // in case they closed the window, then take
  // it as a sign that they want to quit
  case Event.WINDOW_DESTROY:
      System.exit(0);
      break;              // hmmm...


  // just pass these on
  case Event.MOUSE_DOWN:
  case Event.MOUSE_UP:
  case Event.MOUSE_DRAG:
  case Event.KEY_PRESS:
  case Event.KEY_ACTION:
  case Event.KEY_RELEASE:
  case Event.KEY_ACTION_RELEASE:
  case Event.GOT_FOCUS:
  case Event.LOST_FOCUS:
```

```
  case Event.MOUSE_ENTER:
  case Event.MOUSE_EXIT:
  case Event.MOUSE_MOVE:
    return false;
  }


  return true;
}
```

The setEdit() method takes care of disabling buttons such as the Next, Previous, New, Edit, and Delete buttons, enabling the Save and Cancel buttons, and setting every field on the form (except ID) to be editable. This is called from handleEvent(), when the user clicks on the New or Edit button. The handleEvent() method will specifically enable the ID field only when the New button was pressed.

```
/**
 * setEdit()
 *
 * prepare the form for editing/adding
 *
 */
public protected void setEdit () {

  // disable all these buttons

  next.disable();
  previous.disable();
  newrow.disable();
  edit.disable();
  delete.disable();

  // set everything except the ID to be editable
  txt_name.setEditable(true);
  txt_address.setEditable(true);
  txt_city.setEditable(true);
```

**Continued**

```
        txt_state.setEditable(true);
        txt_zip.setEditable(true);
        txt_country.setEditable(true);
        txt_phone.setEditable(true);

        // enable these two buttons

        save.enable();
        cancel.enable();
    }
```

The setBrowse() method sets things up when the user goes from edit or add mode to browsing mode. It enables the Next, Previous, New, Edit, and Delete buttons, disables the Save and Cancel buttons, and disables every field on the form. This is called from handleEvent(), when the user clicks the Save or Cancel button.

```
/**
 * setBrowse()
 *
 * prepare the form for viewing
 *
 */
public protected void setBrowse() {

    // enable all these buttons

    next.enable();
    previous.enable();
    newrow.enable();
    edit.enable();
    delete.enable();

    // disable the fields

    txt_name.setEditable(false);
```

```
     txt_address.setEditable(false);
     txt_city.setEditable(false);
     txt_state.setEditable(false);
     txt_zip.setEditable(false);
     txt_country.setEditable(false);
     txt_phone.setEditable(false);
     txt_id.setEditable(false);


     // disable these two buttons


     save.disable();
     cancel.disable();
   }
```

The getRow() method issues an SQL Select statement, using the ID value for the current row contained in the cardfileKeys Vector. If the cardfileKeys Vector is empty, it simply clears the form and returns. Because I'm lazy, I associated each form element with a column name using columnmap. To show each field, I simply need to iterate over each column name, as retrieved from the MsqlResult.ListFields() method. Using each column name, I can obtain a reference to the corresponding TextField object with:

```
columnmap.get(col_name)
```

This needs to be cast to TextField, and then I can invoke any TextField-specific properties, such as setText().

```
/**
 * getRow()
 *
 * retrieve a row from the table, using the one indicated by
 * cardfileKeys.elementAt(currentRow)
 *
 */
public protected void getRow() {

  // if there are no rows to process, just clear
  // the form and return...
```

**Continued**

```
        if (cardfileKeys.isEmpty()) {
          clearForm();
          return;
        }

        try {

            // issue a SELECT statement to get the row that is
            // pointed to by currentRow. Unless we have an
            // integrity violation, this should be only one
            // row.

            MsqlResult    result = msql.Query("select * from cardfile where id = " +
                       "'" +
                       cardfileKeys.elementAt(currentRow) +
                       "'");

            // ahhh... catalog data. Because each textfield is
            // represented in the columnmap hash, keyed by
            // the column name to which it corresponds, I
            // can use the array of column names to map each
            // column in the result set to the fields on the
            // form.

            MsqlFieldDesc field[]  = result.ListFields();

            // get the number of columns

            int cols = result.NumFields();

            // retrieve the row

            String row[];
            row = result.FetchRow();
```

```
    // loop over each column, up until the number indicated
    // by the call the NumFields()

    for(int i=0; i < cols; i++) {

        // get the name of the column from field[i].FieldName()

        String col_name = field[i].FieldName();

        // this gets the object from columnmap (a TextField), which
        // is keyed by the name of the column in col_name
        // here, we simply call the setText() method of that TextField
        // object to the value of the column.

        ((TextField) columnmap.get(col_name)).setText(row[i]);

    }

}
catch (MsqlException e) {
  e.printStackTrace();
}
catch (ArrayIndexOutOfBoundsException e) {
  // ahhh, just ignore it!
}
}
```

The delRow() method issues an SQL DELETE statement to delete the current row, then removes the corresponding Vector element to delete it from the cardfileKeys Vector. Then, the currentRow is set to 0, and getRow() is invoked.

```
/**
 * delRow()
 *
 * deletes the current row.
```

**Continued**

```
 *
 */
public protected void delRow() {

  try {

    // issue the query to delete the row

    MsqlResult    result = msql.Query("delete from cardfile where id = " +
               "'" +
               cardfileKeys.elementAt(currentRow) +
               "'");

    // Oh yeah, don't forget to remove the element from
    // cardfileKeys.

    cardfileKeys.removeElement(cardfileKeys.elementAt(currentRow));

    // let's just be lazy and return to row 0...

    currentRow = 0;

    // call getRow() to refresh the form with the current record.

    getRow();

  }
  catch (MsqlException e) {
    e.printStackTrace();
  }
}
```

Finally, the `main()` method takes care of instantiating the CardFile object. Because it's pretty self-sufficient, it only needs to be constructed in order to run.

```
// our little friend main, who makes it all happen

public static void main(String[] args) {

    // make a new CardFile
    CardFile cardfile = new CardFile();

}

}
```

This simple example demonstrates much of the functionality that is needed to assemble simple database applications using MsqlJava. In the next chapter, I'll revisit the CardFile class; you will watch helplessly as I rearrange its components, with the express intent of designing an abstract class. The CardFileAbstract class will provide all of the functionality of the CardFile, except all of the data access methods will be removed. Any functional subclass of CardFileAbstract will need to define the data access methods, such as retrieving a row, inserting, updating, or deleting a row.

# Chapter 10

# Reimplementing the CardFile Application as an Abstract Class

In Chapter 9, you examined the CardFile application, which demonstrated a simple database application using mSQL and MsqlJava. CardFile provides some fairly generic database functionality. It includes some visual components and some functional components, including insert, update, and delete. However, as generic as this program may be, it still is bound to one particular database server.

One of the primary goals of a database access standard such as ODBC or JDBC is to provide database-independence. This allows the developer to concentrate on the functionality of the application and not worry too much about how databases are to be accessed. This also provides an enormous scalability benefit; if one database server turns out to be undesirable, an application can be quickly modified to work with a different product.

When I finished writing Chapter 9, I realized that I wanted to change the CardFile application to be more generic. At first, I decided to rewrite the chapter using CardFileAbstract. But, I remembered that this had happened before, in real-world situations. I have had many assignments that have included tasks similar to this; the client tells me, "Our system can handle only a limited set of cases; can you make it handle hundreds?" This has happened to me so many times, you wouldn't believe it. So, I decided that I'd let you watch the gruesome butchery that has to go on to make this happen, as you watch CardFile being transformed into an abstract class, CardFileAbstract. An Abstract Class is a special sort of class in Java. It cannot be directly instantiated, as some or all of its methods are not defined in the class definition.

The CardFileAbstract class will not define any of the database access methods. These must be defined in a class that subclasses CardFileAbstract. This will make it easier to isolate the database-dependent components, which will make it easier to implement a CardFile application with another database product. In the CardFileAbstract class, you must define how the form looks and how the buttons and fields behave, but you don't define any of the database access methods.

When it's time to implement the CardFile, it's simply a matter of subclassing it. To use the subclass, the developer must define all the methods that were not defined in the abstract class. In this chapter, CardFile will become CardFileAbstract, and the mSQL implementation will be `MsqlCardFile`.

The following listing shows the changes that were made to CardFile in order to implement it as an abstract class. Not much has really changed, except that the `login()`, `getRow()`, `delRow()`, `nextRow()`, `prevRow()`, `save()`, and `update()` methods are defined as abstract methods:

# CardFileAbstract.java

```
import java.awt.*;
import java.lang.*;
import java.util.*;


public abstract class CardFileAbstract extends Frame {
```

Instead of using java.awt.TextField directly, you must use the myTextField class. myTextField is defined further on in the code, and it provides a feature that will make it easier to work with other tools that might translate empty strings into SQL NULLs. An SQL NULL is a special state that a column or variable may have; it reflects the absence of value, rather than a particular type of value. For the purposes of the CardFile application, it is better to have empty strings default to blank values.

```
    // the myTextField objects for each column

    myTextField txt_name, txt_address, txt_city, txt_state,
```

```
             txt_zip, txt_country, txt_phone, txt_id;

String formstate; // indicates whether we are adding or editing

//  String    name, address, city, state, zip, country, phone;

// a layout manager for the Frame

GridBagLayout layoutmangler = new GridBagLayout();

// each of the buttons and a panel to hold them

Button next, previous, quit, save, newrow, edit, cancel, delete;
Panel actionbuttons;

// this hash is used to map column names to the
// corresponding objects (the myTextFields)

Hashtable columnmap = new Hashtable();

// the default constructor

public CardFileAbstract() {

  // set the layout for the frame
  this.setLayout(layoutmangler);

  // this is the offset within the GridBagLayout. If
  // I want the next object on a different line, I
  // postincrement. If not, I don't.
  int i = 0;

  // the name field
  //
  // first, I add an anonymous text label to the Frame using
  // the AddToFrame method. Note that it uses column 0, and
```

**Continued**

```
// row i (currently zero). I don't want the textfield
// to appear on a different row, so I don't postincrement i.

AddToFrame(new Label("Name:"), 0, i);

// now, I instantiate txt_name. This is a textfield with 20
// spaces. Then, I add it to the frame and insert a reference
// to it in the columnmap, keyed by 'name', which is the name
// of the column in the CardFile table

txt_name = new myTextField(20);
txt_name.setEditable(false);
AddToFrame(txt_name, 1, i++);
columnmap.put("name", txt_name);

// the rest of the fields. Everything is pretty much the same as above.
//
// the address field

AddToFrame(new Label("Address:"), 0, i);
txt_address = new myTextField(35);
txt_address.setEditable(false);
AddToFrame(txt_address, 1, i++);
columnmap.put("address", txt_address);

// the city field
// don't postincrement i, so state will show up
// on the same row.

AddToFrame(new Label("City:"), 0, i);
txt_city = new myTextField(20);
txt_city.setEditable(false);
AddToFrame(txt_city, 1, i);
columnmap.put("city", txt_city);

// the state field
```

```
AddToFrame(new Label("State:"), 2, i);
txt_state = new myTextField(2);
txt_state.setEditable(false);
AddToFrame(txt_state, 3, i++);
columnmap.put("state", txt_state);

// the zip field

AddToFrame(new Label("Zip:"), 0, i);
txt_zip = new myTextField(11);
txt_zip.setEditable(false);
AddToFrame(txt_zip, 1, i++);
columnmap.put("zip", txt_zip);

// the country field

AddToFrame(new Label("Country:"), 0, i);
txt_country = new myTextField(25);
txt_country.setEditable(false);
AddToFrame(txt_country, 1, i++);
columnmap.put("country", txt_country);

// the phone field

AddToFrame(new Label("Phone:"), 0, i);
txt_phone = new myTextField(20);
txt_phone.setEditable(false);
AddToFrame(txt_phone, 1, i++);
columnmap.put("phone", txt_phone);

// the ID field.

AddToFrame(new Label("Id:"), 0, i);
txt_id = new myTextField(4);
txt_id.setEditable(false);
```

**Continued**

```
AddToFrame(txt_id, 1, i++);
columnmap.put("id", txt_id);

// create the button panel and give it a new FlowLayout

actionbuttons = new Panel();
actionbuttons.setLayout(new FlowLayout(FlowLayout.CENTER, 5, 5));

// The constraints for the button panel are a little
// more complex than the constraints for the labels
// and textfields, so we'll set it up here and add
// the actionbuttons panel

GridBagConstraints c = new GridBagConstraints();
c.gridwidth = 3; c.gridheight = 1;
c.fill = GridBagConstraints.NONE;
c.anchor = GridBagConstraints.CENTER;
c.weightx = 0.0; c.weighty = 0.0;
c.gridx = 0; c.gridy = i;
((GridBagLayout)this.getLayout()).setConstraints(actionbuttons, c);
this.add(actionbuttons);

// instantiate and add each of the buttons

previous = new Button("Previous");
actionbuttons.add(previous);

next = new Button("Next");
actionbuttons.add(next);

quit = new Button("Quit");
actionbuttons.add(quit);

newrow = new Button("New");
actionbuttons.add(newrow);
```

```
edit = new Button("Edit");
actionbuttons.add(edit);

delete = new Button("Delete");
actionbuttons.add(delete);

// save and cancel are disabled until the user
// is adding or editing.

save = new Button("Save");
actionbuttons.add(save);
save.disable();

cancel = new Button("Cancel");
actionbuttons.add(cancel);
cancel.disable();

login();

// call getRow() to display the first row in the table.

getRow();

}
```

Here are all the abstract classes. They must be defined in any class that implements Card-FileAbstract, or that class itself will become an abstract class:

```
public abstract void login();
public abstract void getRow();
public abstract void delRow();
public abstract void nextRow();
public abstract void prevRow();
public abstract void save();
public abstract void update();
```

**Continued**

```
/**
 * clearForm()
 *
 * Clear all of the input fields
 *
 */
public protected void clearForm () {

  // blank the name field
  txt_name.setText("");

  // blank the address field
  txt_address.setText("");

  // blank the city field
  txt_city.setText("");

  // blank the state field
  txt_state.setText("");

  // blank the zip field
  txt_zip.setText("");

  // blank the country field
  txt_country.setText("");

  // blank the phone field
  txt_phone.setText("");

  // blank the id field
  txt_id.setText("");

}

/**
```

```
 * AddToFrame()
 *
 * A convenient method to wrap the living hell
 * that is GridBagConstraints()
 *
 */
public protected void AddToFrame (Component item, int x, int y) {

   // some sane layout defaults.

   GridBagConstraints c = new GridBagConstraints();
   c.gridwidth = 1; c.gridheight = 1;
   c.fill = GridBagConstraints.NONE;
   c.anchor = GridBagConstraints.NORTHWEST;
   c.weightx = 0.0; c.weighty = 0.0;

   // set the grid coordinates

   c.gridx = x; c.gridy = y;

   // set the constraints, and add the item to the layout

   ((GridBagLayout)this.getLayout()).setConstraints(item, c);
   this.add(item);

}
```

Here's the slightly modified `handleEvent()` method. Note that the handlers for Next and Previous no longer perform any processing whatsoever. This functionality must be entirely encapsulated within the `nextRow()` and `prevRow()` methods.

```
/**
 * handleEvent
 *
 * Deal with things the user did...
```

**Continued**

```java
*/
public boolean handleEvent(Event event) {

  switch(event.id) {

  // deal with action buttons

  case Event.ACTION_EVENT:

    if (event.target == next) {
      nextRow();
    }

    if (event.target == previous) {
      prevRow();
    }

    if (event.target == delete) {
      delRow();
    }

    // if the user pressed quit, then let's get out of here!

    if (event.target == quit) {
      System.exit(0);
    }

    // if the user wants to edit the current row,
    // then set the formstate as appropriate, and
    // call the setEdit() method.

    if (event.target == edit) {
      formstate = "edit";
      setEdit();
    }
```

```
// in case the user presses the new button, I
// want to 1) clear the form, 2) set the formstate
// to "new," 3) let them modify the ID field, and
// 4) call setEdit()

if (event.target == newrow) {
  clearForm();
  formstate = "new";
  txt_id.setEditable(true);

  setEdit();
}


// in case the user hits the Save button, I need
// to distinguish between "new" and "edit" mode,
// so I know whether to call save() or update().
// Also, I need
if (event.target == save) {
  if (formstate.equals("new")) {
    save();
    txt_id.setEditable(false); // make the ID field uneditable
  }
  if (formstate.equals("edit")) {
    update();
  }

  // set the formstate to "browse", and call setBrowse()
  formstate = "browse";
  setBrowse();
}


// if the user pressed cancel, return the formstate to browse

if (event.target == cancel) {

  // if it was new, make sure that they can't edit the
```

**Continued**

```
          // ID field...

      if (formstate.equals("new")) {
        txt_id.setEditable(false);
      }


      // return the formstate to browse, call getRow()
      // to retrieve the row they were looking at
      // before editing or adding, and call setBrowse()

      formstate = "browse";
      getRow();
      setBrowse();
    }

  break;

// in case they closed the window, then take
// it as a sign that they want to quit
case Event.WINDOW_DESTROY:
    System.exit(0);
    break;              // hmmm...

// just pass these on
case Event.MOUSE_DOWN:
case Event.MOUSE_UP:
case Event.MOUSE_DRAG:
case Event.KEY_PRESS:
case Event.KEY_ACTION:
case Event.KEY_RELEASE:
case Event.KEY_ACTION_RELEASE:
case Event.GOT_FOCUS:
case Event.LOST_FOCUS:
case Event.MOUSE_ENTER:
case Event.MOUSE_EXIT:
case Event.MOUSE_MOVE:
```

```
      return false;
   }

   return true;
}

/**
 * setEdit()
 *
 * prepare the form for editing/adding
 *
 */
public protected void setEdit () {

   // disable all these buttons

   next.disable();
   previous.disable();
   newrow.disable();
   edit.disable();
   delete.disable();

   // set everything except the ID to be editable
   txt_name.setEditable(true);
   txt_address.setEditable(true);
   txt_city.setEditable(true);
   txt_state.setEditable(true);
   txt_zip.setEditable(true);
   txt_country.setEditable(true);
   txt_phone.setEditable(true);

   // enable these two buttons

   save.enable();
   cancel.enable();
}
```

**Continued**

```java
/**
 * setBrowse()
 *
 * prepare the form for viewing
 *
 */
public protected void setBrowse() {

    // enable all these buttons

    next.enable();
    previous.enable();
    newrow.enable();
    edit.enable();
    delete.enable();

    // disable the fields

    txt_name.setEditable(false);
    txt_address.setEditable(false);
    txt_city.setEditable(false);
    txt_state.setEditable(false);
    txt_zip.setEditable(false);
    txt_country.setEditable(false);
    txt_phone.setEditable(false);
    txt_id.setEditable(false);

    // disable these two buttons

    save.disable();
    cancel.disable();
}

}
```

Here's the myTextField class. It supports a single constructor, which corresponds to TextField(int). Note that the only method that is overriden is the getText() method. If TextField.getText() returns a blank value, it is translated to a single space. This will prevent some database APIs from automatically converting values to an SQL NULL:

```
class myTextField extends TextField {

  public myTextField(int size) {
    super( size );
  }

  public String getText() {

    String retval = super.getText();
    if (retval.equals("")) {
      return " ";
    } else {
      return retval;
    }
  }
}
```

Here's the MsqlCardFile.java implementation of CardFileAbstract. You will find many of the methods to be identical to those found in the original CardFile class, with the exception of nextRow() and prevRow(). The nextRow() and prevRow() methods include code that was originally found in CardFile.handleEvents().

# MsqlCardFile.java

```
import java.awt.*;
import java.lang.*;
import java.util.*;

public class MsqlCardFile extends CardFileAbstract {
```

**Continued**

```
    Msql msql;
    int currentRow;
    Vector cardfileKeys;

    public MsqlCardFile() {

      super();

    }

    public void login () {

      // instantiate a new Msql object

      msql = new Msql();

      // the Vector holds the primary key (customer ID) for
      // each row in the table. currentRow holds the index
      // of the one we are currently viewing

      currentRow = 0;
      cardfileKeys = new Vector();

      // connect to the localhost and use the database
      // named 'sample'

      try {
        msql.Connect("localhost");
        msql.SelectDB("sample");
      }
      catch(MsqlException e ) {
        e.printStackTrace();
      }

      // call getKeys() to populate cardfileKeys with unique identifiers
      // for all the keys in the table
```

```
  getKeys();

}

/**
 * getRow()
 *
 * retrieve a row from the table, using the one indicated by
 * cardfileKeys.elementAt(currentRow)
 *
 */
public protected void getRow() {

  // if there are no rows to process, just clear
  // the form and return...

  if (cardfileKeys.isEmpty()) {
    clearForm();
    return;
  }

  try {

    // issue a select statement to get the row that is
    // pointed to by currentRow. Unless we have an
    // integrity violation, this should be only one
    // row.

    MsqlResult    result = msql.Query("select * from cardfile where id = " +
                  "'" +
                  cardfileKeys.elementAt(currentRow) +
                  "'");

    // ahhh... catalog data. Because each textfield is
    // represented in the columnmap hash, keyed by
```

**Continued**

```
// the column name to which it corresponds, I
// can use the array of column names to map each
// column in the result set to the fields on the
// form.

MsqlFieldDesc field[]  = result.ListFields();

// get the number of columns

int cols = result.NumFields();

// retrieve the row

String row[];
row = result.FetchRow();

// loop over each column, up until the number indicated
// by the call the NumFields()

for(int i=0; i < cols; i++) {

   // get the name of the column from field[i].FieldName()

   String col_name = field[i].FieldName();

   // this gets the object from columnmap (a TextField) which
   // is keyed by the name of the column in col_name
   // here, we simply call the setText() method of that TextField
   // object to the value of the column.

   ((TextField) columnmap.get(col_name)).setText(row[i]);

  }

}
catch (MsqlException e) {
```

```
      e.printStackTrace();
  }
  catch (ArrayIndexOutOfBoundsException e) {
    // ahhh, just ignore it!
  }
}



/**
 * getKeys()
 *
 * This populates the cardfileKeys Vector with unique identifiers
 * for all of the rows in the cardfile table. This lets us buffer
 * all of the rows, without storing the values for each column.
 * As a result, we only have to worry about dirty data if someone
 * changes a key, which of course, you would *never* do...
 *
 * now, if someone else deletes or inserts a row, that's a
 * different problem. Handling that is an exercise left to
 * the reader...
 */
public protected void getKeys() {

  try {

    // delete all the elements in cardfileKeys

    cardfileKeys.removeAllElements();

    // execute a query to get the ID column for each of the
    // rows. Then, process each row and add the ID column
    // to cardfileKeys

    MsqlResult    result = msql.Query("select ID from cardfile");
    String row[];
    while(( row = result.FetchRow()) != null){
```

**Continued**

```
            cardfileKeys.addElement(row[0]);
      }


   }
   catch (MsqlException e) {
      e.printStackTrace();
   }
}


/**
 *
 * save()
 *
 * Save the record we are editing to the table
 *
 */
public protected void save() {

   // construct an INSERT statement, with values for each
   // column, including ID. Teaching this system to auto-
   // increment ID in a multiuser environment is an exercise
   // left up to the reader.
   //
   // Assuming, of course, that bambi hasn't released a version
   // of mSQL that supports this natively :-)

   String sql = "insert into cardfile " +
                "    (name, address, city, state, zip, country, phone, id)" +
                "    values ( " +
                            "'" + txt_name.getText() + "', " +
                            "'" + txt_address.getText() + "', " +
                            "'" + txt_city.getText() + "', " +
                            "'" + txt_state.getText() + "', " +
                            "'" + txt_zip.getText() + "', " +
                            "'" + txt_country.getText() + "', " +
                            "'" + txt_phone.getText() + "', " +
```

```
                                "'" + txt_id.getText() + "' " +
                    ")";

        try {

            // if the query doesn't throw an exception, we can add the newly
            // created ID to the cardfileKeys Vector, and set the currentRow
            // to the element that points to the new record

            MsqlResult    result = msql.Query(sql);
            cardfileKeys.addElement(txt_id.getText());
            currentRow = cardfileKeys.indexOf(txt_id.getText());

            // call getRow() to refresh the form. This really shouldn't
            // be necessary, but it lets us know that the record was
            // saved correctly. Or not, as the case may be :-)

            getRow();

        }
        catch(MsqlException e ) {
            e.printStackTrace();
        }

    }

    /**
     *
     * update()
     *
     * Send an update to the mSQL server.
     *
     */
    public protected void update() {

        // construct an update string for each of the columns
```

```
      // except for the ID. This is used as the criteria
      // for the update, so we probably don't want to
      // update it...

      String sql = "update cardfile " +
                   " set name    = '" + txt_name.getText() + "', " +
                   "     address = '" + txt_address.getText() + "', " +
                   "     city    = '" + txt_city.getText() + "', " +
                   "     state   = '" + txt_state.getText() + "', " +
                   "     zip     = '" + txt_zip.getText() + "', " +
                   "     country = '" + txt_country.getText() + "', " +
                   "     phone   = '" + txt_phone.getText() + "' " +
                   " where id = '" + txt_id.getText() + "'";
      try {

        // send the query

        MsqlResult    result = msql.Query(sql);

        // call getRow() to refresh the form. This really shouldn't
        // be necessary, but it lets us know what the update did.

        getRow();
      }
      catch(MsqlException e ) {
        e.printStackTrace();
      }

  }


  // if the next button was pushed, then I want to
  // increment currentRow. But, if that would push
  // it out past cardfileKeys.size(), I will just
  // wrap around to the beginning (zero).
  public void nextRow() {
```

```
    if (currentRow + 1 == cardfileKeys.size()) {
      currentRow = 0;
    } else {
      currentRow++;
    }

    // call getRow() to update the form
    getRow();
  }


// if the user pushed the previous button, then
// I want to decrement currentRow. If currentRow is
// already zero, then decrementing further would
// probably throw some evil exception, so I'll
// set it to cardfileKeys.size() - 1, which is the
// index of the last element.
public void prevRow() {
  if (currentRow  == 0) {
    currentRow = cardfileKeys.size() - 1;
  } else {
    currentRow--;
  }

  // call getRow() to update the form
  getRow();
}



/**
 * delRow()
 *
 * deletes the current row.
 *
 */
public protected void delRow() {
```

**Continued**

```
    try {

        // issue the query to delete the row

        MsqlResult    result = msql.Query("delete from cardfile where id = " +
                        "'" +
                      cardfileKeys.elementAt(currentRow) +
                        "'");

        // Oh yeah, don't forget to remove the element from
        // cardfileKeys.

        cardfileKeys.removeElement(cardfileKeys.elementAt(currentRow));

        // let's just be lazy and return to row 0...

        currentRow = 0;

        // call getRow() to refresh the form with the current record.

        getRow();

    }
    catch (MsqlException e) {
        e.printStackTrace();
    }
}

// our little friend main, who makes it all happen

public static void main(String[] args) {

    // make a new MsqlCardFile, pack() it and show() it.
    MsqlCardFile cardfile = new MsqlCardFile();
    cardfile.pack();
    cardfile.show();
```

```
    }

}
```

You may compile MsqlCardFile with javac compiler and run it with the java interpreter. It requires no arguments. CardFileAbstract is a simple abstract class that can be implemented with a variety of database APIs.

# Chapter 11

# Connecting to Databases Using Applets

You may have noticed a conspicuous absence of any discussion concerning applets in this book. This is not because I despise applets, but merely because of some inherent limitations in the state of the art as far as JDBC is concerned. One of the major limitations is the fact that a Java applet may not load native code. Because JDBC drivers such as the JDBC-ODBC bridge require native libraries, this can be a significant restriction. Also, because applets are prevented from writing to the local filesystem, the tinySQL engine would not work within an applet; not that this would be of much use, since you would want each applet to write to a database on some server to share information.

## Pure Java JDBC Drivers

Eventually, most vendors will supply JDBC drivers in 100 percent Java, with no native code. In some cases, this will be a little complicated, as connectivity libraries such as DB-Lib (which are used with Sybase and Microsoft SQL Server) are not currently available in Java, but instead are provided as libraries that can be linked to with native code, usually C and C++. Nevertheless, as time goes on, more drivers will appear that are implemented using only Java. When this occurs, the techniques shown in this book will work as well with these drivers as with those that use native code.

# Burns, Busts, and Bummers (No Rip-offs)

Some drivers may never be implemented in such a fashion. Although you've seen an implementation of tinySQL that uses DBF files, there is one difficulty in providing a JDBC driver for such packages as dBase, FoxPro, or Excel. All of these products are inherently single-tier. Database servers, such as Oracle, Sybase, and Microsoft SQL Serve, are multiple-tier. A single-tier database product relies on the fact that all client applications, such as something you might implement in FoxPro or Access, have direct access to the database files and can at least read them, if not modify them. As such, any JDBC driver for such products requires the same sort of access. In contrast, a multiple-tier database product allows access from any client that can connect over the network and provide the correct username and password.

Because a product like Microsoft SQL Server allows clients to connect over a socket, it would be possible for an applet to connect from anywhere in the world, provided that applet was loaded from a Web server running on the same machine as the data server. Not so for data sources such as FoxPro, dBase, or Access; unless the client applet can get access to the underlying files, there's no way to read or write them. No database server is serving up these files. Of course, as with most needs, someone usually rushes in to fill them. Products such as WebLogic's jdbcKona/T3 (described later) provide a means of proxying JDBC connections. This allows all the platform-dependent stuff to reside on your server, and applets can use a Java-only JDBC driver to connect to the proxy server.

Other products, such as DataRamp, JDesignerPro, and JetConnect (all of which are described later) provide remote ODBC connectivity, which can be quite useful, as well.

# mSQL JDBC and Applets

One candidate for an SQL engine to use with applets is mSQL. The mSQL JDBC driver is written entirely without native methods, and it should work fine in an applet context. However, it's important to keep in mind another applet restriction; it cannot open a network connection to any computer other than the host from which it was loaded. This means that if you are using the mSQL JDBC driver within your applets, you must ensure that the Web server that serves the applets is running on the same host as the mSQL daemon.

# Weblogic's jdbcKona/T3

In addition to supplying the first (to my knowledge) commercially available JDBC drivers for Oracle, Sybase, and Microsoft SQL Server, WebLogic (http://www.weblogic.com) provides a product known as jdbcKona/T3. jdbcKona/T3 is made up of several components; your favorite JDBC driver, WebLogic's T3Server, and its T3Client.

WebLogic's T3Server is a Java application that you can run on your Web server; applets served up from your Web server can then connect to the T3Server. The T3Server acts as a JDBC proxy, making JDBC connections on behalf of your applet. To interact with the T3Server, your applet must instantiate a T3Client and construct a Properties object that includes the T3Client object, a username, password, server name, and other information. The following example, taken from the jdbcKona/T3Client documentation, shows how a T3Client is instantiated and how that object is used to request that the T3Server make a connection to an Oracle dataserver. The server makes the connection using WebLogic's Oracle JDBC driver, but the applet that is using the T3Client object simply uses the T3Client JDBC driver. Because the T3Server proxies all of the T3Client's requests, it doesn't matter that the JDBC driver used on the server is implemented using native methods; the T3Client JDBC driver is Java only.

```
T3Client t3=null;
t3 = new T3Client("weblogic.t3://bigbox:7001");
t3.connect();

Properties props = new Properties();
props.put("user",     "scott");
props.put("password", "tiger");
props.put("server",   "t:bigbox:DEMO20");
props.put("t3url",    "jdbc:weblogic.oracle");
props.put("t3driver", "weblogic.jdbc.oci.Driver");
props.put("t3client", t3);

Class.forName("weblogic.jdbc.t3client.Driver");

Connection conn = DriverManager.getConnection("jdbc:weblogic:t3client", props);
```

It may be a little difficult to understand what the T3Server does. Because applets cannot load native methods, they must use classes that are written in Java only. However, the T3Server is a Java application that runs on your Web server, and it is not bound by these restrictions. After your Web server has sent one of your applets to someone's browser, that applet makes a connection to the T3Server using the T3Client JDBC driver. To the applet, the T3Client looks and feels like any other JDBC driver; however, every database request gets sent to the T3Server, which makes the "real" connection to the data server on behalf of the applet.

# JetConnect from XDB Systems

XDB Systems (`http://www.xdb.com/`) provides an ODBC proxy server that allows you to develop ODBC-enabled applets and applications. JetConnect provides full ODBC functionality, which includes scrolling cursors, row- and column-wise binding, multiple connection mechanisms, and all three ODBC execution models. At the time of this writing, JetConnect is not available as a JDBC driver, but XDB has plans to include JDBC support in the future. ODBC actually provides more features than JDBC; therefore, a product that provides most, if not all, of the ODBC API such as JetConnect may be preferable in some cases to JDBC.

Like WebLogic's jdbcKona/T3, JetConnect provides a proxy server that runs on the same machine as the Web server and makes ODBC connections on behalf of your applets.

# JDP

JDesignerPro (JDP), from Bulletproof (`http:/www.bulletproof.com`) is part of an integrated suite of tools that also provide ODBC proxying capabilities. JDP relies on the JAGG engine, which is a CGI executable that makes ODBC connections on behalf of a Java applet or application. In addition, JDP provides a high-level interface for developing front ends to your data, and it provides database-oriented widgets, such as a grid control. The demonstrations I've seen at their Web site have impressed me, and JDP seems to load even complicated GUI interfaces quite quickly over the network. JAGG and JDP seem to be a good means of connecting front ends to ODBC data sources, and they seem to allow for rapid development as well.

# DataRamp

DataRamp (`http://www.dataramp.com`) provides another ODBC proxy solution with some neat twists. The DataRamp server is a socket-based server that allows remote connections to use ODBC data sources installed on the server. One of the DataRamp clients is an ODBC driver installed on the client machine. DataRamp provides a JDBC client as well. DataRamp can provide proxying for any ODBC-enabled application, as well as JDBC-enabled Java applications and applets, which makes it an attractive solution for dealing with all of your ODBC proxying problems; you can now provide ODBC proxying for a front-end product such as Access, as well as for your Java programs.

# It's Never Really the End

And so the juggernaut rolls on. While JDBC provides an excellent, developer-friendly API for database development, in some cases, particularly with single-tier ODBC connectivity, it might need some helping along. At the very least, some of these third-party products amount to database servers for single-tier database products, which is quite a feat in and of itself. I've contributed more than my fair share to legacy applications written in single-tier packages, so it's right that I explain some way of connecting them to Java.

# MsqlJava API Reference by Example

The MsqlJava API is a very simple API; it reflects the underlying simplicity of the mSQL engine. Despite their austerity, mSQL and MsqlJava can be used to develop sophisticated, SQL-backed Java applications and applets. The following describes the MsqlJava API, providing examples and explanations for each method.

## Constructing the Msql Object

The MsqlJava API provides two methods for instantiating an Msql object. The first, Msql(), really doesn't do anything for you; after you've instantiated it, you still need to use the Connect() method to make a connection to the server. The second, Msql(String msqlServer), instantiates the Msql object and makes the connection with some sane defaults.

### public Msql()

```
Msql msql = new Msql();
```

This instantiates a new Msql object, but it does not make a connection to a server; you must still use one of the Connect() methods to make a connection.

## public Msql(String msqlServer)

```
Msql msql = new Msql("some.msql.server.com");
```

This instantiates a new Msql object and connects as the user "nobody."

# Connecting to the mSQL Server

The MsqlJava API provides several methods that allow you to connect to the server. If you used the Msql() method to create an Msql object (without the host name), you will need to use one of these methods to connect to the server.

## public void Connect (String msqlServer, String userName)

```
msql.Connect("some.msql.server.com", "bjepson");
```

This makes a connection to the specified mSQL server with the username "bjepson." This method assumes that the mSQL server is listening on the root port (1112), rather than the mortal port (4333).

## public void Connect(String msqlServer, String userName, boolean rootServer)

```
msql.Connect("some.msql.server.com", "bjepson", true);
```

This makes a connection to the specified mSQL server with the username "bjepson," using the root port (1112).

```
msql.Connect("some.msql.server.com", "bjepson", false);
```

This makes a connection to the specified mSQL server with the username "bjepson," using the mortal port (4333).

## public void Connect(String msqlServer)

```
msql.Connect("some.msql.server.com");
```

This makes a connection to the specified mSQL server with the default username "nobody," using the root port (1112).

## public void Connect
## (String msqlServer, boolean rootServer)

```
msql.Connect("some.msql.server.com", true);
```

This makes a connection to the specified mSQL server with the default username "nobody," using the root port (1112).

```
msql.Connect("some.msql.server.com", false);
```

This makes a connection to the specified mSQL server with the default username "nobody," using the mortal port (4333).

# Selecting a Database:
# public void SelectDB(String db)

```
msql.SelectDB("master");
```

mSQL, like other SQL Servers, supports multiple databases, each of which contains tables. The above example selects a database named "master."

# Issuing a Query:
# public MsqlResult Query (String s)

```
MsqlResult rs = msql.Query("SELECT * FROM people");
```

The SQL SELECT statement is executed, which returns an MsqlResult object rs.

```
msql.Query("INSERT INTO people (name, id) VALUES ('Brian', 300)");
```

The SQL INSERT statement is executed, but since it is a statement that does not generate a result, no result set is created. Such SQL statements return null anyhow, so there wouldn't be much sense in instantiating a MsqlResult object.

# Working with Result Sets:
# public String [] FetchRow()

```
String row[];
while(( row = rs.FetchRow()) != null){
  // do something here...
}
```

This returns the next row in the database as an array of Strings. You can repeatedly call this until it returns null, at which time you know you have exhausted all the rows.

## public MsqlFieldDesc FetchField()

```
MsqlFieldDesc f = rs.FetchField();
```

This returns an MsqlFieldDesc object containing information about each field in the result set. You can call this method until it returns null to process each field. See "Getting Column Metadata for a Particular Table" for information on how to work with MsqlFieldDesc objects.

## public int NumRows()

```
int numrows = rs.NumRows();
```

This returns the number of rows in the result set.

## public int NumFields()

```
int numcols = rs.NumFields();
```

This returns the number of columns in the result set.

## Getting a String Array of All Databases on the Server: public String[] ListDBs()

```
String dbs[] = msql.ListDBs();
```

This returns an array of Strings containing the names of all the databases on the mSQL server.

## Getting a String Array of All Tables in the Database: public String[] ListTables()

```
String tables[] = msql.ListTables();
```

This returns an array of Strings containing the names of all the tables in the database that was selected by SelectDB().

## Getting Column Metadata for a Particular Table: public MsqlFieldDesc[] ListFields(String s)

```
MsqlFieldDesc columns[] = msql.ListFields("people");
```

This returns an array of MsqlFieldDesc objects containing information about all of the fields (also known as columns) in the "people" table. The MsqlFieldDesc object offers the following methods for getting at the metadata information.

## public String TableName();

```
String table = columns[i].TableName();
```

This returns the name of the table to which the column at the specified index belongs.

## public String FieldName();

```
String field = columns[i].FieldName();
```

This returns the name of the column.

## public int FieldType();

```
int type = columns[i].FieldType();
```

This returns the datatype of the column. An INTEGER column type is signified by 1, CHAR by 2, and REAL by 3. If the column is NULL, the datatype is returned as 5.

## public int FieldLength();

```
int len = columns[i].FieldLength();
```

This returns the length (display width) of the column.

## public boolean NonNull();

```
int nullok = columns[i].NonNull();
```

This returns true if the column can accept NULLs, false if not.

## public boolean IsKey();

```
int iskey = columns[i].IsKey();
```

This returns true if the column is the Primary Key.

# Closing the Connection:
# public void Close()

```
msql.Close();
```

This closes the connection to the mSQL server.

# JDBC API Reference

This appendix includes references for the JDBC Driver API, which is exposed to anyone using a JDBC driver. For information on developing drivers, you may find Chapter 7 instructive. Because a JDBC driver consists of implementing each of the methods contained herein, this appendix will no doubt prove useful as well.

## Instantiating a Driver

To instantiate a driver, you must first register it with the JDBC driver manager by loading the class with Class.forName, as shown below, in an example that loads the JDBC-ODBC bridge driver:

```
Class.forName("jdbc.odbc.JdbcOdbcDriver");
```

Because `Class.forName()` can throw a java.lang.ClassNotFoundException, you should be sure to include this statement in a try...catch clause as appropriate. To request that the JDBC driver manager instantiate a class, you must call the static method `getConnection()` with a JDBC URL that is supported by one of the drivers you loaded with `Class.forName()`, and with a username and password, which may be blank, if not required:

```
String url = "jdbc:odbc:MSSQL";
String user = "javatest";
String pwd = "javatest";
// make a connection to the specified URL
//
Connection con = DriverManager.getConnection(url, user, pwd);
```

getConnection() can throw a java.sql.SQLException, so you should include the appropriate try...catch handling. The Connection object returned by the driver manager is your gateway into the fun world of JDBC.

# Using a Connection

A Connection object is obtained using DriverManager.getConnection() and provides the ability to create various statement objects.

## Statement createStatement() throws SQLException

This creates a Statement object that can be used to execute SQL statements.

```
Statement stmt = con.createStatement();
```

## PreparedStatement prepareStatement (String sql) throws SQLException

This creates a PreparedStatement object that can be used to precompile and execute SQL statements. This is good if you plan on executing the same statement many times over within the same connection. You can specify positional parameters, which can be set multiple times in your program.

```
String sql = "INSERT INTO authors " +
             "(au_id, au_fname, au_lname, phone, contract)" +
             "VALUES(?, ?, ?, ?, ?)";
```

```
PreparedStatement pstmt = con.prepareStatement(sql);

pstmt.setString(1, "000-12-4567");    // au_id
pstmt.setString(2, "Brian");          // au_fname
pstmt.setString(3, "Jepson");         // au_lname
pstmt.setString(4, "(401) 555-5555"); // phone
pstmt.setBoolean(5, true);            // contract flag

pstmt.executeUpdate();
```

# CallableStatement prepareCall(String sql) throws SQLException

This creates a CallableStatement object that is used to execute stored procedures that return values. It inherits all of the positional parameter features of the PreparedStatement and adds support for OUT (or OUTPUT) parameters, which are simply parameters that are returned back to your Java program that called the stored procedure. Here's a simple stored procedure written in Transact-SQL (the SQL dialect used by SQL Server), which uses an OUTPUT parameter:

```
CREATE PROCEDURE max_price
   @pattern VARCHAR(50),
   @retval  VARCHAR(10) OUTPUT
AS
BEGIN

   DECLARE @max_price money

   DECLARE @like_pattern VARCHAR(51)
   SELECT @like_pattern = RTRIM(@pattern) + '%'

   SELECT @max_price=MAX(price)
      FROM titles
      WHERE title LIKE @like_pattern
```

```
SELECT @retval = CONVERT(VARCHAR(10), @max_price)

END
```

The following Java code will execute the stored procedure shown above and will retrieve the OUTPUT parameter:

```
// set up a call to the max_price stored proc as a
// callable statement with two parameters.
//
String sql = "{call max_price(?, ?)}";
CallableStatement cstmt = con.prepareCall(sql);

cstmt.setString(1, "S");              // all titles starting with S

// register the VARCHAR output parameter
//
cstmt.registerOutParameter(2, java.sql.Types.VARCHAR);

cstmt.executeUpdate();

// get the output parameter
//
System.out.println( cstmt.getString(2) );
```

# void setAutoCommit(boolean autoCommit) throws SQLException

AutoCommit determines whether statements sent to the database server are automatically committed. The default is true. If you set AutoCommit to false, you should explicitly commit each set of statements with the commit() method. This feature is meaningful only if your database supports transactions.

```
con.setAutoCommit(true);
con.setAutoCommit(false);
```

# boolean getAutoCommit()
# throws SQLException

This returns the current setting of AutoCommit. This feature is meaningful only if your database supports transactions.

```
boolean autocommit_val = con.getAutoCommit();
```

# void rollback() throws SQLException

If AutoCommit is set off, all of the SQL statements you issue are implicitly wrapped in a transaction that can be committed or rolled back. The following example shows an update that is executed but rolled back. This causes the original value to be retained when the value is subsequently read. This feature is meaningful only if your database supports transactions.

```
// make a connection to the specified URL
//
Connection con = DriverManager.getConnection(url, user, pwd);

// set auto-commit mode off; it is on by default.
//
con.setAutoCommit(false);

// get a statement object
//
Statement stmt = con.createStatement();

String sql = "UPDATE authors SET au_id = '000-00-0000' " +
             "WHERE  au_lname = 'Jepson'";
stmt.executeUpdate(sql);

// issue the rollback
//
con.rollback();

// get a new connection because the last one was closed
```

**Continued**

```
// (not all drivers are capable of disabling autoclose)
//
con = DriverManager.getConnection(url, user, pwd);

// get a new statement, since the last one was closed
//
stmt = con.createStatement();

// execute a query to check the value of au_id
//
ResultSet rs = stmt.executeQuery("SELECT au_id FROM authors " +
                                 "WHERE au_lname = 'Jepson'");

rs.next();
System.out.println( rs.getString(1) );

stmt.close();
con.close();
```

## void commit()
## throws SQLException

This commits all uncommitted statements. The following example shows an update that is executed and committed. In contrast to the previous example, commit() causes the new value to be available when the value is subsequently read. This feature is meaningful only if your database supports transactions.

```
// make a connection to the specified URL
//
Connection con = DriverManager.getConnection(url, user, pwd);

// set auto-commit mode off; it is on by default.
//
```

```
con.setAutoCommit(false);

// get a statement object
//
Statement stmt = con.createStatement();

String sql = "UPDATE authors SET au_id = '999-99-9999' " +
                "WHERE  au_lname = 'Jepson'";
stmt.executeUpdate(sql);

// issue the commit
//
con.commit();

// get a new connection because the last one was closed
// (not all drivers are capable of disabling autoclose)
//
con = DriverManager.getConnection(url, user, pwd);

// get a new statement, since the last one was closed
//
stmt = con.createStatement();

// execute a query to check the value of au_id
//
ResultSet rs = stmt.executeQuery("SELECT au_id FROM authors " +
                                    "WHERE au_lname = 'Jepson'");

rs.next();
System.out.println( rs.getString(1) );

stmt.close();
con.close();
```

## void close() throws SQLException

This closes the Connection. Once this is done, you can no longer get any of the various statement objects from the Connection.

```
con.close();
```

## boolean isClosed() throws SQLException

This returns true if the Connection is closed.

```
boolean is_it_closed = con.isClosed();
```

## DatabaseMetaData getMetaData() throws SQLException

This returns a DatabaseMetaData object for the database. See the section on this object for more information.

```
DatabaseMetaData dmd = con.getMetaData();
```

## void setReadOnly(boolean readOnly) throws SQLException

This sets the Connection into read-only mode, which may improve the speed of certain operations.

```
con.setReadOnly(true);
con.setReadOnly(true);
```

## boolean isReadOnly() throws SQLException

This returns true if the Connection is in read-only mode, false otherwise.

```
boolean is_it_readonly = isReadOnly();
```

## void setCatalog(String catalog)
## throws SQLException

This sets the current database (or catalog) to the one specified. This seems to generate harmless warnings on SQL Server, so they should be caught and ignored, or logged if necessary.

```
try {

  // switch to the master database
  //
  con.setCatalog("master");

} catch (SQLWarning e) {
  // print out warnings
  //
  SQLWarning w = con.getWarnings();
  while (w != null) {
    System.out.println(w.getMessage());
    w = w.getNextWarning();
  }

}
```

## String getCatalog()
## throws SQLException

This retrieves the current database (or catalog) name.

```
System.out.println( con.getCatalog() );
```

## void setTransactionIsolation(int level)
## throws SQLException

For database servers that support transactions, this method can be used to specify how transactions should behave. Each of the available levels are discussed here.

```
import java.sql.*;
o
con.setTransactionIsolation(Connection.TRANSACTION_NONE);
```

Using the TRANSACTION_NONE isolation level indicates that the database does not support transactions.

```
con.setTransactionIsolation(Connection.TRANSACTION_READ_UNCOMMITTED);
```

The TRANSACTION_READ_UNCOMMITTED mode will allow you to read uncommitted transactions; if one user has issued a:

```
begin transaction
update authors set au_id = "999-99-9999" where au_lname = "Jepson"
```

Then another user can read the new value, even before the `commit()` or `rollback()` has occurred. This is considered a *dirty read*, since the data is uncommitted, and may not be valid; if the first user rolls back the transaction, the second user will have read incorrect data.

```
con.setTransactionIsolation(Connection.TRANSACTION_READ_COMMITTED);
```

Under TRANSACTION_READ_COMMITTED mode, dirty reads are not permitted; in the previous example, the second user would be blocked until the update is committed or the server detects a deadlock and kills one of the processes.

```
con.setTransactionIsolation(Connection.TRANSACTION_REPEATABLE_READ);
```

Setting this transaction isolation level would permit phantom reads, allowing the second user in the above example to read a row from the database while the first user's update was uncommitted. However, rather than reading the uncommitted value as in TRANSACTION_READ_UNCOMMITTED, the second user would read the original value before the update was issued.

```
con.setTransactionIsolation(Connection.TRANSACTION_SERIALIZABLE);
```

TRANSACTION_SERIALIZABLE mode disallows phantom and dirty reads; in the SQL Server implementation of SQL, it has the same effect as issuing a HOLDLOCK in all SQL statements, blocking any updates until the statement is committed. This may vary in other implementations of SQL.

# int getTransactionIsolation() throws SQLException

This returns the current transaction isolation level.

```
int foo = con.getTransactionIsolation();
if (foo == Connection.TRANSACTION_SERIALIZABLE) {
  System.out.println(
    "Transactions are serializable, whatever that means.");
}
```

# SQLWarning getWarnings() throws SQLException

This returns the first SQLWarning in the chain of warnings for this Connection.

```
// print out warnings
//
SQLWarning w = con.getWarnings();
while (w != null) {
  System.out.println(w.getMessage());
  w = w.getNextWarning();
}
```

# void clearWarnings() throws SQLException

This clears this Connection's chain of warnings.

```
con.clearWarnings();
```

# Working with a Statement

A Statement object is obtained from the Connection object's `createStatement()` method.

## ResultSet executeQuery(String sql) throws SQLException

This executes an SQL statement, usually a SELECT or a stored procedure that returns rows of one or more tables. The `execute()` method should be used where multiple result sets are expected.

```
ResultSet rs = stmt.executeQuery("SELECT au_id FROM authors " +
                                 "WHERE au_lname = 'Jepson'");
```

## int executeUpdate(String sql) throws SQLException

This is used to execute an SQL statement where no results are expected, as with an INSERT or UPDATE statement. See `getUpdateCount()` for a means of determining how many rows were affected.

```
String sql = "UPDATE authors SET au_id = '000-00-0000' " +
             "WHERE  au_lname = 'Jepson'";
stmt.executeUpdate(sql);
```

## void close() throws SQLException

This closes the current Statement.

```
stmt.close();
```

## int getMaxFieldSize() throws SQLException

This returns the current limit on field (column) sizes. If a query attempts to return a column whose width exceeds the value returned by this method, it is truncated without warning or exception. If this value is zero, then no limits are in effect.

```
int maxsize = stmt.getMaxFieldSize();
```

## void setMaxFieldSize(int max) throws SQLException

This sets the maximum field size.

```
stmt.setMaxFieldSize(254);
```

## int getMaxRows() throws SQLException

This returns the current limit on the number of rows a query may return. If this value is exceeded, the excess rows are not included in the result set, without warning or exception. If this value is zero, then no limits are in effect.

```
int maxrows = stmt.getMaxRows();
```

## void setMaxRows(int max) throws SQLException

This sets the limit on the number of rows a query may return.

```
stmt.setMaxRows(2048);
```

## void setEscapeProcessing(boolean enable) throws SQLException

If the JDBC driver supports escape processing, this allows you to turn it on and off. It is set on by default. Escape processing will convert escaped ODBC SQL to the dialect used by the database server. See the CallableStatement prepareCall(String sql) example shown previously for an example that uses the escaped "call" keyword, which is mapped to "exec" under SQL Server.

```
stmt.setEscapeProcessing(true);
stmt.setEscapeProcessing(false);
```

## int getQueryTimeout() throws SQLException

The query timeout is the number of seconds the driver will wait for a statement to finish executing. An SQLException is thrown when this is exceeded. Zero implies no limit.

```
int timeout = stmt.getQueryTimeout();
```

## void setQueryTimeout(int seconds) throws SQLException

This sets the query timeout.

```
stmt.setQueryTimeout(180);
```

## void cancel() throws SQLException

This can be used by one thread to cancel a query that is being executed by another thread.

```
stmt.cancel();
```

## SQLWarning getWarnings() throws SQLException

This returns the first SQLWarning in the chain of warnings for this statement.

```
// print out warnings
//
SQLWarning w = stmt.getWarnings();
while (w != null) {
  System.out.println(w.getMessage());
  w = w.getNextWarning();
}
```

## void clearWarnings() throws SQLException

This clears this Statement's chain of warnings.

```
stmt.clearWarnings();
```

## void setCursorName(String name) throws SQLException

This sets the cursor name for this statement. This cursor name can be referenced by positioned updates and deletes.

```
stmt.setCursorName("C_FOOBAR");
```

## int getUpdateCount() throws SQLException

This discovers the number of rows affected by the last update executed on this Statement.

```
// execute an update that affects multiple rows
//
String sql = "UPDATE authors SET zip = '12345' WHERE city = 'Oakland'";
stmt.executeUpdate(sql);

System.out.println( stmt.getUpdateCount() + " rows affected.");
```

## boolean execute(String sql) throws SQLException; ResultSet getResultSet() throws SQLException; boolean getMoreResults() throws SQLException

These methods are used to manage SQL statements (usually stored procedure calls) that produce multiple result sets. Here's a Transact-SQL stored procedure that produces two result sets.

```
DROP PROCEDURE multi_sample
GO

CREATE PROCEDURE multi_sample
AS
```

```
BEGIN

  /* Result Set 1 */
  SELECT DISTINCT au_lname, au_fname, "RICH BASTARD" category
    FROM authors, titleauthor, roysched, titles
    WHERE authors.au_id = titleauthor.au_id
    AND   titles.title_id = titleauthor.title_id
    AND   roysched.title_id = titleauthor.title_id
    AND   roysched.hirange IN (SELECT MAX(hirange) FROM roysched)
    ORDER BY au_lname, au_fname

  /* Result Set 2 */
  SELECT DISTINCT au_lname, au_fname, "PAUPER" category
    FROM authors, titleauthor, roysched, titles
    WHERE authors.au_id = titleauthor.au_id
    AND   titles.title_id = titleauthor.title_id
    AND   roysched.title_id = titleauthor.title_id
    AND   roysched.hirange IN (SELECT MIN(hirange) FROM roysched)
    ORDER BY au_lname, au_fname

END
GO
```

The following Java code will execute the stored procedure shown above and display all of its results.

```
// get a statement object
//
Statement stmt = con.createStatement();

// execute a stored procedure
//
stmt.execute("exec multi_sample");

// get the first result set
//
```

```
ResultSet rs = stmt.getResultSet();

// if the first result set wasn't null,
// the program should try to get the next
// result set
//
boolean more_results;
if (rs != null) {
  more_results = true;
} else {
  more_results = false;
}

// keep getting results until there are no more
// result sets to process
//
while(more_results) {

  // get each row and print it
  //
  boolean seen = false;
  while( rs.next() ) {

    String au_fname = rs.getString(1);
    String au_lname = rs.getString(2);
    if (!seen) {
      System.out.println("ALL THE " + rs.getString(3) + "S.");
    }
    System.out.println("    " + au_fname.trim() + " " + au_lname.trim());
    seen = true;

  }

  // try to get another result set
  //
  more_results = stmt.getMoreResults();
```

**Continued**

```
    if (more_results) {
      rs = stmt.getResultSet();
    }


  }
```

# Working with a ResultSet object

A ResultSet object is created by a Statement's executeQuery() or getResultSet() method, as well as other methods in the java.sql package.

## boolean next() throws SQLException

This advances to the next row in the result set. This should be called before attempting to read data from the first row, as shown in this example:

```
  while( rs.next() ) {
    String au_fname = rs.getString(1);
  }
```

## void close() throws SQLException

This closes the current result set.

```
  rs.close();
```

## boolean wasNull() throws SQLException

This will tell you if the last column read performed with one of the getXXX() methods returned an SQL NULL.

```
  while( rs.next() ) {
    String au_fname = rs.getString(1);
    if (rs.wasNull()) {
      au_fname = 'NULL';
    }
  }
```

## String getString(int columnIndex) throws SQLException

This gets a column value by index (first column is 1, second is 2) as a String object.

```
String au_fname = rs.getString(1);
```

## boolean getBoolean(int columnIndex) throws SQLException

This gets a column value by index as a boolean value.

```
boolean contract = rs.getBoolean(1);
```

## byte getByte(int columnIndex) throws SQLException

This gets a column value by index as a byte value.

```
byte contract = rs.getByte(1);
```

## short getShort(int columnIndex) throws SQLException

This gets a column value by index as a short value.

```
short hirange = rs.getShort(1);
```

## int getInt(int columnIndex) throws SQLException

This gets a column value by index as an int value.

```
int hirange = rs.getInt(1);
```

## long getLong(int columnIndex) throws SQLException

This gets a column value by index as a long value.

```
long hirange = rs.getLong(1);
```

## float getFloat(int columnIndex) throws SQLException

This gets a column value by index as a float value.

```
float hirange = rs.getFloat(1);
```

## double getDouble(int columnIndex) throws SQLException

This gets a column value by index as a double value.

```
double hirange = rs.getDouble(1);
```

## Bignum getBignum(int columnIndex, int scale) throws SQLException

This gets a column value by index as a Bignum object with the specified scale (precision).

```
Numeric hirange = rs.getBignum(1, 4);
```

## byte[] getBytes(int columnIndex) throws SQLException

This gets a column value by index as an array of bytes.

```
byte[] au_lname = rs.getBytes(1);
```

## java.sql.Date getDate(int columnIndex) throws SQLException

This gets a column value by index as a java.sql.Date object.

```
java.sql.Date birthday = rs.getDate(1);
```

## java.sql.Time getTime(int columnIndex) throws SQLException

This gets a column value by index as a java.sql.Time object.

```
java.sql.Time appointment_start = rs.getTime(1);
```

## java.sql.Timestamp getTimestamp (int columnIndex) throws SQLException

This gets a column value by index as a java.sql.Timestamp object.

```
java.sql.Timestamp timestamp = rs.getTimestamp(1);
```

## java.io.InputStream getAsciiStream (int columnIndex) throws SQLException

This gets a column value by index as an InputStream object. This can be useful for large text values.

```
import java.io.*;
InputStream foo = rs.getAsciiStream(1);
```

## java.io.InputStream getUnicodeStream (int columnIndex) throws SQLException

This gets a column value by index as an InputStream object. This can be useful for large text values containing Unicode data.

```
import java.io.*;
InputStream foo = rs.getUnicodeStream(1);
```

# java.io.InputStream getBinaryStream (int columnIndex) throws SQLException

This gets a column value by index as an InputStream object. This can be useful for large binary values.

```
import java.io.*;
InputStream foo = rs.getBinaryStream(1);
```

# String getString(String columnName) throws SQLException

This gets a named column value as a String object.

```
String au_fname = rs.getString("au_fname");
```

# boolean getBoolean(String columnName) throws SQLException

This gets a named column value as a boolean value.

```
boolean contract = rs.getBoolean("contract");
```

# byte getByte(String columnName) throws SQLException

This gets a named column value as a byte value.

```
byte contract = rs.getByte("contract");
```

# short getShort(String columnName) throws SQLException

This gets a named column value as a short value.

```
short hirange = rs.getShort("hirange");
```

# int getInt(String columnName)
# throws SQLException

This gets a named column value as an int value.

```
int hirange = rs.getInt("hirange");
```

# long getLong(String columnName)
# throws SQLException

This gets a named column value as a long value.

```
long hirange = rs.getLong("hirange");
```

# float getFloat(String columnName)
# throws SQLException

This gets a named column value as a float value.

```
float hirange = rs.getFloat("hirange");
```

# double getDouble(String columnName)
# throws SQLException

This gets a named column value as a double value.

```
double hirange = rs.getDouble("hirange");
```

# Bignum getBignum(String columnName,
# int scale) throws SQLException

This gets a named column value as a Bignum object with the specified scale (precision).

```
Numeric hirange = rs.getBignum("hirange", 4);
```

## byte[] getBytes(String columnName) throws SQLException

Gets a named column value as an array of bytes.

```
byte[] au_lname = rs.getBytes("hirange");
```

## java.sql.Date getDate(String columnName) throws SQLException

Gets a named column value as a java.sql.Date object.

```
java.sql.Date birthday = rs.getDate("birthday");
```

## java.sql.Time getTime(String columnName) throws SQLException

Gets a named column value as a java.sql.Time object.

```
java.sql.Time appointment_start =
rs.getTime("appointment_start");
```

## java.sql.Timestamp getTimestamp (String columnName) throws SQLException

Gets a named column value as a java.sql.Timestamp object.

```
java.sql.Timestamp timestamp = rs.getTimestamp("timestamp");
```

## java.io.InputStream getAsciiStream (String columnName) throws SQLException

Gets a named column value as an InputStream object. This can be useful for large text values.

```
import java.io.*;
InputStream foo = rs.getAsciiStream("au_biography");
```

## java.io.InputStream getUnicodeStream (String columnName) throws SQLException

Gets a named column value as an InputStream object. This can be useful for large text values containing Unicode data.

```
import java.io.*;
InputStream foo = rs.getUnicodeStream("au_biography");
```

## java.io.InputStream getBinaryStream (String columnName) throws SQLException

Gets a named column value as an InputStream object. This can be useful for large binary values.

```
import java.io.*;
InputStream foo = rs.getBinaryStream("au_picture");
```

## SQLWarning getWarnings() throws SQLException

Returns the first SQLWarning in the chain of warnings for this result set.

```
// print out warnings
//
SQLWarning w = rs.getWarnings();
while (w != null) {
  System.out.println(w.getMessage());
  w = w.getNextWarning();
}
```

## void clearWarnings() throws SQLException

Clears this result set's chain of warnings.

```
rs.clearWarnings();
```

# String getCursorName() throws SQLException

This returns the cursor name for this result set, which can be used in subsequent positioned updates and deletes. Positioned updates and deletes are supported by certain database products with the WHERE CURRENT OF clause.

```
String cname = rs.getCursorName();

// execute a useless update on a different statement than the one
// that provided the ResultSet
//
stmt2.executeUpdate("UPDATE test SET name = '*' + name " +
                    "WHERE CURRENT OF " + cname);
```

# ResultSetMetaData getMetaData() throws SQLException

This returns the metadata for this result set. See the ResultSetMetaData object for more information.

```
ResultSetMetaData meta = rs.getMetaData()
```

# Object getObject(int columnIndex) throws SQLException

This returns a column value by column index as a generic Object.

```
String foobar = (String) rs.getObject(1);
```

# Object getObject(String columnName) throws SQLException

This returns a named column value as a generic Object.

```
String foobar = (String) rs.getObject("foobar");
```

## int findColumn(String columnName) throws SQLException

Given a column name, this returns its index.

```
int column_index = rs.findColumn("au_fname");
```

# The ResultSetMetaData Object

The ResultSetMetaData object provides information about the result set. It is instantiated with the ResultSet's `getMetaData()` method.

## int getColumnCount() throws SQLException

This returns the number of columns in the result set.

```
int count = meta.getColumnCount();
```

## boolean isAutoIncrement(int column) throws SQLException

Given a column's index, this will tell you if the column is an "auto increment" column. Such columns automatically increment in value when a new row is inserted and may require special handling for inserts. You should consult your database server's documentation for more information regarding how the server handles these columns.

```
boolean isai = meta.isAutoIncrement(1);
```

## boolean isCaseSensitive(int column) throws SQLException

This returns true if the column's case is significant, false otherwise.

```
boolean is_case_sensitive = meta.isCaseSensitive(1);
```

## boolean isSearchable(int column) throws SQLException

This returns true if the column can be used in a WHERE clause, false otherwise.

```
boolean is_searchable = meta.isSearchable(1);
```

## boolean isCurrency(int column) throws SQLException

This returns true if the column is some sort of money datatype, false otherwise.

```
boolean is_currency = meta.isCurrency(1);
```

## int isNullable(int column) throws SQLException

This returns true if the column can accept SQL NULLs, false otherwise.

```
boolean is_nullable = meta.isNullable(1);
```

## boolean isSigned(int column) throws SQLException

This returns true if the column's datatype is a signed numeric type, false otherwise.

```
boolean is_signed = meta.isSigned(1);
```

## int getColumnDisplaySize(int column) throws SQLException

This returns the column's display size (width).

```
int size = meta.DisplaySize(1);
```

# String getColumnLabel(int column) throws SQLException

This returns the suggested label for the column, which can be used for displays and reports.

```
String label = meta.getColumnLabel(1);
```

# String getColumnName(int column) throws SQLException

This returns the name of the column.

```
String name = meta.getColumnName(1);
```

# String getSchemaName(int column) throws SQLException

This returns the table schema name (in some implementations, this is its owner) for a given column, if applicable.

```
String schema_name = meta.getSchemaName(1);
```

# int getPrecision(int column) throws SQLException

This returns the number of decimal places for the column.

```
int precision = meta.getPrecision(1);
```

# int getScale(int column) throws SQLException

This returns the number of digits to the right of the decimal point for the column.

```
int precision = meta.getScale(1);
```

## String getTableName(int column) throws SQLException

This returns the table name for a given column.

```
String table_name = meta.getTableName(1);
```

## String getCatalogName(int column) throws SQLException

This returns the catalog/database name for a given column.

```
String db_name = meta.getCatalogName(1);
```

## int getColumnType(int column) throws SQLException

This returns the column's data type as contained in java.sql.Types.

```
int type = meta.getColumnType(1);
```

## String getColumnTypeName(int column) throws SQLException

This returns the column's data type as contained in java.sql.Types.

```
int type = meta.getColumnType(1);
```

## boolean isReadOnly(int column) throws SQLException

This returns whether or not the column is read-only.

```
boolean is_readonly = meta.isReadOnly(1);
```

# boolean isWritable(int column) throws SQLException

This returns whether or not the column is writable.

```
boolean is_writable = meta.isWritable(1);
```

# boolean isDefinitelyWritable(int column) throws SQLException

This returns whether or not a write will definitely succeed on this column.

```
boolean is_writable_ya_sure = meta.isDefinitelyWritable(1);
```

# Working with PreparedStatements

The PreparedStatement object is instantiated using the Connection object's `prepareStatement()` method.

## ResultSet executeQuery() throws SQLException

This executes a query using a prepared statement.

```
PreparedStatement pstmt =
    con.prepareStatement("SELECT au_id FROM authors WHERE au_lname = ?");
pstmt.setString(1, "Jepson");
ResultSet rs = pstmt.executeQuery();
rs.next();
System.out.println( rs.getString(1) );
pstmt.close();
```

## int executeUpdate() throws SQLException

This executes a prepared statement that does not return a result set. See the example for PreparedStatement prepareStatement(String sql) under the Connection object.

## void setNull(int parameterIndex, int sqlType) throws SQLException

This sets one of a prepared statement's parameters to NULL, given the index and SQL data type.

```
pstmt.setNull(1, java.sql.Types.CHAR);
```

## void setBoolean(int parameterIndex, boolean x) throws SQLException

This sets one of a prepared statement's parameters to a boolean value.

```
pstmt.setBoolean(1, true);
```

## void setByte(int parameterIndex, byte x) throws SQLException

This sets one of a prepared statement's parameters to a byte value.

```
pstmt.setByte(1, 1);
```

## void setShort(int parameterIndex, short x) throws SQLException

This sets one of a prepared statement's parameters to a short value.

```
pstmt.setShort(1, 112);
```

## void setInt(int parameterIndex, int x) throws SQLException

This sets one of a prepared statement's parameters to an int value.

```
pstmt.setInt(1, 1024);
```

## void setLong(int parameterIndex, long x) throws SQLException

This sets one of a prepared statement's parameters to a long value.

```
pstmt.setLong(1, 1024);
```

## void setFloat(int parameterIndex, float x) throws SQLException

This sets one of a prepared statement's parameters to a float value.

```
pstmt.setFloat(1, 1.024);
```

## void setDouble(int parameterIndex, double x) throws SQLException

This sets one of a prepared statement's parameters to a double value.

```
pstmt.setDouble(1, 1024);
```

## void setBignum(int parameterIndex, Bignum x) throws SQLException

This sets one of a prepared statement's parameters to a value derived from a java.sql.Bignum object.

```
pstmt.setBignum(1, new Bignum(100, 2));
```

## void setString(int parameterIndex, String x) throws SQLException

This sets one of a prepared statement's parameters to a value derived from a String object.

```
pstmt.setString(1, "Hello");
```

## void setBytes(int parameterIndex, byte x[]) throws SQLException

This sets one of a prepared statement's parameters to a byte array.

```
byte[] b = new byte[10];
some_random_file.readFully(b);
pstmt.setBytes(1, b);
```

## void setDate(int parameterIndex, java.sql.Date x) throws SQLException

This sets one of a prepared statement's parameters to a value derived from a java.sql.Date object.

```
pstmt.setDate(1, new java.sql.Date("1996-01-01"));
```

## void setTime(int parameterIndex, java.sql.Time x) throws SQLException

This sets one of a prepared statement's parameters to a value derived from a java.sql.Time object.

```
pstmt.setTime(1, new java.sql.Time("10:10:00"));
```

## void setTimestamp(int parameterIndex, java.sql.Timestamp x) throws SQLException

This sets one of a prepared statement's parameters to a value derived from a java.sql.Time object.

```
pstmt.setTimestamp(1, new java.sql.Timestamp(1996, 0, 1, 10, 10,
                                              0, 0))
```

## void setAsciiStream(int parameterIndex, java.io.InputStream x, int length) throws SQLException

This sets one of a prepared statement's parameters to ASCII values read from an Input-Stream.

```
pstmt.setAsciiStream(1, System.in, 11);
```

## void setUnicodeStream(int parameterIndex, java.io.InputStream x, int length) throws SQLException

This sets one of a prepared statement's parameters to Unicode values read from an Input-Stream.

```
pstmt.setUnicodeStream(1, System.in, 11);
```

## void setBinaryStream(int parameterIndex, java.io.InputStream x, int length) throws SQLException

This sets one of a prepared statement's parameters to values read from a binary input stream.

```
pstmt.setBinaryStream(1, System.in, 11);
```

## void clearParameters() throws SQLException

This clears all of the parameters of the prepared statement.

```
pstmt.clearParameters();
```

## void setObject(int parameterIndex, Object x, int targetSqlType, int scale) throws SQLException

This sets a prepared statement's parameter to accept input from a generic Object, including a value for the precision.

```
pstmt.setObject(1, new Float(100.2), java.sql.Types.NUMERIC, 4)
```

## void setObject(int parameterIndex, Object x, int targetSqlType) throws SQLException

This sets a prepared statement's parameter to accept input from a generic Object.

```
pstmt.setObject(1, new String("Hello"), java.sql.Types.CHAR);
```

## void setObject(int parameterIndex, Object x) throws SQLException

This sets a prepared statement's parameter to accept input from a generic Object.

```
pstmt.setObject(1, new String("Hello"));
```

## boolean execute() throws SQLException

This executes a prepared statement, returning no results.

```
pstmt.execute();
```

# Working with the CallableStatement

The callable statement is instantiated using the Connection object's `prepareCall()` method. It provides extensions to the prepared statement that include OUT or OUTPUT parameters. An exhaustive example is included in the Connection section.

## void registerOutParameter (int parameterIndex, int sqlType) throws SQLException

This registers an output parameter given a specific SQL type.

```
cstmt.registerOutParameter(2, java.sql.Types.VARCHAR);
```

## void registerOutParameter (int parameterIndex, int sqlType, int scale) throws SQLException

This registers an output parameter given a specific SQL type and scale.

```
cstmt.registerOutParameter(2, java.sql.Types.NUMERIC, 3);
```

## Other Methods

The following methods resemble some of the methods in ResultSet, except they operate on OUT parameters rather than columns in a result set. If your callable statement has a mixture of OUT and ordinary parameters, as is the case with the example shown in the section on the Connection class, you should keep in mind that all parameters (OUT and IN) are indexed; if you mistakenly retrieve a parameter that is purely input, you will probably retrieve the value you originally sent to the server.

```
boolean wasNull() throws SQLException
String getString(int parameterIndex) throws SQLException
boolean getBoolean(int parameterIndex) throws SQLException
byte getByte(int parameterIndex) throws SQLException
short getShort(int parameterIndex) throws SQLException
int getInt(int parameterIndex) throws SQLException
long getLong(int parameterIndex) throws SQLException
float getFloat(int parameterIndex) throws SQLException
double getDouble(int parameterIndex) throws SQLException
```

**Continued**

```
Bignum getBignum(int parameterIndex, int scale) throws SQLException
byte[] getBytes(int parameterIndex) throws SQLException
java.sql.Date getDate(int parameterIndex) throws SQLException
java.sql.Time getTime(int parameterIndex) throws SQLException
java.sql.Timestamp getTimestamp(int parameterIndex) throws SQLException
Object getObject(int parameterIndex) throws SQLException
```

# DatabaseMetaData

A DatabaseMetaData object contains a vast amount of information about the driver and the database server. It is instantiated using the `getMetaData()` method in the Connection class. Some of the methods here return a result set that can be manipulated as shown in the section on the ResultSet class.

## boolean allProceduresAreCallable() throws SQLException

This returns true if all of the procedures returned by `getProcedures()` (see below) can be called by the current user; it returns false otherwise.

```
boolean b = dmd.allProceduresAreCallable();
```

## boolean allTablesAreSelectable() throws SQLException

This returns true if all of the tables returned by `getTables()` (see below) can be queried by the current user; it returns false otherwise.

```
boolean b = dmd.allTablesAreSelectable();
```

## String getURL() throws SQLException

This returns the URL used to connect to the database.

```
String url = dmd.getUrl();
```

# String getUserName() throws SQLException

This returns the current username.

```
String user = dmd.getUserName();
```

# boolean isReadOnly() throws SQLException

This returns true if the database is in read-only mode, false otherwise.

```
boolean ro = dmd.isReadOnly();
```

# boolean nullsAreSortedHigh() throws SQLException

This returns true if NULL values are sorted high, false otherwise.

```
boolean nulls_high = dmd. nullsAreSortedHigh();
```

# boolean nullsAreSortedLow() throws SQLException

This returns true if NULL values are sorted low, false otherwise.

```
boolean nulls_low = dmd. nullsAreSortedLow();
```

# boolean nullsAreSortedAtStart() throws SQLException

This returns true if NULL values are sorted at the start of a result set (irrespective of sort order), false otherwise.

```
boolean nulls_at_start = dmd. nullsAreSortedAtStart();
```

## boolean nullsAreSortedAtEnd()
## throws SQLException

This returns true if NULL values are sorted at the end of a result set (irrespective of sort order), false otherwise.

```
boolean nulls_at_end = dmd. nullsAreSortedAtEnd();
```

## String getDatabaseProductName()
## throws SQLException

This returns the database product name.

```
String product = dmd.getDatabaseProductName();
```

## String getDatabaseProductVersion()
## throws SQLException

This returns the database product version.

```
String version = dmd.getDatabaseProductVersion();
```

## String getDriverName()
## throws SQLException

This returns the name of this JDBC driver.

```
String driver_name = dmd.getDriverName();
```

## String getDriverVersion()
## throws SQLException

This returns the version of this JDBC driver.

```
String driver_version = dmd.getDriverVersion();
```

# int getDriverMajorVersion()

This returns the major version of this JDBC driver.

```
int major_version = dmd.getDriverMajorVersion();
```

# int getDriverMinorVersion()

This returns the minor version of this JDBC driver.

```
int minor_version = dmd.getDriverMinorVersion();
```

# boolean usesLocalFiles()
# throws SQLException

This returns true if the database stores its tables in local files, false otherwise.

```
boolean local_files = dmd.usesLocalFiles();
```

# boolean usesLocalFilePerTable()
# throws SQLException

This returns true if the database stores each table in a separate file, false otherwise.

```
boolean one_file = dmd.usesLocalFilePerTable();
```

# boolean supportsMixedCaseIdentifiers()
# throws SQLException

This returns true if the database supports mixed case unquoted SQL identifiers, false otherwise.

```
boolean b = dmd.supportsMixedCaseIdentifiers();
```

### boolean storesUpperCaseIdentifiers() throws SQLException

This returns true if the database stores mixed case unquoted SQL identifiers in uppercase, false otherwise.

```
boolean b = dmd.storesUpperCaseIdentifiers();
```

### boolean storesLowerCaseIdentifiers() throws SQLException

This returns true if the database stores mixed case unquoted SQL identifiers in lowercase, false otherwise.

```
boolean b = dmd.storesLowerCaseIdentifiers();
```

### boolean storesMixedCaseIdentifiers() throws SQLException

This returns true if the database stores mixed case unquoted SQL identifiers in mixed case, false otherwise.

```
boolean b = dmd.storesMixedCaseIdentifiers();
```

### boolean supportsMixedCaseQuotedIdentifiers() throws SQLException

This returns true if the database supports mixed case quoted SQL identifiers, false otherwise.

```
boolean b = dmd.supportsMixedCaseQuotedIdentifiers();
```

### boolean storesUpperCaseQuotedIdentifiers() throws SQLException

This returns true if the database stores mixed case quoted SQL identifiers in uppercase.

```
boolean b = dmd.storesUpperCaseQuotedIdentifiers();
```

## boolean storesLowerCaseQuotedIdentifiers() throws SQLException

This returns true if the database stores mixed case quoted SQL identifiers in lowercase.

```
boolean b = dmd.storesLowerCaseQuotedIdentifiers();
```

## boolean storesMixedCaseQuotedIdentifiers() throws SQLException

This returns true if the database stores mixed case quoted SQL identifiers in mixed case.

```
boolean b = dmd.storesMixedCaseQuotedIdentifiers();
```

## String getIdentifierQuoteString() throws SQLException

This returns the string used to quote SQL identifiers and returns a single space if identifier quoting isn't supported. JDBC compliant drivers use the double quote character.

```
String qs = dmd.getIdentifierQuoteString()
```

## String getSQLKeywords() throws SQLException

This returns a comma-delimited list of SQL keywords that are not SQL92 keywords.

```
String keywords = dmd.getSQLKeywords();
```

## String getNumericFunctions() throws SQLException

This returns a comma-delimited list of numeric functions.

```
String funcs = dmd.getNumericFunctions();
```

## String getStringFunctions() throws SQLException

This returns a comma-delimited list of string functions.

```
String funcs = dmd.getStringFunctions();
```

## String getSystemFunctions() throws SQLException

This returns a comma-delimited list of system functions.

```
String funcs = dmd.getSystemFunctions();
```

## String getTimeDateFunctions() throws SQLException

This returns a comma-delimited list of time and date functions.

```
String funcs = dmd.getTimeDateFunctions();
```

## String getSearchStringEscape() throws SQLException

This returns the string that can be used to escape "_" or "%" in LIKE clauses.

```
String esc = dmd.getSearchStringEscape();
```

## String getExtraNameCharacters() throws SQLException

This gets any non-alphanumeric (beyond A-Z, a-z, 0-9, and _) that can be used in unquoted identifier names.

```
String extra = dmd.getExtraNameCharacters();
```

## boolean supportsAlterTableWithAddColumn() throws SQLException

This returns true if the ALTER TABLE command supports adding columns to a table.

```
boolean b = dmd.supportsAlterTableWithAddColumn();
```

## boolean supportsAlterTableWithDropColumn() throws SQLException

This returns true if the ALTER TABLE command supports dropping columns from a table.

```
boolean b = dmd.supportsAlterTableWithDropColumn();
```

## boolean supportsColumnAliasing() throws SQLException

This returns true if the SELECT statement supports column aliasing using the AS clause.

```
boolean b = dmd.supportsColumnAliasing();
```

## boolean nullPlusNonNullIsNull() throws SQLException

This returns true if any concatenations involving a NULL and non-NULL values returns NULL.

```
boolean b = dmd.nullPlusNonNullIsNull();
```

## boolean supportsConvert() throws SQLException

This returns true if the SQL CONVERT function is supported.

```
boolean b = dmd.supportsConvert();
```

## boolean supportsConvert(int fromType, int toType) throws SQLException

This returns true if the SQL CONVERT function is supported between the specified types.

```
boolean b = dmd.supportsConvert(java.sql.Types.INTEGER,
                                java.sql.Types.CHAR);
```

## boolean supportsTableCorrelationNames() throws SQLException

This returns true if table correlation names are supported.

```
boolean b = dmd.supportsTableCorrelationNames();
```

This feature allows you to specify a table alias in SELECT statements as in:

```
SELECT auth.au_lname FROM authors auth WHERE auth.au_lname = 'Jepson'
```

## boolean supportsDifferentTableCorrelation-Names() throws SQLException

This returns true if table correlation names must be different from the table's name.

```
boolean b = dmd.supportsDifferentTableCorrelationNames();
```

## boolean supportsExpressionsInOrderBy() throws SQLException

This returns true if you may include expressions in an ORDER BY clause.

```
boolean b = dmd.supportsExpressionsInOrderBy();
```

## boolean supportsOrderByUnrelated() throws SQLException

If the database allows you to include columns in an ORDER BY clause that are not included in the SELECT list, this will return true.

```
boolean b = dmd.supportsOrderByUnrelated();
```

# boolean supportsGroupBy()
## throws SQLException

This returns true if the database supports the GROUP BY clause.

```
boolean b = dmd.supportsGroupBy();
```

# boolean supportsGroupByUnrelated()
## throws SQLException

If the database allows you to include columns in a GROUP BY clause that are not included in the SELECT list, this will return true.

```
boolean b = dmd.supportsGroupByUnrelated();
```

# boolean supportsGroupByBeyondSelect()
## throws SQLException

This is a slight variation on supportsGroupByUnrelated().

```
boolean b = dmd.supportsGroupByBeyondSelect();
```

If, having included all of the columns in the SELECT list, the database allows you to include columns in an GROUP BY clause that are not included in the SELECT list, this will return true, as in:

```
SELECT city, AVG(age)
   FROM census
   GROUP BY city, country
```

# boolean supportsLikeEscapeClause()
## throws SQLException

This returns true if you may include JDBC/ODBC escape clauses within LIKE expressions.

```
boolean b = dmd.supportsLikeEscapeClause();
```

## boolean supportsMultipleResultSets() throws SQLException

This returns true if the database and driver support multiple result sets.

```
boolean b = dmd.supportsMultipleResultSets();
```

## boolean supportsMultipleTransactions() throws SQLException

This returns true if it is possible to have multiple transactions open across different connections.

```
boolean b = dmd.supportsMultipleTransactions();
```

## boolean supportsNonNullableColumns() throws SQLException

This returns true if it is possible to define a column that does not accept NULLs.

```
boolean b = dmd.supportsNonNullableColumns();
```

## boolean supportsMinimumSQLGrammar() throws SQLException

This returns true if the ODBC Minimum Grammar is supported by this driver.

```
boolean b = dmd.supportsMinimumSQLGrammar();
```

## boolean supportsCoreSQLGrammar() throws SQLException

This returns true if the ODBC Core Grammar is supported by this driver.

```
boolean b = dmd.supportsCoreSQLGrammar();
```

# boolean supportsExtendedSQLGrammar() throws SQLException

This returns true if the ODBC Extended Grammar is supported by this driver.

```
boolean b = dmd.supportsExtendedSQLGrammar();
```

# boolean supportsANSI92EntryLevelSQL() throws SQLException

This returns true if the ANSI92 Entry Level SQL grammar is supported by the database, which is required for JDBC compliance.

```
boolean b = dmd. supportsANSI92EntryLevelSQL();
```

# boolean supportsANSI92IntermediateSQL() throws SQLException

This returns true if the ANSI92 Intermediate SQL grammar is supported by the database.

```
boolean b = dmd.supportsANSI92IntermediateSQL();
```

# boolean supportsANSI92FullSQL() throws SQLException

This returns true if the full ANSI92 SQL grammar is supported by the database.

```
boolean b = dmd. supportsANSI92FullSQL();
```

# boolean supportsIntegrityEnhancement Facility() throws SQLException

This returns true if the database supports the SQL Integrity Enhancement Facility.

```
boolean b = dmd.supportsIntegrityEnhancementFacility();
```

# boolean supportsOuterJoins()
# throws SQLException

This returns true if outer joins are supported by the database.

```
boolean b = dmd.supportsOuterJoins();
```

# boolean supportsFullOuterJoins()
# throws SQLException

This returns true if full outer joins are supported by the database.

```
boolean b = dmd.supportsFullOuterJoins();
```

# boolean supportsLimitedOuterJoins()
# throws SQLException

This returns true if only limited support for outer joins is provided.

```
boolean b = dmd.supportsLimitedOuterJoins();
```

# String getSchemaTerm() throws SQLException

This returns the database vendor's preferred term for an SQL schema (in SQL Server, this is the table's owner).

```
String schema_term = dmd.getSchemaTerm();
```

# String getProcedureTerm()
# throws SQLException

This returns the database vendor's preferred term for a stored procedure.

```
String procedure_term = dmd.getProcedureTerm();
```

# String getCatalogTerm() throws SQLException

This returns the database vendor's preferred term for a catalog (often "database").

```
String procedure_term = dmd.getProcedureTerm();
```

# boolean isCatalogAtStart() throws SQLException

This determines whether or not the catalog name must appear at the beginning of a fully qualified table name (as in pubs.dbo.authors). If this returns false, then the catalog name must appear at the end.

```
boolean b = dmd.isCatalogAtStart();
```

# String getCatalogSeparator() throws SQLException

This returns the separator that must appear between the catalog name and the table name (in SQL Server, it's a period - ".").

```
String sep = dmd.getCatalogSeparator();
```

# boolean supportsSchemasInDataManipulation() throws SQLException

This returns true if you can use a schema name to qualify a table in a data manipulation statement.

```
boolean b = dmd.supportsSchemasInDataManipulation();
```

# boolean supportsSchemasInProcedureCalls() throws SQLException

This returns true if you can use a schema name in a stored procedure call.

```
boolean b = dmd.supportsSchemasInProcedureCalls();
```

### boolean supportsSchemasInTableDefinitions() throws SQLException

This returns true if you can use a schema name in a table definition.

```
boolean b = dmd.supportsSchemasInTableDefinitions();
```

### boolean supportsSchemasInIndexDefinitions() throws SQLException

This returns true if you can use a schema name in an index definition.

```
boolean b = dmd.supportsSchemasInIndexDefinitions();
```

### boolean supportsSchemasInPrivilege Definitions() throws SQLException

This returns true if you can use a schema name in a privilege definition statement.

```
boolean b = dmd.supportsSchemasInPrivilegeDefinitions();
```

### boolean supportsCatalogsInDataManipulation() throws SQLException

This returns true if you can use a catalog to qualify a table in a data manipulation statement.

```
boolean b = dmd.supportsCatalogsInDataManipulation();
```

### boolean supportsCatalogsInProcedureCalls() throws SQLException

This returns true if you can use a catalog in a procedure call.

```
boolean b = dmd.supportsCatalogsInProcedureCalls();
```

# boolean supportsCatalogsInTableDefinitions() throws SQLException

This returns true if you can use a catalog in a table definition.

```
boolean b = dmd.supportsCatalogsInTableDefinitions();
```

# boolean supportsCatalogsInIndexDefinitions() throws SQLException

This returns true if you can use a catalog in an index definition.

```
boolean b = dmd.supportsCatalogsInIndexDefinitions();
```

# boolean supportsCatalogsInPrivilegeDefinitions() throws SQLException

This returns true if you can use a catalog in a privilege definition.

```
boolean b = dmd.supportsCatalogsInPrivilegeDefinitions();
```

# boolean supportsPositionedDelete() throws SQLException

This returns true if the database supports a positioned delete.

```
boolean b = dmd.supportsPositionedDelete();
```

# boolean supportsPositionedUpdate() throws SQLException

This returns true if the database supports a positioned update.

```
boolean b = dmd.supportsPositionedUpdate();
```

## boolean supportsSelectForUpdate() throws SQLException

This returns true if SELECT for UPDATE is supported.

```
boolean b = dmd.supportsSelectForUpdate();
```

## boolean supportsStoredProcedures() throws SQLException

This returns true if stored procedures are supported using the stored procedure escape syntax.

```
boolean b = dmd.supportsStoredProcedures();
```

## boolean supportsSubqueriesInComparisons() throws SQLException

This returns true if expressions may include subqueries in their terms. This is required for JDBC compliance.

```
boolean b = dmd.supportsSubqueriesInComparisons();
```

## boolean supportsSubqueriesInExists() throws SQLException

This returns true if the EXISTS clause may include a subquery.

```
boolean b = dmd.supportsSubqueriesInExists();
```

## boolean supportsSubqueriesInIns() throws SQLException

This returns true if subqueries are supported using the IN clause.

```
boolean b = dmd.supportsSubqueriesInIns();
```

# boolean supportsSubqueriesInQuantifieds() throws SQLException

This returns true if subqueries in quantified expressions are supported.

```
boolean b = dmd.supportsSubqueriesInQuantifieds();
```

# boolean supportsCorrelatedSubqueries() throws SQLException

This returns true if tables and columns in a SELECT may be correlated with tables and columns in a subquery.

```
boolean b = dmd.supportsCorrelatedSubqueries();
```

# boolean supportsUnion() throws SQLException

This returns true if the UNION clause is supported.

```
boolean b = dmd.supportsUnion();
```

# boolean supportsUnionAll() throws SQLException

This returns true if the UNION ALL clause is supported.

```
boolean b = dmd.supportsUnionAll();
```

# boolean supportsOpenCursorsAcrossCommit() throws SQLException

This returns true if a cursor may remain open across transaction commits.

```
boolean b = dmd.supportsOpenCursorsAcrossCommit();
```

# boolean supportsOpenCursorsAcrossRollback() throws SQLException

This returns true if a cursor may remain open across transaction rollbacks.

```
boolean b = dmd.supportsOpenCursorsAcrossRollback();
```

# boolean supportsOpenStatementsAcross Commit() throws SQLException

This returns true if statements can remain open after commits.

```
boolean b = dmd.supportsOpenStatementsAcrossCommit();
```

# boolean supportsOpenStatementsAcross Rollback() throws SQLException

This returns true if statements can remain open after rollbacks.

```
boolean b = dmd.supportsOpenStatementsAcrossRollback();
```

# int getMaxBinaryLiteralLength() throws SQLException

This returns the maximum number of characters allowed in a literal binary value that is contained in an SQL statement.

```
int i = dmd.getMaxBinaryLiteralLength();
```

# int getMaxCharLiteralLength() throws SQLException

This returns the maximum number of characters allowed in a literal character value that is contained in an SQL statement.

```
int i = dmd.getMaxCharLiteralLength();
```

## int getMaxColumnNameLength()
## throws SQLException

This returns the maximum permitted size of a column name.

```
int i = dmd.getMaxColumnNameLength();
```

## int getMaxColumnsInGroupBy()
## throws SQLException

This returns the maximum number of columns that may be included in a GROUP BY clause.

```
int i = dmd. getMaxColumnsInGroupBy();
```

## int getMaxColumnsInIndex()
## throws SQLException

This returns the maximum number of columns that may be included in a list of index columns.

```
int i = dmd.getMaxColumnsInIndex();
```

## int getMaxColumnsInOrderBy()
## throws SQLException

This returns the maximum number of columns that may appear in an ORDER BY clause.

```
int i = dmd.getMaxColumnsInOrderBy();
```

## int getMaxColumnsInSelect()
## throws SQLException

This returns the maximum number of columns that may appear in a SELECT statement's select list.

```
int i = dmd.getMaxColumnsInSelect();
```

## int getMaxColumnsInTable() throws SQLException

This returns the maximum number of columns that a table may contain.

```
int i = dmd.getMaxColumnsInTable();
```

## int getMaxConnections() throws SQLException

This returns the maximum number of connections that can be open to the database.

```
int i = dmd.getMaxConnections();
```

## int getMaxCursorNameLength() throws SQLException

This returns the maximum length of a cursor name.

```
int i = dmd.getMaxCursorNameLength();
```

## int getMaxIndexLength() throws SQLException

This returns the maximum length in bytes of an index expression.

```
int i = dmd.getMaxIndexLength();
```

## int getMaxSchemaNameLength() throws SQLException

This returns the maximum size of a schema name.

```
int i = dmd.getMaxSchemaNameLength();
```

## int getMaxProcedureNameLength() throws SQLException

This returns the maximum length of a stored procedure name.

```
int i = dmd.getMaxProcedureNameLength();
```

## int getMaxCatalogNameLength() throws SQLException

This returns the maximum length of a catalog name.

```
int i = dmd.getMaxCatalogNameLength();
```

## int getMaxRowSize() throws SQLException

This returns the maximum length of a row.

```
int i = dmd.getMaxRowSize();
```

## boolean doesMaxRowSizeIncludeBlobs() throws SQLException

This returns true if the value reported by `getMaxRowSize()` includes blobs such as LONGVARCHAR and LONGVARBINARY.

```
boolean b = dmd.doesMaxRowSizeIncludeBlobs();
```

## int getMaxStatementLength() throws SQLException

This returns the maximum size of an SQL statement.

```
int i = dmd.getMaxStatementLength();
```

## int getMaxStatements() throws SQLException

This returns the maximum number of statements that may be open at one time.

```
int i = dmd.getMaxStatements();
```

## int getMaxTableNameLength()
## throws SQLException

This returns the maximum length of a table name.

```
int i = dmd.getMaxTableNameLength();
```

## int getMaxTablesInSelect()
## throws SQLException

This returns the maximum number of tables that may participate in a SELECT statement.

```
int i = dmd.getMaxTablesInSelect();
```

## int getMaxUserNameLength()
## throws SQLException

This returns the maximum length of a username.

```
int i = dmd.getMaxUserNameLength();
```

## int getDefaultTransactionIsolation()
## throws SQLException

This returns the default transaction isolation level as defined in java.sql.Connection.

```
int i = dmd.getDefaultTransactionIsolation();
if (i == Connection.TRANSACTION_READ_UNCOMMITTED) {
  System.out.println("TRANSACTION_READ_UNCOMMITTED");
}
```

## boolean supportsTransactions()
## throws SQLException

This returns true if the database supports transactions.

```
boolean b = dmd.supportsTransactions();
```

# boolean supportsTransactionIsolationLevel (int level) throws SQLException

Given a transaction isolation level as defined in java.sql.Connection, this returns true if the database supports that level.

```
boolean b =
   dmd.supportsTransactionIsolationLevel(Connection.TRANSACTION_READ_COMMITTED);
```

# boolean supportsDataDefinitionAndData ManipulationTransactions() throws SQLException

This returns true if both data definition and data manipulation statements may be included within a transaction.

```
boolean b = dmd.supportsDataDefinitionAndDataManipulationTransactions();
```

# boolean supportsDataManipulation TransactionsOnly() throws SQLException

This returns true if data definition statements only may be included within a transaction.

```
boolean b = dmd.supportsDataManipulationTransactionsOnly();
```

# boolean dataDefinitionCausesTransaction Commit() throws SQLException

This returns true if data definition statements within a transaction cause an implicit commit.

```
boolean b = dmd.dataDefinitionCausesTransactionCommit();
```

## boolean dataDefinitionIgnoredInTransactions() throws SQLException

This returns true if data definition statements are ignored within a transaction.

```
boolean b = dmd.dataDefinitionIgnoredInTransactions();
```

## ResultSet getProcedures(String catalog, String schemaPattern, String procedureNamePattern) throws SQLException

This returns a ResultSet object containing all stored procedures. The catalog and schema pattern may be null. Both the schema pattern and procedure name pattern use the same wildcard and/or regexp features as the LIKE clause of the SQL SELECT statement.

```
ResultSet rs = dmd.getProcedures("master", null, "%");
ResultSetMetaData rm = rs.getMetaData();

while (rs.next()) {

  String row = "";
  for (int i = 1; i <= rm.getColumnCount(); i++) {
    row += rs.getString(i) + "  ";
  }
  System.out.println(row);

}
```

## ResultSet getProcedureColumns(String catalog, String schemaPattern, String procedureNamePattern, String columnNamePattern) throws SQLException

This returns a result set containing information about one or more procedure's columns (input and output parameters).

```
ResultSet rscols = dmd.getProcedureColumns
   ("pubs", null, "max_price", "%");
```

# ResultSet getTables(String catalog, String schemaPattern, String tableNamePattern, String types[]) throws SQLException

Given a catalog, schema pattern, and a tablename pattern, this retrieves a list of tables and information about those tables. The types String array allows you to specify one or more of the following tables types: "TABLE," "VIEW," "SYSTEM TABLE," "GLOBAL TEMPORARY," "LOCAL TEMPORARY," "ALIAS," and/or "SYNONYM."

```
String[] types = { "TABLE", "VIEW" };

ResultSet rs = dmd.getTables("pubs", "dbo", "%", types);
```

# ResultSet getSchemas() throws SQLException

This returns a result set containing all of the schemas in the database.

```
ResultSet rs = dmd.getSchemas();
```

# ResultSet getCatalogs() throws SQLException

This returns a result set that enumerates all of the catalogs in the database.

```
ResultSet rs = dmd.getCatalogs();
```

# ResultSet getTableTypes() throws SQLException

This returns a ResultSet that enumerates the table types supported by the database.

```
ResultSet rs = dmd.getTableTypes();
```

# ResultSet getColumns(String catalog, String schemaPattern, String tableNamePattern, String columnNamePattern) throws SQLException

Given a catalog name, a schema pattern, a table pattern, and a column name pattern, this returns a result set with information about all of all the columns in the tables that match the patterns specified.

```
ResultSet rs = dmd.getColumns("pubs", "dbo", "authors", "%");
```

# ResultSet getColumnPrivileges(String catalog, String schema, String table, String columnNamePattern) throws SQLException

Given a catalog name, a schema pattern, a table pattern, and a column name pattern, this returns a result set with information concerning user access privileges for all the columns in the tables that match the patterns specified.

```
ResultSet rs = dmd.getColumnPrivileges("pubs", "dbo", "authors", "%");
```

# ResultSet getTablePrivileges(String catalog, String schemaPattern, String tableName Pattern) throws SQLException

Given a catalog name, schema pattern, and table name pattern, this returns a result set with information concerning user access privileges for all of all the tables that match the patterns specified.

```
ResultSet rs = dmd.getTablePrivileges("pubs", "dbo", "%");
```

# ResultSet getBestRowIdentifier(String catalog, String schema, String table, int scope, boolean nullable) throws SQLException

This returns a description of the table's optimal set of columns that uniquely identify a row. You may include one of the following values for the scope parameter:

DatabaseMetaData.bestRowTemporary temporary, just while you are using the row

DatabaseMetaData.bestRowTransaction valid for the remainder of the transaction

DatabaseMetaData.bestRowSession valid for the remainder of the current session

```
ResultSet rs = dmd.getBestRowIdentifier
  ("pubs", "dbo", "authors", DatabaseMetaData.bestRowTemporary, true);
```

# ResultSet getVersionColumns(String catalog, String schema, String table) throws SQLException

This returns a result set containing a description of columns that are automatically updated when any value in the row is updated, such as timestamp columns.

```
ResultSet rs = dmd.getVersionColumns ("javadb", "dbo", "invoices");
```

# ResultSet getPrimaryKeys(String catalog, String schema, String table) throws SQLException

This returns a result set that enumerates the primary key columns for the specified table.

```
ResultSet rs = dmd.getPrimaryKeys ("pubs", "dbo", "authors");
```

# ResultSet getImportedKeys(String catalog, String schema, String table) throws SQLException

This returns information concerning primary keys in other tables that are referenced by foreign keys in the specified table.

```
ResultSet rs = dmd.getImportedKeys ("pubs", "dbo", "titleauthor");
```

## ResultSet getExportedKeys(String catalog, String schema, String table) throws SQLException

This returns information concerning foreign keys in other tables that reference primary keys in the specified table.

```
ResultSet rs = dmd.getExportedKeys ("pubs", "dbo", "titleauthor");
```

## ResultSet getCrossReference(String primaryCatalog, String primarySchema, String primaryTable, String foreignCatalog, String foreignSchema, String foreignTable) throws SQLException

Given a fully qualified (catalog, schema, and table) table, this will return information about how the second table's foreign keys relate to the first table's primary keys.

```
ResultSet rs = dmd.getCrossReference
    ("pubs", "dbo", "authors", "pubs", "dbo", "titleauthor");
```

## ResultSet getTypeInfo() throws SQLException

This returns a result set that describes all of the data types available in the database.

```
ResultSet rs = dmd.getTypeInfo();
```

## ResultSet getIndexInfo(String catalog, String schema, String table, boolean unique, boolean approximate) throws SQLException

This returns statistic information about the indexes for the specified table. The unique flag, when true, indicates that only unique indexes should be reported. The approximate flag, when true, indicates that it is acceptable for this method to return approximate or out-of-date statistics.

```
ResultSet rs =
    dmd.getIndexInfo("pubs", "dbo", "titleauthor", false, false);
```

# ODBC/JDBC Escape Processing

I've hinted at and flirted with the concept of ODBC escape processing. Basically, it's a feature that must be provided by the driver to map ODBC/JDBC-specific SQL syntax into vendor-specific SQL. Appendix D includes examples of scalar function calls using the escape syntax; some more examples will be shown here. In order for these to work, the escape syntax must be supported by the driver.

## Outer Joins

An outer join is specified in JDBC with the syntax:

```
table LEFT OUTER JOIN {table | outer-join} ON search-condition
```

This must be enclosed within the JDBC escape syntax:

```
{oj outer_join_syntax}
```

as in:

```
SELECT au_fname, au_lname, title_id
  FROM authors, titleauthor
  {oj titleauthor LEFT OUTER JOIN authors ON authors.au_id = titleauthor.au_id}
```

In SQL Server's Transact-SQL, this would be rendered as:

```
SELECT au_fname, au_lname, title_id
  FROM authors, titleauthor
  WHERE authors.au_id *= titleauthor.au_id
```

Without the outer join, the above query would display only authors who also have titles. With the outer join, all authors are listed; for those authors not having titles, the title_id is returned as NULL.

## Escaping LIKE Characters

The SQL LIKE clause uses the percent character "%" to indicate one or more of any character, like the asterisk "*" used in Unix shell regexps and MS-DOS wildcards. The underscore character "_" is used to indicate any single character, like the question mark "?" used in Unix shell regexps and MS-DOS wildcards.

If you want to include any of these as a literal (i.e., you want to find values containing either of these characters), you should use the escape syntax:

```
SELECT au_lname
  FROM authors
  WHERE au_lname LIKE '%\_' {escape '\'}
```

This tells JDBC that the \ should be used to denote a literal for either "_'" or "%."

## Invoking Stored Procedures

The JDBC escape syntax for invoking a stored procedure is simply:

```
{call procedure_name [parameter 1, parameter 2, ...]}
```

## Time and Date

Because each database product varies in its representation of Time, Date, and Timestamp literals, the following escapes are provided. Dates can be escaped with:

```
{d 'yyyy-mm-dd'}
```

as in:

```
SELECT title, pubdate
  FROM titles
  WHERE pubdate > {d '1991-07-01'}
```

Time expressions can be escaped with:

```
{t 'hh:mm:ss'}
```

as in:

```
SELECT title, pubdate
  FROM titles
  WHERE pubdate > {t '22:00:00'}
```

Datetime expressions can be escaped with:

```
{ts 'yyyy-mm-dd hh:mm:ss'}
```

as in:

```
SELECT title, pubdate
    FROM titles
    WHERE pubdate > {ts '1991-07-01 12:00:00'}
```

# JavaLex and JavaCup Introduction

JavaLex and JavaCup are two tools that perform roughly the same function as the standard Unix tools *lex* and *yacc*. The difference is that lex and yacc produce C code and JavaLex and JavaCup produce Java code. These tools are used to develop *parsers*, which are needed by any program that has to deal with streams of commands that conform to a specific grammar; the parser can be used to analyze the commands and map them to actions that must occur. The *scanner* is produced by JavaLex and takes care of breaking the input into *tokens*, while the parser is produced by JavaCup and determines whether the incoming tokens make some sense in the context of the grammar.

tinySQL uses such a grammar, which is included with the example code for Chapter 6. The file tinySQL.cup contains the JavaCup parser source, and the file scanner.lex contains the JavaLex source. This appendix will provide a quick introduction to both JavaLex and JavaCup by using a version of the JavaCup simple_calc example that has been modified to make JavaCup and JavaLex work together.

Before starting, you should obtain JavaLex from its Web site, at http://www .cs.princeton.edu/~ejberk/JavaLex/JavaLex.html. You should also get JavaCup, at http://www.cc.gatech.edu/gvu/people/Faculty/hudson/java_cup/ home.html. Before continuing, you should install the packages according to their instructions and ensure that the example code works.

# The JavaCup Grammar

A JavaCup grammar consists of several components. The simple_calc example included demonstrates a calculator that can parse input from standard input and perform simple arithmetic. The following expressions are contained in the file calc.input, to give you an idea of what the calculator can parse:

```
1+3*4;
(1+3)*4;
1+(3*4);
(200%4)-30;
```

The first things that get taken care of in the JavaCup specification include any IMPORT statements you might need. You will always need to import the runtime classes for JavaCup, as shown below:

```
// JavaCup specification for a simple expression evaluator (w/ actions)
import java_cup.runtime.*;
```

Secondly, you must also include some information on initializing and invoking the scanner. The scanner class that you will generate later includes a static method called `init()`. This instantiates a scanner object that is a static variable within the scanner class. You must tell JavaCup how to initialize the scanner. This is done by enclosing the necessary Java code between an init with {: and a :}.

Then, you must tell JavaCup how to fetch a token from the scanner. This is done by enclosing the code between a scan with {: and a :}.

```
/* Preliminaries to set up and use the scanner.  */
init with {: scanner.init();              :};
scan with {: return scanner.next_token(); :};
```

The method used to scan (see scan with, above) will return a token to the parser. There are two types of tokens. Terminal tokens are returned by the scanner. Non-terminal tokens are larger grammatical components that are made up of terminal tokens and are generated by the parser itself.

Within each of the two types of tokens, there are three subtypes. A regular token does not have an associated value and is usually simply a word, symbol, or a non-terminal. An integer token (int_token) has a value that is later accessible through its int_val field, and a String token (str_token) has a value accessible through its str_val field.

The token declarations result in a class called sym being generated which contains all of these tokens as constants. You don't ever need to worry about the value of the constants; JavaCup will take care of assigning them.

```
/* Terminals (tokens returned by the scanner). */
terminal token    SEMI, PLUS, MINUS, TIMES, DIVIDE, MOD,  LPAREN, RPAREN;
terminal int_token NUMBER;
```

Non-terminal tokens are generated by the grammar and must be declared as well.

```
/* Non terminals */
non terminal symbol    expr_list, expr_part;
non terminal int_token  expr, term, factor;
```

Here's where it starts to get interesting. The grammar is composed of a series of rules. On the left-hand side is a non-terminal token. In the following example, the non-terminal expr_list (a list of expressions) may consist of either an expr_list followed by an expr_part (this is a recursive definition), or (the pipe "|" symbol is used to denote one or more possible ways to generate this token) simply an expr_part. An expr_part is basically a mathematical expression followed by a semicolon. Note that the semicolon at the end of each grammar entry signifies the end of the definition; the SEMI token is used to signify a semicolon in the actual command input stream.

The expr_list token is composed entirely of non-terminal tokens. A non-terminal is a token that is derived from tokens obtained from the scanner. An expression list, then, can consist of one or more expression parts, which are described next.

```
/* The grammar */
expr_list ::= expr_list expr_part
              |
              expr_part;
```

The expr_part non-terminal token is an expr non-terminal followed by a SEMI token (a semicolon). Note that the expr non-terminal includes a :e after it, followed by a code snippet. The expr token was defined earlier as an int_token, which means it has an integer value available through the int_val field. The :e simply provides you with the ability to reference the token in the code snippet as an object named e. The code snippet is enclosed in {: :}, and defines what happens when an expr non-terminal, followed by a semicolon, is encountered; it simply prints out the int_val associated with it.

```
expr_part ::= expr:e
              {: System.out.println("= " + e.int_val); :}
              SEMI
              ;
```

The following three non-terminals show how the expr object gets its value. Within each possible combination of tokens an object named RESULT is given an integer value. This occurs for the factor non-terminal, the term non-terminal, and the expr non-terminal. The RESULT object is created and made available to any definition that contains the specified non-terminal.

At the very bottom, the factor non-terminal is defined as either a NUMBER token's int_val, a NUMBER token preceded by a minus sign, producing its negative int_val, or an expression grouped in parentheses. This allows for precedence grouping.

The term non-terminal is defined as one of four possibilities; a factor non-terminal, or a term (which now includes a factor, by virtue of the last possibility in the definition) followed by the TIMES, DIVIDE, or MOD token and another factor. Each time, the appropriate operation is performed before returning the int_val.

Because the expr is defined as a term, an expr (which can be a single term) PLUS another term, or an expr MINUS another term, any TIMES, DIVIDE, or MOD arithmetic will be performed first, which fits in with what you might expect in mathematical precedence.

```
expr      ::= expr:e1 PLUS term:e2
              {: RESULT.int_val = e1.int_val + e2.int_val; :}
              |
              expr:e1 MINUS term:e2
```

```
                   {: RESULT.int_val = e1.int_val - e2.int_val; :}

                   |

                   term:e1

                   {: RESULT.int_val = e1.int_val; :}

                   ;


term       ::= term:e1 TIMES factor:e2

                   {: RESULT.int_val = e1.int_val * e2.int_val; :}

                   |

                   term:e1 DIVIDE factor:e2

                   {: RESULT.int_val = e1.int_val / e2.int_val; :}

                   |

                   term:e1 MOD factor:e2

                   {: RESULT.int_val = e1.int_val % e2.int_val; :}

                   |

                   factor:e

                   {: RESULT.int_val = e.int_val; :}

                   ;


factor     ::= NUMBER:n

               {: RESULT.int_val = n.int_val;  :}

               |

               MINUS factor:e

               {: RESULT.int_val = -e.int_val; :}

               |

               LPAREN expr:e RPAREN

               {: RESULT.int_val = e.int_val;  :}

               ;
```

The parser and sym source code can be generated with the following command:

```
java java_cup.Main < parser.cup
```

This will produce parser.java and sym.java; you should compile sym.java before compiling the scanner because it depends on sym.class.

# JavaLex Scanner Specifications

Like the JavaCup specification, the first thing you need to include at the top of your JavaLex specification is any import statements and code that must be included in the generated scanner. This includes the java.util and java.lang packages, as well as the java_cup.runtime package.

```
import java.util.*;
import java.lang.*;
import java_cup.runtime.*;



%%
```

That section is terminated with a %%. Following this, the code that should be included within the scanner class itself is enclosed in a %{ and a }%. This includes the static initializer as well as the static next_token() method.

```
%{
static scanner foo;
public static void init() {
    foo = new scanner(System.in);
}


public static token next_token() throws java.io.IOException {
    return foo.yylex();
}
%}
```

Next, a few directives are included. The %class directive tells JavaLex what class name to generate the scanner as (simply "scanner"). Also, it includes the %type directive to determine which object to use for tokens, which is simply the class token, which is part of the java_cup.runtime package. The %eofval tells JavaLex what action to take when it encounters an end-of-file, which is to simply return a new token object, which is given the value of sym.EOF as its initialization value. This is the first time you've seen the constants in the sym class referenced. These will be used as arguments to the `token()` constructor. Since JavaCup took care of assigning numbers to them, you need only refer to them by their constant name.

```
%class scanner
%type token
%eofval{
return (new token(sym.EOF));
%eofval}
```

The next section is where you can define any symbols that might be needed to produce lexical rules. These are regular expressions; the first is NUMBER, which consists of one or more digits. The second is WHITE_SPACE_CHAR, which can consist of one or more white-space characters.

```
NUMBER=[0-9]+

WHITE_SPACE_CHAR=[\n\ \t\b\012]

%%
```

The remainder of the JavaLex specification involves the lexical rules. A lexical analyzer, or scanner, can have different states; certain tokens may shift into a new state, such as when in the middle of a comment. If you are in the comment state, most of the lexical rules don't apply until you leave that state. In the simple_calc, however, only one state is used—the initial (YYINITIAL) state of the scanner. After each token has been read, it returns to that state.

A token is defined by the state the scanner is in, which is enclosed by the less than/greater than symbols. Then, if it's simply a literal, the literal can be included in double quotes. After that, a Java code snippet is included, which usually consists of nothing more than returning a token. The next eight tokens are literals:

```
<YYINITIAL> ";" { return new token (sym.SEMI); }

<YYINITIAL> "+" { return new token (sym.PLUS); }
```

**Continued**

```
<YYINITIAL> "-" { return new token (sym.MINUS); }

<YYINITIAL> "*" { return new token (sym.TIMES); }

<YYINITIAL> "/" { return new token (sym.DIVIDE); }

<YYINITIAL> "%" { return new token (sym.MOD); }

<YYINITIAL> "(" { return new token (sym.LPAREN); }

<YYINITIAL> ")" { return new token (sym.RPAREN); }
```

The NUMBER token is a little special. It's a non-literal token, and a String object called yytext will be available for all non-literals. You can return an int_token, which is initialized with the token name (sym.NUMBER), and a numeric value. Here, `Integer.parseInt()` is used to convert yytext into an integer. If it were a str_token, you could just use yytext in the `str_token()` constructor without conversion.

```
<YYINITIAL> {NUMBER} { return new int_token (sym.NUMBER, Integer.parseInt(yytext)); }
```

Finally, WHITE_SPACE_CHAR is dealt with and simply ignored; no code is included, no token returned.

```
<YYINITIAL> {WHITE_SPACE_CHAR} { }
```

You can generate the scanner with the following command:

```
java JavaLex scanner.lex
```

This produces the file scanner.lex.java, which may be compiled. After you have compiled that, you should compile parser.java and Main.java. The calculator can be tested with:

```
java Main < calc.input
```

which should produce the following output:

```
= 13
= 16
= 13
= -30
```

The simple_calc example is considerably simpler than the grammar used for the tinySQL engine. If you are planning to embark on a career that involves parsers and scanners, it is highly recommended that you peruse a book such as *lex and yacc* (O'Reilly and Associates), by John R. Levine, Tony Mason, and Doug Brown. Even though there is some difference between the Java tools and their C counterparts, there is enough similarity to make such a book indispensable.

# JDBC/ODBC SQL Reference

Any driver that is truly JDBC compliant will support a great deal of the SQL syntax shown in this appendix. This appendix will cover many of the JDBC SQL statements that you may find useful. Although certain data sources such as SQL Server and Oracle have their own SQL dialect, a fully JDBC-compliant driver will support escape clauses that map JDBC-specific SQL to driver-specific SQL.

## Minimum, Core, and Extended Grammars

A JDBC driver can provide support for some or all of the ODBC SQL grammar. Since JDBC is based on ODBC, this should come as no surprise. There are three levels of conformance, *Minimum*, *Core*, and *Extended*. To determine which level is supported by the driver you are using, you can instantiate a DatabaseMetaData object and check with one of the following methods, which return a boolean value:

```
supportsMinimumSQLGrammar()
supportsCoreSQLGrammar()
supportsExtendedSQLGrammar()
```

If an SQL statement is available in a lower level (starting with Minimum), it will be available in the higher levels as well. Some components of certain SQL statements are available only with higher conformance levels.

# Conventions

Certain conventions are used in each statement's description. For example, items enclosed in greater than or less than signs <> indicate components that will be explained in greater detail or in the section "SQL Components," such as:

```
<select list>
<table name>
```

Items enclosed in braces [] are optional components of the syntax, such as:

```
SELECT <select list>
   FROM <table name>
   [WHERE <search condition list>]
```

The above example indicates that the

```
WHERE <search condition list>
```

component is optional.

An ellipsis ... indicates elements that may repeat. For example,

```
SELECT <select list>
   FROM <table name>
   [WHERE <search condition list>]
   [GROUP BY <column name>[, <column name>]...]
```

This indicates that you may continue adding column names to the GROUP BY clause until you exceed the driver's limit, if any.

A pipe symbol | indicates alternate components. In the following example:

```
CREATE [UNIQUE] INDEX <index name>
   ON <table name>
   (<column name> [ASC | DESC]
   [, <column name> [ASC | DESC]]...)
```

either ASC or DESC may be used, but not both.

The {} curly braces are used to group alternate components in cases where it may not be immediately clear how they are grouped. For example, the following grouping:

```
INSERT INTO <table name>
   [(<column name> [, <column name>]...)]
   { <query specification> | VALUES (<expression> [, <expression>]...)}
```

tells you that the alternating components separated by the | symbol are limited to <query specification> and VALUES clause.

# SQL Statements

The following sections introduce some of the more common SQL statements that you will find useful. The ODBC conformance level for each statement is included immediately before the explanation.

## ALTER TABLE

**Conformance Level: Core**  This statement adds one or more columns to the structure of a table within your data source. The value of the column for each row that existed before you added the column is set to NULL.

```
ALTER TABLE <table name>
   ADD <column name> <data type>
   | ADD (<column name> <data type> [, <column name> <data type>]...)
```

Examples:

```
ALTER TABLE collect
   ADD co_height int
ALTER TABLE collect
   ADD (co_height int, co_width int)
```

## CREATE INDEX

**Conformance Level: Core**  This statement creates a named index on one or more columns in a table.

```
CREATE [UNIQUE] INDEX <index name>
   ON <table name>
   (<column name> [ASC | DESC]
     [, <column name> [ASC | DESC]]...)
```

You can add an index to a table, which can cause certain statements, particularly those with a WHERE clause, potentially to run faster. You may specify one or more columns for the index. Each column may be indexed ascending or descending by specifying one of the optional ASC or DESC keywords. Certain JDBC drivers will respect the usage of the UNIQUE keyword. If an index is created as unique, any attempt to enter duplicate values in the table for the columns named in the index will generate an error.

Example:

```
CREATE UNIQUE INDEX ix_name
    ON collect
    (collector_name ASC)
```

# CREATE TABLE
**Conformance Level: Minimum**  This statement creates a table.

```
CREATE TABLE <table name>
    (<column element> [, <column element>]...)
```

A column element may be either a column definition:

```
<column name> <data type>
    [DEFAULT <expression>]
    [<column constraint> [, <column constraint>]...]
```

or a table constraint definition:

```
    UNIQUE (<column name> [, <column name>]...)
  | PRIMARY KEY (<column name> [, <column name>]...)
  | CHECK (<search condition>)
  | FOREIGN KEY (<referencing column list>)
    REFERENCES <referenced table>  (<referenced column list>)
```

The simplest column element is a column name and a data type, as shown in the following CREATE TABLE statement:

```
CREATE TABLE people
    (pe_name char (10),
    pe_shoesize int,
    pe_IQ int)
```

(The column elements are shown in bold.) A column element may also have a DEFAULT clause, which specifies a value to be used when a row is inserted, but the column name is not included in the insert. Here's an example:

```
CREATE TABLE people
    (pe_name char (10),
    pe_shoesize int DEFAULT 8,
    pe_IQ int)
```

A column constraint definition can consist of any of the following clauses:

```
NOT NULL
| UNIQUE
| PRIMARY KEY
| REFERENCES <referenced table> (<referenced column list>)
| CHECK <search condition>
```

A column may have multiple constraint definitions. The NOT NULL clause specifies that the column must be assigned a value on an insert, and the value cannot be changed to a NULL. A NULL is the absence of any value, and it can cause undesirable (but predictable) behavior in queries. The UNIQUE clause specifies that no two rows in the table may have the same value for the column, and the PRIMARY KEY clause specifies that that column is the primary key for the table.

The REFERENCES clause allows the developer to specify declarative referential integrity. If you have two or more tables that are linked to each other by primary and foreign keys, such as:

```
CREATE TABLE collect
    (collector_name char (25),
    collector_id int)
CREATE TABLE cart
    (cartridge_name char (25),
    cartridge_id int)
CREATE TABLE cartxref
    (cx_cartridge_id_ int,
    cx_collector_id_ int,
    cx_quantity int)
```

In this example, collect is linked to cartxref on collector_id = cx_collector_id_, and cart is linked to cartxref on cartridge_id = cx_cartridge_id_. If your data source supports it, you can explicitly declare this relationship by defining the tables this way:

```
CREATE TABLE collect
    (collector_name char (25),
     collector_id int PRIMARY KEY)
CREATE TABLE cart
    (cartridge_name char(25),
     cartridge_id int PRIMARY KEY)
CREATE TABLE cartxref
    (cx_cartridge_id_ int REFERENCES cart (cartridge_id),
     cx_collector_id_ int REFERENCES collect (collector_id),
     cx_quantity int)
```

Certain data sources can utilize this declarative referential integrity. It can be useful in situations where a user might try to delete rows in the cart table while there are related rows in the cartxref table. The declarative referential integrity can aid in cascading the deletions to the cartxref table or blocking them entirely.

The CHECK clause can be used to prevent insertions based on certain criteria. You can supply a search condition as the argument to the CHECK clause:

```
CREATE TABLE cartxref
    (cx_cartridge_id_ int,
     cx_collector_id_ int,
     cx_quantity int CHECK (cx_quantity >= 0))
```

The above CHECK constraint would prevent you from entering negative values for cartridge quantities.

A table constraint definition is used to define certain table-wide attributes. The UNIQUE clause is used to specify a column or series of columns the values of which, taken collectively, must be unique for a given row. For example, if the columns collector_name and collector_age are defined with a UNIQUE clause such as:

```
UNIQUE (collector_name, collector_age)
```

then no two rows may have the same age and name. Attempting to insert "Brian Jepson" as the collector_name and 28 as the collector_age into more than one row will generate an error. The PRIMARY KEY clause enforces the same criteria, but the column(s) are listed in the system data dictionary as the primary key for that table. The CHECK clause in a table constraint definition is used to reject INSERTs based on certain criteria. For example, the following table definition will reject any attempt to INSERT a person whose IQ is less than his or her shoe size:

```
CREATE TABLE people
    (pe_name char (10),
     pe_shoesize int,
     pe_IQ int,
     CHECK (pe_IQ > pe_shoesize))
```

The FOREIGN KEY clause allows you to specify one or more columns for a foreign key reference, as seen in the column constraint REFERENCES. The example seen earlier could be rewritten with the FOREIGN KEY clause as shown:

```
CREATE TABLE cartxref
    (cx_cartridge_id_ int,
     cx_collector_id_ int,
     cx_quantity  int,
     FOREIGN KEY (cx_cartridge_id_) REFERENCES cart (cartridge_id),
     FOREIGN KEY (cx_collector_id_) REFERENCES collect (collector_id))
```

# DELETE
**Conformance Level: Minimum**  This statement deletes rows matching a search condition.

```
DELETE FROM <table name>
    [WHERE <search condition>]
```

With a search condition, the DELETE statement deletes all rows matching the search condition. Without a search condition, it deletes all records.

Example:

```
DELETE FROM cartxref
    WHERE cx_quantity = 0
```

The above example deletes all rows in the cartxref table that have a zero quantity.

# DROP INDEX
**Conformance Level: Core**  This statement drops (removes) an index.

```
DROP INDEX <index name>
```

or

```
DROP INDEX <index name> ON <table name>
```

Some drivers require that you specify the name of the table to which the index belongs.

Example:

```
DROP INDEX ix_name
   ON collect
```

# DROP TABLE
**Conformance Level: Minimum**  This statement drops (removes) a table.

```
DROP TABLE <table name>
```

Caution: this statement will permanently remove a table!

Example:

```
DROP TABLE collect
```

# INSERT
**Conformance Level: Minimum**  This statement inserts a single row into a table.

```
INSERT INTO <table name>
    [(<column name> [, <column name>]...)]
    VALUES (<expression> [, <expression>]...)
```

The INSERT statement will insert a row into the named table, and it will populate each column specified with the corresponding value. If values are supplied for all columns in the physical order in which they are defined, the column names are not needed.

Example:

```
INSERT INTO cartxref
    (cx_cartridge_id_, cx_collector_id_, cx_quantity)
    VALUES (1, 1, 1)
```

# INSERT

**Conformance Level: Core**  This statement inserts one or more rows into a table.

```
INSERT INTO <table name>
    [(<column name> [, <column name>]...)]
    { query-specification| VALUES (<expression> [, <expression>]...)}
```

Instead of a VALUES clause, you may also supply a query specification (see the SELECT statement), which returns a result set that can be inserted into the table. For each column in the INSERT statement, there must be a corresponding column in the SELECT statement that makes up the query.

Example:

```
INSERT INTO summary
    (su_name, su_quant)
    SELECT collector_name, SUM(cx_quantity)
        FROM collect, cartxref
        WHERE cx_collector_id_ = collector_id
        GROUP BY collector_name
```

# SELECT

**Conformance Level: Minimum, Core**  This statement retrieves a selected set of columns from one or more tables where rows match a specified search condition.

```
SELECT [ALL | DISTINCT] <select list>
    FROM <table reference list>
    WHERE <search condition list>
    [ORDER BY    <column designator> [ASC | DESC]
                [, <column designator> [ASC | DESC]]...]
```

**The Select List**  A select list consists of one or more expressions, which can optionally be followed by an AS clause. The AS clause specifies the name of the column to use in the result set:

```
<expression> [AS <result column name>]
```

An expression can simply be a column name:

```
SELECT collector_name
    FROM collect
```

The AS clause can be used to rename the column in the result set:

```
SELECT collector_name AS name
   FROM collect
```

An expression can also be any valid expression in the ODBC SQL Syntax:

```
SELECT pl_fname + ' ' + pl_lname AS fullname
   FROM players
```

You may also use the * (asterisk) character to specify that all columns from all tables are to be included:

```
SELECT *
   FROM players
```

# The ALL and DISTINCT Keywords

The ALL keyword (this is assumed if neither ALL nor DISTINCT is supplied) retrieves all rows from the result set, regardless of duplicates. The DISTINCT keyword will eliminate duplicate rows, that is, each row will have a unique value for all columns in a result set that uses the DISTINCT clause. The ALL and DISTINCT clauses do not modify one particular column. They affect all columns in the result set, and there may be only one ALL or DISTINCT clause per SELECT statement. If you wanted a list of all unique last names in the players table, you could issue this SELECT statement:

```
SELECT DISTINCT pl_lname
   FROM players
```

# The WHERE Clause

The WHERE clause allows you to specify various filter criteria. A WHERE clause requires a search condition list. Each search condition should return a boolean true or false value and may be separated by AND or OR. A search condition may take several forms. The following predicates are available in drivers that conform to the minimum grammar:

```
<expression> <comparison operator> <expression>
| <expression> LIKE <pattern value>
| <column name> IS [NOT] NULL
```

**The Comparison Predicate of the WHERE Clause**  The comparison predicate is quite simple. You must supply an expression on both sides of the comparison, and each row that the comparison evaluates to true is selected:

```
SELECT *
   FROM cartxref
   WHERE cx_quantity < 10
```

The above example selects all rows that have a quantity of less than 10. You may combine comparison predicates with the and or or clause:

```
SELECT *
   FROM cartxref
   WHERE cx_quantity < 10
      OR cx_quantity > 100
```

The above example selects all rows that have a quantity of either less than 10 or greater than 100. The comparison predicate is also used to join one or more tables. In order to ensure that you get the collector name lined up with the correct cartridge IDs, you must join cartxref to collect with the expression cx_collector_id_ = collector_id:

```
SELECT *
   FROM cartxref, collect
   WHERE cx_quantity < 10
   AND    cx_collector_id_ = collector_id
```

The above example will select all rows from cartxref for which the quantity is less than 10. All of the columns from collect are included, but only those rows for which collector_id is equal to the cx_collector_id_ on cartxref will be selected. That makes sure that cartridge assignments are retrieved with the correct collector name.

**The Like Predicate of the WHERE Clause**  The LIKE predicate is similar to the comparison, except that the right-hand side of the expression must be a pattern value. A pattern value is a string literal that can contain wildcard characters. Within a pattern value, the character '%' (percent) will match zero or more occurrences of any character, and the character '_' (underscore) will match one single character:

```
SELECT *
   FROM cartxref, collect
   WHERE cx_quantity < 10
```

```
AND    cx_collector_id_ = collector_id
AND    collector_name LIKE 'B%'
```

This will select all cartridge assignments and collector names for which the quantity is less than 10 and the collector's name starts with the letter B.

**The NULL Predicate of the WHERE Clause** The NULL predicate is used to include or exclude all rows based on whether a particular column is NULL. A column is said to be NULL if it contains no value, and a blank value (zero or the empty string) is not considered NULL. This will select all cartridge assignments that have no quantity assigned, rather than zero:

```
SELECT *
    FROM cartxref, collect
    WHERE cx_quantity IS NULL
```

**Core Grammar WHERE Predicates** In addition to the above predicates, the following predicates are available to drivers conforming to the core grammar:

```
<expression> BETWEEN <expression> AND <expression>
| EXISTS ( <subquery> )
| <expression> [NOT] IN (subquery)
| <expression> <comparison operator> {ALL | ANY} <subquery>
```

**The Between Predicate of the WHERE Clause** The BETWEEN predicate allows you to specify values that fall between a specific range:

```
SELECT *
    FROM cartxref
    WHERE cx_quantity BETWEEN 10 AND 100
```

**The Exists Predicate of the WHERE Clause** The EXISTS predicate allows you to specify a subquery (another SQL SELECT) and evaluates to true only if there is at least one row returned by the subquery. This is often used with a correlated subquery. A correlated subquery is a SELECT statement that contains references to fields contained in tables other than the tables included in that SELECT's table list:

```
SELECT collector_name
    FROM collect
    WHERE EXISTS
        (SELECT *
```

```
    FROM cartxref
    WHERE cartxref.cx_collector_id_ = collect.collector_id)
```

The above SELECT statement correlates the subquery to the top-level query on cartxref.cx_collector_id_ = collect.collector_id. Note that the collect table is not included in the subquery's table list.

**The In Predicate of the WHERE Clause**   The IN predicate is used to compare values in one query with values in a subquery. It allows you to select all rows for which a given expression's value is (or is not) contained within another query:

```
SELECT cartridge_name
    FROM cart
    WHERE cartridge_id IN
        (SELECT cx_cartridge_id_
            FROM cartxref
            WHERE cx_quantity > 10)
```

The above example will select all cartridge names whose IDs can be found in the subquery, which selects all cartridge IDs that have a quantity greater than 10 assigned to a collector. This can be restated as:

```
SELECT DISTINCT cartridge_name
    FROM cart, cartxref
    WHERE cartridge_id = cx_cartridge_id_
    AND cx_quantity > 10
```

The DISTINCT clause is needed because there may be more than one cartridge/collector assignment that exceeds 10 in quantity for a particular cartridge. Typically, IN clauses that use the NOT keyword cannot be restated as shown above.

```
SELECT cartridge_name
    FROM cart
    WHERE cartridge_id NOT IN
        (SELECT cx_cartridge_id_
            FROM cartxref
            WHERE cx_quantity > 10)
```

This query will select only those cartridges that have no collector/cartridge assignment such that one collector owns 10 of the cartridges. If collector A owns 12 of the Missile

Command cartridges, and collector B owns 2, the Missile Command cartridge is excluded. However, the following query will not exclude this cartridge because at least one record will be found that is less than 10, so modifying the query not to use a subquery *does not work*, even if you reverse the quantity filter condition:

```
SELECT DISTINCT cartridge_name
    FROM cart, cartxref
    WHERE cartridge_id = cx_cartridge_id_
    AND cx_quantity <= 10
```

This example does not work the same way as the NOT IN example shown previously; despite the fact that collector A owns 12 copies of Missile Command, which does not satisfy 'AND cx_quantity <= 10'. Because collector B owns 2, it satisfies the condition.

**The Subquery Comparison Predicate of the WHERE Clause** The subquery comparison predicate performs a similar function, but it can be used with the comparison operator. The ANY keyword specifies that the comparison must evaluate to true for any of the rows in the subquery. The following SELECT will retrieve all collector names who have at least one cartridge, the quantity of which is equal to that of any quantity of any cartridge owned by T. Johnson:

```
SELECT DISTINCT collector_name
    FROM cartxref, collect
    WHERE cx_collector_id_ = collector_id
    AND cx_quantity = ANY
        (SELECT cx_quantity
            FROM cartxref, collect
            WHERE cx_collector_id_ = collector_id
            AND collector_name = 'T. Johnson')
```

The ALL keyword specifies that the comparison must evaluate to true for all of the rows in the subquery. The following SELECT will retrieve all collector names who have at least one cartridge, the quantity of which is greater than that of any quantity of any cartridge owned by T. Johnson:

```
SELECT DISTINCT collector_name
    FROM cartxref, collect
    WHERE cx_collector_id_ = collector_id
    AND cx_quantity > ALL
```

```
(SELECT cx_quantity
    FROM cartxref, collect
WHERE cx_collector_id_ = collector_id
AND collector_name = 'T. Johnson')
```

# The ORDER BY Clause

The ORDER BY clause allows you to specify how the SELECT statement is to order its results. You can optionally specify ASC or DESC to control whether the results are ordered for that column ascending or descending. You may specify the name(s) of the column(s) to order by, as in:

```
SELECT cx_collector_id_, cx_cartridge_id_
    FROM cartxref
    ORDER BY cx_collector_id_, cx_cartridge_id_
```

or you may specify an integer value for each column's position in the result set:

```
SELECT cx_collector_id_, cx_cartridge_id_
    FROM cartxref
    ORDER BY 1, 2
```

**Core Grammar Extensions to the SELECT Statement**  In addition to Core grammar WHERE clauses, several other SELECT statement clauses are supported by the Core Grammar:

```
SELECT [ALL | DISTINCT] <select list>
    FROM <table reference list>
    WHERE <search condition list>
    [GROUP BY <column name> [, <column name>]...]
    [HAVING <search condition>]
    [UNION <subquery>]
    [ORDER BY    <column designator> [ASC | DESC]
                [, <column designator> [ASC | DESC]]...]
```

# The GROUP BY Clause

The GROUP BY clause is used to generate summary values. You are allowed to choose which columns are used to produce distinct values by which the summary values are generated. For example, to see a sum total of all cartridges owned by each collector, you could issue:

```
SELECT collector_name, SUM(cx_quantity)
   FROM collect, cartxref
   WHERE cx_collector_id_ = collector_id
   GROUP BY collector_name
```

This will produce one record for each collector, followed by a column containing the sum total of all cartridges that the collector owns. You can also use an aggregate function without the GROUP BY clause:

```
SELECT SUM(cx_quantity)
   FROM cartxref
```

This will give you the sum of all carts owned. The HAVING clause works in conjunction with the aggregate functions. To get a sum total of all cartridges owned by each collector, but only for those collectors having more than two, you could use the following select statement:

```
SELECT collector_name, SUM(cx_quantity)
   FROM collect, cartxref
   WHERE cx_collector_id_ = collector_id
   GROUP BY collector_name
   HAVING SUM(cx_quantity) > 2
```

The following aggregate functions are available:

AVG()     Average of values

COUNT()   Count of records that match criteria

MIN()     Minimum value

MAX()     Maximum value

SUM()     Sum of values

# The UNION Clause

The UNION clause allows you to combine one or more queries into a result set. The number of columns and data types of each corresponding column must match, or an error will result. Here's a UNION that combines the minimum number of any given cart and maximum number of any given cartridge owned by each collector:

```
SELECT collector_name,
       'MAX' AS type,
       MAX(cx_quantity)
   FROM collect, cartxref
   WHERE cx_collector_id_ = collector_id
   GROUP BY collector_name
   UNION
   SELECT collector_name,
          'MIN' AS type,
          MIN(cx_quantity)
      FROM collect, cartxref
      WHERE cx_collector_id_ = collector_id
      GROUP BY collector_name
```

# UPDATE

**Conformance Level: Minimum** This statement updates the columns within a table.

```
UPDATE <table name>
   SET   <column name> = {<expression> | NULL}
         [,<column name> = {<expression> | NULL}]...
   WHERE <search condition>
```

The UPDATE statement is used to update the values of certain columns within a table. You can specify which columns to update using a search condition, which follows the same criteria as the WHERE clause of the SELECT statement. You may specify any number of columns to update, and you may include an expression to assign to those columns, or NULL.

To change the spelling of a single name within the collector table:

```
UPDATE collect
   SET collector_name = 'Brian Jepson'
   WHERE collector_id = 2
```

To make all of the names within the collector table uppercase:

```
UPDATE collect
   SET collector_name = {fn UCASE(collector_name)}
```

# ODBC Scalar Functions

In the last example above (the UPDATE statement), you saw the use of the UCASE function to uppercase a value. In general, ODBC Scalar functions, such as UCASE, should be enclosed in the *ODBC Extended Escape delimiters*, { and }. The fn keyword tells ODBC that a function name is expected. This ensures that even if the ODBC driver's syntax for a particular function differs, you can use the ODBC scalar function name, without having to modify your code for each driver. This makes it easier to write cross-platform code.

## String Functions

The following functions can be used to manipulate string expressions. Most drivers should support some or all of these, but you may need to check the documentation for each driver you use.

**ASCII(<string>)** This function returns as an integer value the ASCII code of the leftmost character of the argument <string>:

```
SELECT {fn ASCII(collector_name)}
    FROM collect
```

**CHAR(<integer>)** The CHAR function returns the character that has the ASCII value specified in <integer>:

```
SELECT {fn CHAR(collector_id + 64)}
    FROM collect
```

**CONCAT(<string1>, <string2>)** CONCAT returns a single string value that is the result of concatenating the arguments <string1> and <string2>:

```
SELECT {fn CONCAT(pl_fname, pl_lname)}
    FROM players
```

**INSERT(<string1>, <integer1>, <integer2>, <string2>)** This replaces <integer2> characters within <string1>, starting at the character position represented by <integer1>. The first character position is 1. The value of <string2> is inserted as a replacement string:

```
SELECT {fn INSERT(pl_fname, 2, 4, pl_lname)}
    FROM players
```

**LCASE(<string>)**  This function returns the lowercased string value of <string>:

```
SELECT {fn LCASE(pl_lname)}
    FROM players
```

**LEFT(<string>, <integer>)**  The LEFT function returns a string consisting of the <integer> leftmost characters from <string>:

```
SELECT {fn LEFT(pl_fname, 3)}
    FROM players
```

**LENGTH(<string>)**  This returns an integer value consisting of the number of characters in <string>, ignoring any trailing blanks:

```
SELECT {fn LENGTH(pl_fname)}
    FROM players
```

**LOCATE(<string1>, <string2> [, <integer>)**  This returns the offset in <string2> of the first occurrence of <string1>. You may optionally supply a position to begin searching, with <integer>.

```
SELECT {fn LOCATE('on', pl_lname)}
    FROM players
```

**LTRIM(<string>)**  This function returns a string consisting of the <string> with leading blanks removed:

```
SELECT {fn LTRIM(pl_fname)}
    FROM players
```

**REPEAT(<string>, <integer>)**  REPEAT returns a string composed of <string> repeated <integer> times:

```
SELECT {fn REPEAT(pl_fname, 2)}
    FROM players
```

**REPLACE(<string1>, <string2>, <string3>)**  This returns a string created by replacing all occurrences of <string2> within <string1> with <string3>:

```
SELECT {fn REPLACE(pl_fname, 'e', 'o')}
    FROM players
```

**RIGHT(<string>, <integer>)** This returns a string consisting of the <integer> rightmost characters from <string>:

```
SELECT {fn RIGHT(pl_fname, 3)}
    FROM players
```

**RTRIM(<string>)** The RTRIM function returns a string consisting of the <string> with trailing blanks removed:

```
SELECT {fn RTRIM(pl_fname)}
    FROM players
```

**SUBSTRING(<string>, <integer1>, <integer2>)** This returns a substring of <string> that begins at <integer1> position within <string> and continues for <integer2> characters:

```
SELECT {fn SUBSTRING(pl_fname, 3, 3)}
    FROM players
```

**UCASE(<string>)** This returns the uppercased string value of <string>:

```
SELECT {fn UCASE(pl_lname)}
    FROM players
```

# Numeric Functions

The following functions can be used to manipulate numeric expressions. Most drivers should support some or all of these, but you may need to check the documentation for each driver you use.

**ABS(<numeric>)** ABS returns the absolute value of the integer or float value specified by <numeric>:

```
SELECT {fn ABS(profit_loss)}
    FROM portfolio
```

**ACOS(<float>)** This function returns the arccosine of the value specified by <float> expressed as an angle in radians:

```
SELECT {fn ACOS(roof_angle)}
    FROM dimensions
```

**ASIN(<float>)**  This returns the arcsine of the value specified by <float> expressed as an angle in radians:

```
SELECT {fn ASIN(roof_angle)}
   FROM dimensions
```

**ATAN(<float>)**  ATAN returns the arctangent of the value specified by <float> expressed as an angle in radians:

```
SELECT {fn ATAN(roof_angle)}
   FROM dimensions
```

**ATAN2(<float1>, <float2>)**  The ATAN2 function returns the arctangent of the x and y coordinates specified by <float1> (x) and <float2> (y), expressed as an angle in radians:

```
SELECT {fn ATAN(point_x, point_y)}
   FROM dimensions
```

**CEILING(<numeric>)**  This returns the smallest integer that is greater than or equal to the float or integer value expressed by <numeric>:

```
SELECT {fn CEILING(roof_angle)}
   FROM dimensions
```

**COS(<float>)**  This returns the cosine of the value specified by <float> expressed as an angle in radians:

```
SELECT {fn COS(roof_angle)}
   FROM dimensions
```

**EXP(<float>)**  EXP returns the exponential value of the value specified by <float>:

```
SELECT {fn EXP(length * width * height)}
   FROM dimensions
```

**FLOOR(<numeric>)**  This returns the largest integer that is less than or equal to the float or integer value expressed by <numeric>:

```
SELECT {fn FLOOR(roof_angle)}
   FROM dimensions
```

**LOG(<float>)**  This returns the natural logarithm of the value expressed by <float>:

```
SELECT {fn LOG(roof_angle)}
    FROM dimensions
```

**MOD(&lt;integer1&gt;, &lt;integer2&gt;)** The modulus arithmetic function returns the remainder of &lt;integer1&gt; divided by &lt;integer2&gt;:

```
SELECT {fn MOD(length, height)}
    FROM dimensions
```

**PI()** This returns the constant floating point value of pi:

```
SELECT {fn PI() * (radius * radius)}
    FROM dimensions
```

**RAND([&lt;integer&gt;])** The RAND function returns a pseudo-random floating point value, optionally seeding the random number generator with the value of &lt;integer&gt;:

```
SELECT {fn RAND(collector_id)}
    FROM collect
```

**SIGN(&lt;numeric&gt;)** SIGN returns the sign (1, 0, or -1) of the integer or float value specified by &lt;numeric&gt;:

```
SELECT {fn SIGN(profit_loss)}
    FROM portfolio
```

**SIN(&lt;float&gt;)** SIN returns the sine of the value specified by &lt;float&gt; expressed as an angle in radians:

```
SELECT {fn SIN(roof_angle)}
    FROM dimensions
```

**SQRT(&lt;float&gt;)** This returns the square root of the value specified by &lt;float&gt;:

```
SELECT {fn SQRT(length + width + height)}
    FROM dimensions
```

**TAN(&lt;float&gt;)** This returns the tangent of the value specified by &lt;float&gt; expressed as an angle in radians:

```
SELECT {fn TAN(roof_angle)}
    FROM dimensions
```

# Date and Time Functions

The following functions can be used to manipulate date and time expressions. Most drivers should support some or all of these, but you may need to check the documentation for each driver you use.

**CURDATE()** This returns the current date, expressed as a date value:

```
SELECT {fn CURDATE()}, collector_name
    FROM collect
```

**CURTIME()** This returns the current time, expressed as a time value:

```
SELECT {fn CURTIME()}, collector_name
    FROM collect
```

**DAYOFMONTH(<date>)** This function returns the day of the month of <date>. It is expressed as an integer value between 1 and 31:

```
SELECT {fn DAYOFMONTH(sh_date)}, sh_py_id_
    FROM shows
```

**DAYOFWEEK(<date>)** This function returns the day of the week of <date>. It is expressed as an integer value between 1 and 7. Sunday is represented by 1:

```
SELECT {fn DAYOFWEEK(sh_date)}, sh_py_id_
    FROM shows
```

**DAYOFYEAR(<date>)** The DAYOFYEAR function returns the day of the year of <date>. It is expressed as an integer value between 1 and 366:

```
SELECT {fn DAYOFYEAR(sh_date)}, sh_py_id_
    FROM shows
```

**HOUR(<time>)** This returns the hour of the time value <time>, expressed as an integer between 0 and 23:

```
SELECT {fn HOUR({fn CURTIME()})}, collector_name
    FROM collect
```

**MINUTE(<time>)** This returns the minute of the time value <time>, expressed as an integer between 0 and 59:

```
SELECT {fn MINUTE({fn CURTIME()})}, collector_name
    FROM collect
```

**MONTH(&lt;date&gt;)** This returns the month of &lt;date&gt;. It is expressed as an integer value between 1 and 12:

```
SELECT {fn MONTH(sh_date)}, sh_py_id_
    FROM shows
```

**NOW()** This returns the current date and time, expressed as a timestamp value:

```
SELECT {fn NOW()}, collector_name
    FROM collect
```

**QUARTER(&lt;date&gt;)** QUARTER returns the quarter of &lt;date&gt;. It is expressed as an integer value between 1 and 4:

```
SELECT {fn QUARTER(sh_date)}, sh_py_id_
    FROM shows
```

**SECOND(&lt;time&gt;)** This returns the second of the time value &lt;time&gt;, expressed as an integer between 0 and 59:

```
SELECT {fn SECOND({fn CURTIME()})}, collector_name
    FROM collect
```

**WEEK(&lt;date&gt;)** This function returns the week number of &lt;date&gt;. It is expressed as an integer value between 1 and 53:

```
SELECT {fn WEEK(sh_date)}, sh_py_id_
    FROM shows
```

# SQL Components

This section describes each component available within the various SQL statements. Each includes an example, where the component is shown in **bold**.

## &lt;column element&gt;

See the documentation for CREATE TABLE.

## &lt;column designator&gt;

This returns the name of a column or an integer representing the position of a column in a SELECT statement.

Example:

```
SELECT collector_name, collector_id
    FROM collect
    ORDER BY 1, collector_id
```

# <column element>

See the documentation for CREATE TABLE.

# <column name>

This returns a valid column name (usually alphanumeric).

Example:

```
SELECT collector_name FROM collect
```

# <comparison operator>

This is an operator that returns a true or false (boolean) value. Several comparison operators are available:

```
x = y  x is equal to y
x <> y x is not equal to y
x > y  x is greater than y
x < y  x is less than y
x >= y x is greater than or equal to y
x <= y x is less than or equal to y
```

The comparison operator can compare an expression, which may consist of any combination of column names, literal values, or other operators. Examples:

```
SELECT *
    FROM cartxref
    WHERE cx_quantity < 10
```

The above example selects every record from the cartxref table where the quantity is less than 10.

```
SELECT pe_name
    FROM people
    WHERE pe_IQ > (pe_shoesize * 2)
```

The previous example selects every record from the people table where the person's IQ is greater than his or her shoe size multiplied by 2.

# <data type>

This returns any one of the data types supported by your ODBC driver. It can include optional column width.

Example:

```
CREATE TABLE collect
    (collector_id float,
     collector_name char (40))
```

# <expression>

This returns any well-formed combination of column names, operators, literal values, and scalar functions.

Example:

```
SELECT cx_collector_id_
    FROM cartxref
    WHERE SQRT(cx_quantity * 8) = 18
```

# <index name>

This returns the name of an index.

```
CREATE INDEX ix_name
    ON collect
    (collector_name)
```

# <pattern value>

This returns a string value used for pattern matches. See the documentation for the SELECT statement.

# <query specification>

This is a valid SQL SELECT statement. This can be embedded in other statements, such as INSERT.

```
INSERT INTO summary
    (su_name, su_quant)
```

```
SELECT collector_name, SUM(cx_quantity)
    FROM collect, cartxref
    WHERE cx_collector_id_ = collector_id
    GROUP BY collector_name
```

# <referenced column list>

See documentation for CREATE TABLE.

# <referenced table>

See <table name>.

# <referencing column list>

See documentation for CREATE TABLE.

# <search condition>

This isn expression used to filter results in a query. It can consist of literal values as well as column names. The keywords AND and OR can be used as well

Example:

```
SELECT cx_collector_id_
    FROM cartxref
    WHERE cx_quantity > 10
```

See the documentation on the SELECT statement for more information.

# <search condition list>

One or more search conditions, joined with the AND or OR keywords. See the documentation on the SELECT statement for more information.

# <table name>

This is the name of a table within your data source.

Example:

```
SELECT * FROM collect
```

# <table reference list>

This is a list of tables within a SELECT statement. It may consist of table names or view names. Each table or view name is separated by a comma. The . (dot) notation shown below allows you to explicitly state to which table a certain column belongs:

```
SELECT collect.collector_name, cartxref.cx_quantity
    FROM collect, cartxref
    WHERE cartxref.cx_collector_id_ = collect.collector_id
```

Also, a local alias may be included in the table reference list, which allows you to specify an alternate table name within the query:

```
SELECT a.collector_name, b.cx_quantity
    FROM collect a, cartxref b
    WHERE b.cx_collector_id_ = a.collector_id
```

# Index

## A

ABS(<numeric>), 464
acceptsURL(), 190-191
ACOS(<float>), 464
addNode(), 96-98
    subclassed version, 102
AddToFrame(), 303, 311
ALL keyword, 454
ALTER TABLE, 447
API, consistent, 2
Applets, 353-357
ASCII(<string>), 462
AS clause, 454
ASIN(<float>), 465
ATAN(<float>), 465
ATAN2(<float1>, <float2>), 465

## B

boolean allProceduresAreCallable(), 404
boolean allTablesAreSelectable(), 404
boolean dataDefinitionCausesTransactionCommit(), 247
boolean dataDefinitionIgnoredInTransactions(), 428
boolean doesMaxRowSizeIncludeBlobs(), 425
boolean execute(), 402
boolean execute(String sql), 381-384
boolean getAutoClose(), 377
boolean getAutoCommit(), 370-371
boolean getBoolean(int columnIndex), 385

boolean getBoolean(String columnName), 388
boolean getMoreResults(), 381-384
boolean isAutoIncrement(int column), 393
boolean isCaseSensitive(int column), 393
boolean isCatalogAtStart(), 417
boolean isClosed(), 373
boolean isCurrency(int column), 394
boolean isDefinitelyWritable(int column), 397
boolean isReadOnly(), 374, 405
boolean isReadOnly(int column), 396
boolean isSearchable(int column), 394
boolean isSigned(int column), 394
boolean isWritable(int column), 397
boolean next(), 384
boolean nullPlusNonNullIsNull(), 411
boolean nullsAreSortedAtEnd(), 406
boolean nullsAreSortedAtStart(), 405
boolean nullsAreSortedHigh(), 405
boolean nullsAreSortedLow(), 405
boolean storesLowerCaseIdentifiers, 408
boolean storesLowerCaseQuotedIdentifiers(), 409
boolean storesMixedCaseIdentifiers, 408
boolean storesMixedCaseQuotedIdentifiers(), 409
boolean storesUpperCaseIdentifiers, 408
boolean storesUpperCaseQuotedIdentifiers(), 408
boolean supportsAlterTableWithAddColumn(), 411
boolean supportsAlterTableWithDropColumn(), 411

**473**

boolean supportsANSI92EntryLevelSQL(), 415

boolean supportsANSI92FullSQL(), 415

boolean supportsANSI92IntermediateSQL(), 415

boolean supportsCatalogsInDataManipulation(), 418

boolean supportsCatalogsInIndexDefinitions(), 419

boolean supportsCatalogsInPrivilegeDefinitions(), 419

boolean supportsCatalogsInProcedureCalls(), 418

boolean supportsCatalogsInTableDefinitions(), 419

boolean supportsColumnAliasing(), 411

boolean supportsConvert(), 411

boolean supportsConvert(int from Type, int to Type), 412

boolean supportsCoreSQLGrammar(), 414-415

boolean supportsCorrelatedSubqueries(), 421

boolean supportsDataDefinitionAndDataManipulationTransactions(), 247

boolean supportsDataManipulationTransactionsOnly(), 247

boolean supportsDifferentTableCorrelationNames(), 412

boolean supportsExpressionsInOrderBy(), 412

boolean supportsExtendedSQLGrammar(), 415

boolean supportsFullOuterJoins(), 416

boolean supportsGroupBy(), 413

boolean supportsGroupByBeyondSelect(), 413

boolean supportsGroupByUnrelated(), 413

boolean supportsIntegrityEnhancementFacility(), 415-416

boolean supportsLikeEscapeClause(), 413-414

boolean supportsLimitedOuterJoins(), 416

boolean supportsMinimumSQLGrammar(), 414

boolean supportsMixedCaseIdentifiers(), 407

boolean supportsMixedCaseQuotedIdentifiers(), 408

boolean supportsMultipleResultSets(), 414

boolean supportsMultipleTransactions(), 414

boolean supportsNonNullabelColumns(), 414

boolean supportsOpenCursorsAcrossCommit(), 421

boolean supportsOpenCursorsAcrossRollback(), 422

boolean supportsOpenStatementsAcrossCommit(), 422

boolean supportsOpenStatementsAcrossRollback(), 422

boolean supportsOrderByUnrelated(), 412-413

boolean supportsOuterJoins(), 416

boolean supportsPositionedDelete(), 419

boolean supportsPositionedUpdate(), 419

boolean supportsSchemasInDataManipulation(), 417

boolean supportsSchemasInIndexDefinitions(), 418

boolean supportsSchemasInPrivilegeDefinitions(), 418

boolean supportsSchemasInProcedureCalls(), 417

boolean supportsSchemasInTableDefinitions(), 418

boolean supportsSelectForUpdate(), 420

boolean supportsStoredProcedures(), 420

boolean supportsSubqueriesInComparisons(), 420

boolean supportsSubqueriesInExists(), 420

boolean supportsSubqueriesInIns(), 420

boolean supportsSubqueriesInQuantifieds(), 421

boolean supportsTableCorrelationNames(), 412

boolean supportsTransactionIsolationLevel(int level), 247

boolean supportsTransactions(), 426-247

boolean supportsUnion(), 421

boolean supportsUnionAll(), 421

boolean usesLocalFiles(), 407

boolean usesLocalFilesPerTable(), 407

boolean wasNull(), 384

byte getByte(int columnIndex), 385

byte[] getBytes(int columnIndex), 386

byte[] getBytes(String columnName), 390

byte getByte(String columnName), 388

**C**

CallableStatement, 53-56

CallableStatement prepareCall(String sql), 369-370

cancel(), 219

CardFileAbstract, 59-79

    abstract classes, 327-328, 333

    installation, 62-63

    public abstract void delRow();, 66, 77-78

    public abstract void getRow();, 64-66, 70-72

public abstract void login();, 63–64, 67–69
public abstract void nextRow();, 66, 76
public abstract void prevRow();, 66, 76–77
public abstract void save();, 66, 73–74
public abstract void update();, 67–78
CardFileAbstract.java, 327–341
CardFile.java, 301–325
    AddToFrame(), 303, 311
    clearForm(), 310–311
    delRow(), 323–324
    getKeys(), 303–304, 308–310
    getRow(), 304–308, 321–323
    handleEvent(), 315–319
    main(), 324–325
    Msql.Connect(), 303
    Msql.Query(), 312–313
    Msql.SelectDB(), 303
    save(), 312
    setBrowse(), 320–321
    setEdit(), 319–320
    update(), 313–314
cardfileKeys, 303–304
CEILING(<numeric>), 465
CHAR(<integer>), 462
CHECK clause, 450–451
Class.forName(), 367–368
CLASSPATH, 30, 32–33, 62–63
clearForm(), 310–311
clearWarnings(), 206–207, 219–220, 250
close(), 173, 202, 214, 224
ColSize(), 173–174
ColType(), 174
<column designator>, 468–469
<column element>, 468
columnmap Hashtable, 303
<column name>, 469
commit(), 201
<comparison operator), 469–470
CONCAT(<string1>, <string2>), 462
connect(), 88, 109–110, 189–190
Connection, opening, 36–38
Connectivity, to database servers, 2
COS(<float>), 465
CREATE INDEX, 447–448
createStatement(), 199
CreateTable(), 155–156, 166–167

CREATE TABLE, 448–451
CURDATE(), 467
CURTIME(), 467

**D**

Data:
    adding to tables, 16–18
    dynamic structures, 4–7
    hierarchical, 82–86
    normalization, 10
    updating in tables, 23–24
Database:
    definition, 9
    design, 9–14
    first normal form, 10–12
    second normal form, 12–13
    third normal form, 13–14
    independence, 29–30
    mSQL, 296
    MsqlJava API, 361
    opening a connection, 36–38
    servers, connectivity to, 2
DatabaseMetaData, 57, 404–432
DatabaseMetaData get MetaData(), 374
DataRamp, 357
<data type>, 470
Date, escapes, 434
DAYOFMONTH(<date>), 467
DAYOFWEEK(<date>), 467
DAYOFYEAR(<date>), 467
dbfFile, 265–268
dbfFileConnection, 285–287
dbfFileDriver, 282–285
    test program, 287–289
dbfFileTable, 269–282
DDL.java, 59–62
DELETE, 451
DeleteCol(), 176
DeleteRow(), 176–177, 182
DELETE statement, 24–25
DeleteStatement(), 152–153
delFile(), 169–170
delRow(), 323–324
Dirty read, 376
disableAutoClose(), 206

DISTINCT clause, 457–458
DISTINCT keyword, 454
double getDouble(int columnIndex), 386
double getDouble(String columnName), 389
Drivers:
    discovering capabilities, 57
    getting, 31
    picking, 32
    registering, 35
DROP INDEX, 452
DropTable(), 155, 168–169
DROP TABLE, 452

## E

elem, 92–97
Escape processing, 433–434
Escape syntax, 56
Execute permission, 29
executeQuery(), 212
executetinySQL(), 207
executeUpdate(), 39, 212
EXP(<float>), 465
<expression>, 470
expr_list token, 437
expr_part non-terminal token, 438

## F

finalize(), 89
findColumn(), 248–249
findTableForColumn(), 150–151
float getFloat(int columnIndex), 386
float getFloat(String columnName), 389
FLOOR(<numeric>), 465
FOREIGN KEY clause, 451

## G

getAsciiStream(), 236, 246
getBinaryStream(), 237, 247
getBoolean(), 226–227, 242
getByte(), 226, 241–242
getBytes(), 232–233, 244–245
getCatalog(), 204–205, 258
GetCol(), 176–180
getColumnCount(), 252

getColumnDisplaySize(), 115, 255
getColumnLabel(), 255–256
getColumnName(), 256
getColumnType(), 258–259
getColumnTypeName(), 259–260
getConnection(), 193, 195–196
getCursorName(), 237
getDate(), 233–234, 245
getDouble(), 230–231, 244
getFloat(), 230, 243–244
getInt(), 228–229, 242–243
getKeys(), 72–73, 303–304, 308–310
getLong(), 229, 243
getMajorVersion(), 192
getMaxFieldSize(), 216
getMaxRows(), 217
getMetaData(), 203, 237–238, 251
getMinorVersion(), 192–193
getMoreResults(), 215–216
getNumeric(), 231–232, 244
getObject(), 238–241, 247–248
getPrecision(), 257
getPropertyInfo(), 191–192
getQueryTimeout(), 218
getResultSet(), 213–215
getRow(), 64–66, 304–308, 321–323
getScale(), 257
getSchemaName(), 256
getShort(), 227–228, 242
getString(), 225, 241
getTable(), 156, 168
getTableName(), 257–258
getTime(), 234, 245
getTimestamp(), 235–236, 245–246
get_tinySQL(), 207–209
getTransactionIsolation(), 205–206
getUnicodeStream(), 236, 246
getUpdateCount(), 42, 215
getWarnings(), 206, 219, 250
GoTop(), 175–176
Grids, 106–122
    connect(), 109–110
    getColumnDisplaySize(), 115
    getData(), 113
    handleEvents(), 117–118
    jdbcMlGrid, 106–110
    layoutGrid(), 112

main(), 106-108
prepareGrid(), 111
ResultSetMetaData, 114-115
rows vector, 116-117
SQL UPDATE statement, 118-121
GROUP BY clause, 459-460

# H

handleEvent(), 315-319, 335-340
handleEvents(), 117-118
Hashtable, 4-5, 65
columnmap, 303
elem, 92-97
rs_cached, 90-92, 94-95
tinySQL, 127-133
HAVING clause, 24
Hierarchical data, 82-86
HOUR(<time>), 467

# I

<index name>, 470
INSERT, 452-453
INSERT(<string1>, <integer1>, <integer2>,
<string2>), 462
Inserts, positioned, 17
INSERT Statement, 16-18
InsertStatement(), 155
Installation, 30
CardFileAbstract, 62-63
JDBC-ODBC bridge, 34-35
mSQL, 33-34
tinySQL, 32-33
int executeUpdate(), 397
int executeUpdate(String sql), 378
int findColumn(String columnName), 393
int getColumnCount(), 393
int getColumnDisplaySize(int column), 394
int getColumnType(int column), 396
int getDefaultTransactionIsolation(), 426
int getDriverMajorVersion(), 407
int getDriverMinorVersion(), 407
int getInt(int columnIndex), 385
int getInt(String columnName), 389
int getMaxBinaryLiteralLength(), 422

int getMaxCatalogNameLength(), 425
int getMaxCharLiteralLength(), 422
int getMaxColumnNameLength(), 423
int getMaxColumnsInGroupBy(), 423
int getMaxColumnsInIndex(), 423
int getMaxColumnsInOrderBy(), 423
int getMaxColumnsInSelect(), 423
int getMaxColumnsInTable(), 424
int getMaxConnections(), 424
int getMaxCursorNameLength(), 424
int getMaxFieldSize(), 378-379
int getMaxIndexLength(), 424
int getMaxProcedureNameLength(), 424-425
int getMaxRows(), 379
int getMaxRowSize(), 425
int getMaxSchemaNameLength(), 424
int getMaxStatementLength(), 425
int getMaxStatements(), 425
int getMaxTableNameLength(), 426
int getMaxTablesInSelect(), 426
int getMaxUserNameLength(), 426
int getPrecision(int column), 395
int getQueryTimeout(), 380
int getScale(int column), 395
int getTransactionIsolation(), 376-377
int getUpdateCount(), 381
int isNullable(int column), 394
isCaseSensitive(), 253
isClosed(), 202-203
isCurrency(), 253-254
isNullable(), 254
isReadOnly(), 204, 260
isSearchable(), 253
isSigned(), 254
isWritable(), 260-261

# J

JavaCup, 435-439
java.io.InputStream getAsciiStream(int columnIndex), 387
java.io.InputStream getAsciiStream(String column-
Name), 390
java.io.InputStream getBinaryStream(int
columnIndex), 388

java.io.InputStream getBinaryStream(String columnName), 391

java.io.InputStream getUnicodeStream(int columnIndex), 387–388

java.io.InputStream getUnicodeStream(String columnName), 391

JavaLex, 435
    scanner specifications, 440–443

java.sql.Date getDate(int columnIndex), 387

java.sql.Date getDate(String columnName), 390

java.sql.DriverManager, 35

java.sql.Time getTime(int columnIndex), 387

java.sql.Time getTime(String columnName), 390

java.sql.Timestamp getTimestamp(int columnIndex), 387

java.sql.Timestamp getTimestamp(String columnName), 390

JDBC, 28–57
    database independence, 29–30
    escape syntax, 56
    getting and installing, 30

jdbc_callable.java, 53–56

jdbcCardFile, 67, 79

jdbcCompliant(), 193

JDBC driver:
    ALL keyword, 454
    ALTER TABLE, 447
    conventions, 446–447
    CREATE INDEX, 447–448
    CREATE TABLE, 448–451
    DELETE, 451
    DISTINCT keyword, 454
    DROP INDEX, 452
    DROP TABLE, 452
    GROUP BY clause, 459–460
    INSERT, 452–453
    minimum, core, and extended grammars, 445
    ODBC scalar functions, 462–468
    ORDER BY clause, 459
    pure Java, 353
    SELECT, 453–454
    UNION clause, 460–461
    UPDATE, 461
    WHERE clause, 454–459
    *see also* tinySQL JDBC driver

JDBC Driver API, 367–434

JDBC interface, 187–188

jdbcKona/T3, 354–356

jdbcMlGrid, 106–110

JDBC-ODBC bridge, 31–32, 38
    installation, 34–35

jdbc_prepared_statement.java, 49–52

jdbc_query.java, 45–47

jdbc_update.java, 39–42

jdbc_update2.java, 42–44

JDBC URL, 38

JDesginerPro, 356

JDP, 356

JetConnect, 356

**L**

layoutGrid(), 112

LCASE(<string>), 463

LEFT(<string>, <integer>), 463

LENGTH(<string>), 463

lex, 435

LOCATE(<string1>, <string2> [, <integer>), 463

LOG(<float>), 465–466

login(), 63–64, 67–68

long getLong(int columnIndex), 386

long getLong(String columnName), 389

LTRIM(<string>), 463

**M**

main(), 78, 99–100, 102–104, 106–108, 170–171, 324–325

Maintenance, ease of, 2

Microsoft SQL Server, 354

MINUTE(<time>), 467

mkDataDirectory(), 169

MlGridEvent object, 118

MOD(<integer1>, <integer2>), 466

MONTH(<date>), 468

msql, 296

mSQL, 291
    building and installing, 292–295
    command-line tools, 295–296
    getting, 292
    paying for, 295
    starting, 295

msqladmin, 295–296

MsqlCardFile.java, 341–350

Msql class, 300-301
Msql.Connect( ), 303
MsqlJava:
    getting and installing, 297-298
    testing installation, 297-299
MsqlJava API, 359-365
    closing connection, 365
    connecting to mSQL server, 360-361
    database selection, 361
    issuing a query, 362
    working with result sets, 362-365362
mSQL-JDBC, 354
mSQL JDBC driver, 31, 38
    installation, 33-34
Msql object:
    constructing, 359-360
    instantiating and initializing, 300
Msql.Query( ), 312-313
Msql.SelectDB( ), 303
mSQL server, connecting to MsqlJava API,
    360-361
myFrame.java, 104-106
myTextField, 328, 341

# N

nativeCall( ), 200-201
next( ), 44-45, 223-224
Normal form, 10
    first, 10-12
    second, 12-13
    third, 13-14
NOW( ), 468
Numeric getNumeric(int columnIndex, int scale),
    386
Numeric getNumeric(String columnName, int
    scale), 389

# O

object, instantiating and initializing, 300
Object getObject(int columnIndex), 392
Object getObject(String columnName), 392
ODBC, 28
ODBC date and time functions, 467-468
    CURDATE( ), 467
    CURTIME( ), 467
    DAYOFMONTH(<date>), 467
    DAYOFWEEK(<date>), 467
    DAYOFYEAR(<date>), 467
    HOUR(<time>), 467
    MINUTE(<time>), 467
    MONTH(<date>), 468
    NOW( ), 468
    QUARTER(<date>), 468
    SECOND(<time>), 468
    WEEK(<date>), 468
ODBC escape processing, 433-434
ODBC scalar functions, 462-468
    ABS(<numeric>), 464
    ACOS(<float>), 464
    ASCII(<string>), 462
    ASIN(<float>), 465
    ATAN(<float>), 465
    ATAN2(<float1>, <float2>), 465
    CEILING(<numeric>), 465
    CHAR(<integer>), 462
    CONCAT(<string1>, <string2>), 462
    COS(<float>), 465
    EXP(<float>), 465
    FLOOR(<numeric>), 465
    INSERT(<string1>, <integer1>, <integer2>,
        <string2>), 462
    LCASE(<string>), 463
    LEFT(<string>, <integer>), 463
    LENGTH(<string>), 463
    LOCATE(<string1>, <string2> [, <integer>),
        463
    LOG(<float>), 465-466
    LTRIM(<string>), 463
    MOD(<integer1>, <integer2>), 466
    numeric functions, 464-466
    PI( ), 466
    RAND([<integer>]), 466
    REPEAT(<string>, <integer>), 463
    REPLACE(<string1>, <string2>, <string3>), 463
    RIGHT(<string>, <integer>), 464
    RTRIM(<string>), 464
    SIGN(<numeric>), 466
    SIN(<float>), 466
    SQRT(<float>), 466
    string functions, 462-464
    SUBSTRING(<string>, <integer1>, <integer2>),
        464

TAN(<float>), 466
UCASE(<string>), 464
ORDER BY clause, 459
Outer joins, 433
outline.java, 86–100
outlineMITree.java, 100–106

# P

Parsers, 435
<pattern value>, 470
PI(), 466
prepareCall(), 200
PreparedStatement, 48–52
PreparedStatement prepareStatement(String sql),
    368–369
prepareGrid(), 111
prepareStatement(), 199–200
Primary key, 12
PRIMARY KEY clause, 451
Primary key column, 116
Prototyping, 2
public abstract void delRow();, 66, 77–78
public abstract void getRow();, 64–66, 70–72
public abstract void login();, 63–64, 67–69
public abstract void nextRow();, 66, 76
public abstract void prevRow();, 66, 76–77
public abstract void save();, 66, 73–74
public abstract void update();, 67–78
public boolean IsKey();, 365
public boolean NonNull();, 364
public int FieldLength();, 364
public int FieldType();, 364
public int NumFields(), 363
public int NumRows(), 363
public Msql(), 359–360
public MsqlFieldDesc FetchField(), 362
public MsqlFieldDesc[] ListFields(String s),
    363–364
public MsqlResult Query, 362
public String [] FetchRos(), 362
public String FieldName();, 364
public String[] ListDBs(), 363
public String[] ListTables(), 363
public String TableName();, 364
public void Close(), 365

public void Connect, 360–361
public void SelectDB, 361

# Q

QUARTER(<date>), 468
Queries, issuing, 300–301
<query specification>, 470–471

# R

RAND([<integer>]), 466
readColumnInfo(), 172–173, 183–185
<referenced column list>, 471
<referenced table>, 471
REFERENCES clause, 449
<referencing column list>, 471
Registering, drivers, 35
Relational model, 10–12
REPEAT(<string>, <integer>), 463
REPLACE(<string1>, <string2>, <string3>), 463
ResultSet, pitfalls, 47–48
ResultSet executeQuery(), 397
ResultSet executeQuery(String sql), 378
ResultSet getBestRowIdentifier(String catalog,
    String schema, String table, int scope, boolean
    nullable), 430–431
ResultSet getCatalogs(), 429
ResultSet getColumnPrivileges(String catalog,
    String schema, String table, String column-
    NamePattern), 430
ResultSet getColumns(String catalog, String
    schemaPattern, String tableNamePattern, String
    columnNamePattern), 430
ResultSet getCrossReference(String primaryCata-
    log, String primarySchema, String primary-
    Table, String foreignCatalog, String
    foreignSchema, String foreignTable), 432
ResultSet getExportedKeys(String catalog, String
    schema, String table), 432
ResultSet getImportedKeys(String catalog, String
    schema, String table), 431
ResultSet getIndexInfo(String catalog, String
    schema, String table, boolean unique, boolean
    approximate), 432

ResultSet getPrimaryKeys(String catalog, String schema, String table), 431

ResultSet getProcedureColumns(String catalog, String schemaPattern, String procedure-NamePattern, String columnNamePattern), 428-429

ResultSet getProcedures(String catalog, String schemaPattern, String procedureNamePattern), 428

ResultSet getResultSet(), 381-384

ResultSet getSchemas(), 429

ResultSet getTablePrivileges(String catalog, String schemaPattern, String tableNamePattern), 430

ResultSet getTables(String catalog, String schema-Pattern, String tableNamePattern, String types[]), 429

ResultSet getTableTypes(), 429

ResultSet getTypeInfo(), 432

ResultSet getVersionColumns(String catalog, String schema, String table), 431

ResultSetMetaData, 57, 114-115
    getMetaData(), 392
    object, 393-397

RIGHT(<string>, <integer>), 464

rollback(), 202

Rows, deleting from tables, 24-25

Rows vector, 116

rs_cached, 90-92, 94-95

RTRIM(<string>), 464

## S

save(), 312

Scanner, JavaCup, 436

Scanner.lex, 435

<search condition>, 471

<search condition list>, 471

SECOND(<time>), 468

SELECT, 453-454

Select List, 453

SELECT Statement, 19-23
    core grammar extensions, 459

SelectStatement(), 133-134

setAutoCommit(), 201

setBrowse(), 320-321

setCatalog(), 204

setCursorName(), 220

setEdit(), 319-320

setEscapeProcessing(), 217-218

setMaxFieldSize(), 216-217

setMaxRows(), 217

setQueryTimeout(), 218-219

setReadOnly(), 203

setTransactionIsolation(), 205

short getShort(int columnIndex), 385

short getShort(String columnName), 388-389

SIGN(<numeric>), 466

SIN(<float>), 466

SQL, 14-25

sql(), 127

SQL:
    adding data to tables, 16-18
    creating tables, 14-16
    deleting rows from tables, 24-25
    querying tables, 19-23
    updating data in tables, 23-24

SQL components:
    <column designator>, 468-469
    <column element>, 468
    <column name>, 469
    <comparison operator), 469-470
    <data type>, 470
    <expression>, 470
    <index name>, 470
    <pattern value>, 470
    <query specification>, 470-471
    <referenced column list>, 471
    <referenced table>, 471
    <referencing column list>, 471
    <search condition>, 471
    <search condition list>, 471
    <table name>, 471
    <table reference list>, 472

sqlexec(), 125-127

SQL LIKE clause, escaping, 433-434

SQL SELECT statement, 134-146

SQLStreamInputStream, 125

SQL UPDATE statement, 118-121

SQLWarning getWarnings(), 377, 380, 391

SQRT(<float>), 466

Statement createStatement(), 368

static next_token(), 440

Stored procedures, 29
  invoking, 434
String getCatalog(), 375
String getCatalogName(int column), 396
String getCatalogSeparator(), 417
String getCatalogTerm(), 417
String getColumnLabel(int column), 395
String getColumnName(int column), 395
String getColumnTypeName(int column), 396
String getCursorName(), 392
String getDatabaseProductName(), 406
String getDatabaseProductVersion(), 406
String getDriverName(), 406
String getDriverVersion(), 406
String getExtraNameCharacters(), 410
String getIdentifierQuoteString(), 409
String getNumericFunctions(), 409
String getProcedureTerm(), 416
String getSchemaName(int column), 395
String getSchemaTerm(), 416
String getSearchStringEscape(), 410
String getSQLKeywords, 409
String getString(int columnIndex), 385
String getString(String columnName), 388
String getStringFunctions(), 410
String getSystemFunctions(), 410
String getTableName(int column), 396
String getTimeDateFunctions(), 410
String getURL(), 404
String getUserName(), 405
    Structured Query Language. *See* SQL
Subquery, 24
SUBSTRING(<string>, <integer1>, <integer2>),
    464
sym.java, 439

# T

Table:
    adding data to, 16–18
    creating, 14–16
    definition, 9
    deleting rows, 24–25
    querying, 19–23
    updating data, 23–24
    working with, 300–301

<table name>, 471
<table reference list>, 472
TAN(<float>), 466
TestResult(), 146–150
testTextFile.java, 261–263
TextField object, 65
textFile.java, 165–171
textFileConnection.java, 208–209
textFileDriver.java, 194–196
textFileTable.java, 171–185
textFile tinySQL driver, installation, 32–33
Time, escapes, 434
Timestamp, escapes, 434
tinySQL, 31, 123–185
    close(), 173
    ColSize(), 173–174
    ColType(), 174
    CreateTable(), 155–156, 166–167
    dbfFile, 265–268
    dbfFileConnection, 285–287
    dbfFileDriver, 282–285
    dbfFileTable, 269–282
    debugging, 160–161
    DeleteRow(), 176–177, 182
    DeleteStatement(), 152–153
    delFile(), 169–170
    DropTable(), 155, 168–169
    findTableForColumn(), 150–151
    GetCol(), 176–180
    getTable(), 156, 168
    GoTop(), 175–176
    Hashtable, 127–133
    InsertStatement(), 155
    installation, 32–33
    main(), 170–171
    NextRecord(), 176
    readColumnInfo(), 172–173, 183–185
    SelectStatement(), 133–134
    sql(), 127
    sqlexec(), 125–127
    TestResult(), 146–150
    tiers, 124
    tsColumn, 156–157
    tsResultSet, 158–160
    tsRow, 157–158
    UpdateCol(), 176–177, 180–181

UpdateCurrentRow(), 174-175
UpdateStatement(), 153-155
tinySQLConnection.java, 196-208
tinySQL.cup, 435
tinySQL driver, 38
tinySQLDriver.java, 189-193
tinySQLException.java, 161-162
tinySQL JDBC driver, 31, 187-263
  acceptsURL(), 190-191
  cancel(), 219
  clearWarnings(), 206-207, 219-220, 250
  close(), 202, 214, 224
  commit(), 201
  connect(), 189-190
  createStatement(), 199
  disableAutoClose(), 206
  executeQuery(), 212
  executetinySQL(), 207
  executeUpdate(), 212
  findColumn(), 248-249
  getAsciiStream(), 236, 246
  getBinaryStream(), 237, 247
  getBoolean(), 226-227, 242
  getByte(), 226, 241-242
  getBytes(), 232-233, 244-245
  getCatalog(), 204-205, 258
  getColumnCount(), 252
  getColumnDisplaySize(), 255
  getColumnLabel(), 255-256
  getColumnName(), 256
  getColumnType(), 258-259
  getColumnTypeName(), 259-260
  getConnection(), 193, 195-196
  getCursorName(), 237
  getDate(), 233-234, 245
  getDouble(), 230-231, 244
  getFloat(), 230, 243-244
  getInt(), 228-229, 242-243
  getLong(), 229, 243
  getMajorVersion(), 192
  getMaxFieldSize(), 216
  getMaxRows(), 217
  getMetaData(), 203, 237-238, 251
  getMinorVersion(), 192-193
  getMoreResults(), 215-216

  getNumeric(), 231-232, 244
  getObject(), 238-241, 247-248
  getPrecision(), 257
  getPropertyInfo(), 191-192
  getQueryTimeout(), 218
  getResultSet(), 213-215
  getScale(), 257
  getSchemaName(), 256
  getShort(), 227-228, 242
  getString(), 225, 241
  getTableName(), 257-258
  getTime(), 234, 245
  getTimestamp(), 235-236, 245-246
  get_tinySQL(), 207-209
  getTransactionIsolation(), 205-206
  getUnicodeStream(), 236, 246
  getUpdateCount(), 215
  getWarnings(), 206, 219, 250
  isCaseSensitive(), 253
  isClosed(), 202-203
  isCurrency(), 253-254
  isNullable(), 254
  isReadOnly(), 204, 260
  isSearchable(), 253
  isSigned(), 254
  isWritable(), 260-261
  jdbcCompliant(), 193
  nativeCall(), 200-201
  next(), 223-224
  prepareCall(), 200
  prepareStatement(), 199-200
  rollback(), 202
  setAutoCommit(), 201
  setCatalog(), 204
  setCursorName(), 220
  setEscapeProcessing(), 217-218
  setMaxFieldSize(), 216-217
  setMaxRows(), 217
  setQueryTimeout(), 218-219
  setReadOnly(), 203
  setTransactionIsolation(), 205
  testTextFile.java, 261-263
  textFileConnection.java, 208-209
  textFileDriver.java, 194-196
  tinySQLResultSet.java, 220-250

tinySQLResultSetMetaData.java, 250–251
tinySQLStatement.java, 210–220
wasNull(), 224–225
tinySQLResultSet, constructor, 251–252
tinySQLResultSet.java, 220–250
tinySQLResultSetMetaData.java, 250–251
tinySQLStatement.java, 210–220
tinySQLTABLE, 269
tinySQLTable.java, 162–165
Token:
    declaration, 437
    fetching from scanner, 436
    JavaLex, 440–441
traverseTree(), 89–90
tsColumn, 156–157
tsResultSet, 158–160
tsRow, 157–158

# U

UCASE(<string>), 464
UNION clause, 460–461
UNIQUE clause, 450
UPDATE, 461
update(), 67–78, 313–314
UpdateCol(), 176–177, 180–181
UpdateCurrentRow(), 174–177
UPDATE statement, 23–25
UpdateStatement(), 153–155
Update statement, issuing, 39–44
URL, 38, 83–86

# V

void cancel(), 380
void clearParameters(), 401
void clearWarnings(), 377–378, 380–381, 391
void close(), 373, 378, 384
void commit(), 372–373
void registerOutParameter(int parameterIndex, int
    sqlType), 403
void registerOutParameter(int parameterIndex, int
    sqlType, int scale), 403
void rollback(), 371–372
void setAsciiStream(int parameterIndex,
    java.io.InputStream x, int length), 401
void setAutoClose(boolean autoClose), 377

void setAutoCommit(boolean autoCommit), 370
void setBinaryStream(int parameterIndex,
    java.io.InputStream x, int length), 401
void setBoolean(int parameterIndex, boolean x),
    397
void setByte(int parameterIndex, byte x), 397
void setBytes(int parameterIndex, byte x[]), 400
void setCatalog(String catalog), 374–375
void setCursorName(String name), 381
void setDate(int parameterIndex, java.sql.Date x),
    400
void setDouble(int parameterIndex, double x),
    399
void setEscapeProcessing(boolean enable), 379
void setFloat(int parameterIndex, float x), 399
void setInt(int parameterIndex, int x), 397
void setLong(int parameterIndex, long x), 399
void setMaxFieldSize(int max), 379
void setMaxRows(int max), 379
void setNull(int parameterIndex, int sqlType), 397
void setNumeric(int parameterIndex, Numeric x),
    399
void setObject(int parameterIndex, Object x), 402
void setObject(int parameterIndex, Object x, int
    targetSqlType), 402
void setObject(int parameterIndex, Object x, int
    targetSqlType, int scale), 402
void setQueryTimeout(int seconds), 380
void setReadOnly(boolean readOnly), 374
void setShort(int parameterIndex, short x), 397
void setString(int parameterIndex, String x), 399
void setTime(int parameterIndex, java.sql.Time
    x), 400
void setTimestamp(int parameterIndex,
    java.sql.Timestamp x), 400
void setTransactionIsolation(int level), 375–376
void setUnicodeStream(int parameterIndex,
    java.io.InputStream x, int length), 401

# W

wasNull(), 224–225
Weblogic, jdbcKona/T3, 354–356
WEEK(<date>), 468
WHERE clause, 19–, 2421, 454–459
    between predicates, 456
    comparison predicate, 455

core grammar predicates, 456
exists predicates, 456-457
IN predicate, 457-458
like predicate, 455-456
NULL predicate, 456
subquery comparison predicate, 458-459
Widgets, 81-122
definition, 81
grids, 106-122
hierarchical data, 82-86

outline.java, 86-100
outlineMITree.java, 100-106

## X

XDB Systems, JetConnect, 356

## Y

yacc, 435

# About the Web Site

This book's accompanying Web site contains all the example code included in the book.

It may be downloaded from `http://www.wiley.com.compbooks/`. In addition

to listing all the example code, this Web page also contains:

- Links to the FAQ document (Frequently Asked Questions)
- mSQL databases
- JDBC components
- tinySQL, a generic and extendible SQL engine written in Java
- The tinySQL JDBC driver
- Customizable Java database code
- Other items of interest

Should you have any trouble with this site, or if you simply have questions concerning the book or software, Brian Jepson welcomes your e-mail at `bjepson@ids.net`.